The Past in Visual Culture

D1603143

The Past in Visual Culture

*Essays on Memory, Nostalgia
and the Media*

EDITED BY
JILLY BOYCE KAY, CAT MAHONEY
AND CAITLIN SHAW

McFarland & Company, Inc., Publishers
Jefferson, North Carolina

ISBN (print) 978-1-4766-6380-7
ISBN (ebook) 978-1-4766-2689-5

LIBRARY OF CONGRESS CATALOGUING DATA ARE AVAILABLE

BRITISH LIBRARY CATALOGUING DATA ARE AVAILABLE

© 2017 Jilly Boyce Kay, Cat Mahoney and Caitlin Shaw.
All rights reserved

*No part of this book may be reproduced or transmitted in any form
or by any means, electronic or mechanical, including photocopying
or recording, or by any information storage and retrieval system,
without permission in writing from the publisher.*

Front cover image © 2017 iStock; (on screen) Astronaut Buzz Aldrin
on the moon during the *Apollo 11* mission on July 20, 1969 (NASA)

Printed in the United States of America

*McFarland & Company, Inc., Publishers
Box 611, Jefferson, North Carolina 28640
www.mcfarlandpub.com*

Acknowledgments

It has been deeply rewarding to work on a collection that covers such a broad array of scholarship and that features essays that engage with mediations of memory, history, and nostalgia in diverse and exciting ways. The editors would therefore like to thank each of the contributors for their hard work, patience and dedication during the book's development and for their unique and engaging essays. We would also like to thank Charley Meakin, who was integral to this book's inception and early progression, as well as our copy editor Danielle Shepherd, who helped us to see it through to completion with wonderful professionalism and dedication. Thanks must also go to the Cinema and Television History (CATH) Research Centre at De Montfort University in Leicester, United Kingdom, and to everyone involved in the 2014 conference "Mediated Pasts: Visual Culture and Collective Memory," the inspiration for this collection.

Table of Contents

Introduction

JILLY BOYCE KAY, CAT MAHONEY
and CAITLIN SHAW

As the information age wears on and the accessibility, diversity, and pervasiveness of media exponentially grow, the question of visual culture's role in contemporary retrospective practices becomes ever more apropos. The last ten years have seen a wave of academic research in the area, from theoretical works like José van Dijck's *Mediated Memories in the Digital Age* (2007) to edited volumes like Katharina Niemeyer's *Media and Nostalgia: Yearning for the Past, Present and Future* (2014). The present collection, which works alongside but also builds upon recent publications, is inspired by the conference "Mediated Pasts: Visual Culture and Collective Memory" held at De Montfort University in Leicester, United Kingdom, in June 2014. Headed by keynote speaker Amy Holdsworth, author of *Television, Memory and Nostalgia* (2011), the conference considered the dynamics at play between popular visual culture, history, nostalgia, and memory in journalistic, filmic, televisual, and artistic contexts.

The aim of this collection is to further explore some of the key questions raised at the conference, around the intersections between memory, history, and varied manifestations of nostalgia across multiple media outlets. While debates around mediation and contemporary relationships to the past are not new, they have thus far most often been divided by medium; it is this division that this book seeks to complicate through its consideration of multiple media forms. The emphasis in the scholarship on media and memory has tended to be on period and historical fiction cinema, in part due to the broad impact of work published in the late 1980s and early 1990s by theorists like Fredric Jameson (1991), which saw the postmodern tendency to imitate past styles and modes in period cinema as signaling the receding value of "genuine historicity" (Jameson, 1991, p. 18) in the era of late-capitalist commodification.

2   Introduction

In their introduction to the edited volume *On Media Memory: Collective Memory in the New Media Age* (2011), Oren Meyers, Motti Neiger and Eyal Zandberg address the disproportionate favoring of period screen fiction in academic work, arguing that the notion of "imagined collective memory" has been more traditionally associated with "fictional outlets" and has not been sufficiently investigated in areas like journalism and documentary, which are considered "closely related to 'true' historiography" (2011, p. 7). While work has certainly been done on the interplay between memory and television news, including that of Hayden White (1996) and Andrew Hoskins (2001), more often there is a tendency to align non-fiction media genres with "history," linear time, and facticity, while cinematic fiction is seen to affiliate more easily to the subjective and affective qualities of "memory."

While cinematic texts have enjoyed a privileged position in this regard, it is increasingly the case that important academic work is emerging on the relationships between television, memory, affect, and intimacy. Television has historically been a medium embedded and experienced in the domestic sphere—and indeed, this continues largely to be so, despite the profound technological transformations of recent years. Scholars of television have conducted empirical and theoretical research that has consistently underlined the inextricability of the medium from the histories, structures, and textures of everyday domestic life, both in a material and symbolic sense (see, for example, Spigel, 1992; Silverstone, 1994). Furthermore, Helen Wheatley (2007, p. 2) has pointed out how, within television studies, research has long attended to questions of temporality; the foundational importance of Raymond Williams' (1974) concept of "flow" attests to the centrality of time and temporality in studies of the medium. While television has often been dismissed or derided in academic and journalistic discourse as a medium that works against the possibility of memory— and even as one that induces cultural amnesia—scholars such as Holdsworth have argued that these accounts are reductive, and instead point to more complex, nuanced, and generative relationships between television and memory. As such, television as an object of analysis, and television studies as a mode of analysis, together provide a particularly rich terrain for the study of memory, allowing specific insights into the realms of intimacy, domesticity, and the gendered temporalities of the everyday. For example, Hazel Collie's (2013) work on the memories of women viewers in Britain suggests that television should not be understood as undermining memory, but rather as generative of, and entwined with, the recollection of events across the life course. However, notwithstanding these valuable interventions into the field, the assessment of Meyers, Neiger and Zandberg remains fair: special attention continues to be paid to period screen fictions, possibly because these productions so explicitly recall, reorganize, and reassess familiar pasts. This unevenness can also be understood as part of broader context in which cultural value and historical significance are ascribed to cinematic period fiction texts and genres, in contrast to the texts of television, newspapers, and magazines, which are persistently associated with the quotidian, the ephemeral, and the forgettable.

In *On Media Memory*, the editors' response to this unevenness in focus is to prioritize questions of memory in non-fiction media. While this works valuably toward balancing the field of research, it nonetheless continues to encourage division and to discourage analyses into intersections of and exchanges between fiction and non-fiction media. We believe that considering such junctures and interactions—not just between fiction and non-fiction media but also between films, television, online media, print media, visual art, video games, and other visual cultures—is crucial. As the media continue to converge, fictional stories more and more often unfold across a variety of media platforms, current events now develop rapidly and simultaneously across online, televisual, and print media, and factual entertainment genres such as reality television increasingly take on the "scripted" qualities of fiction. It is therefore exceedingly important to recognize the ways in which visual media co-exist and are explicitly or implicitly in dialogue with one another. The impacts of these intersections on retrospective and memory practices demand consideration, and some literature is beginning to do so; noteworthy examples include Jerome de Groot's *Consuming History: Historians and Heritage in Contemporary Popular Culture* (2008), which considers contemporary uses of history in a variety of mediated contexts, and Niemeyer's aforementioned collection *Media and Nostalgia*, which includes several case studies from both fiction and non-fiction media.

The present work continues this project, with case studies examining mediations of the past in fiction and documentary cinema, dramatic and journalistic television, online media, magazines, visual art, museums, and ephemera. Several essays also explore the interplay between media: between period film and visual art; traditional mass media and online platforms; classic cinema and contemporary documentary production; television culture and gendered magazine culture; and television archives, television news, and the museum.

In addition, this collection embraces different facets of retrospection. Rather than focusing solely on fact-focused histories, on the more subjective territories of memory, or on the daydreams and commodities that form the worlds of nostalgia, heritage, and retro, *The Past in Visual Culture* reflects on their interrelatedness. We understand visual media concurrently as carriers and producers of history and memory, receptacles of and channels for nostalgic yearning, and participators in the heritage and retro industries. This necessarily involves recognizing ongoing debates around the place of history, memory, and nostalgia in the visual media. The position of "history" has long been contested in the context of media cultures; as mass purveyors of known and new histories, the media participate in and highlight the processes of selection, exclusion, and invention inherent in any retelling of previous events. In doing so, they draw criticism from some historians for their lack of factual integrity, and praise from others (see, for instance, Rosenstone, 1995; White, 1996) for their ability to deconstruct and reassess existing historical narratives and to prevent false narratives from developing. This collection does not seek to resolve such contestations and debates, but rather to hold these positions in productive tension throughout the diverse themes and essays of the volume. In doing so, we seek to foreground the media as perhaps the key site of contemporary memory practices.

As producers and recyclists of memories on a global scale, the media call into question how we define memory. The media increasingly reach into the most intimate zones of our lives, so that they are deeply imbricated in everyday experience; they are therefore inescapably implicated in the productions and recollections of biographical and personal memory (see, for example, O'Sullivan, 1991). This begs one to ask whether individual memories can be distinguished from so-called collective memories and, if so, how we define "collective." The notion of "collective memory" as it may or may not pertain to mediation has been contested; Allison Landsberg (2003), for instance, regards it as a "geographically specific" way to "reinforce and naturalize a group's identity" (2003, p. 149), and therefore different from what she calls "prosthetic memory": the recollection of events experienced only through mediation, made possible by "new technologies of memory on the one hand and commodification on the other" (2003, p. 146). Hoskins instead sees the meaning of the "collective" as changing, arguing that it is now "forged, or at least *mediated*, at a global level" (2001, p. 334). In a world where it is possible to posit or conceptualize a *global* collective memory, the ideas, values, and perspectives expressed in mediations and remediations with a transnational reach demand reflection.

Finally, as outlets for cultural longing, and producers and distributors of heritage and retro commodities, the media have provoked seemingly endless debates around the meaning and value (or lack thereof) of nostalgia. Significant discrepancies exist around conceptualizations of nostalgia; Paul Grainge (2000) usefully divides these into those that regard it as a "mood," or a socio-cultural desire brought on by present insecurities for a more authentic, sincere, and stable past, and those that theorize it as a "mode," or the stylistic by-product of "a world of media image, temporal breakdown, and cultural amnesia" (2000, p. 28). "Nostalgia" etymologically suggests a longing for home and was defined this way in early usage (Boym, 2001, p. 3); however, whether it continues to signify emotions of yearning and dissatisfaction when applied to pop cultural reappropriations of past styles, objects, and ephemera is debatable. Also in contention is whether nostalgia must be read as inherently regressive and/or blankly commodified and, if not, to what extent it can be progressive. While early postmodern theorists like Jameson often viewed nostalgia as evidence of capitalism's conquest of historicity, more recent academics have sought to recover nostalgia. Among those who see it as an individual or collective state of being, Svetlana Boym (2001) distinguishes between "reflective" and "restorative" nostalgias, the former progressively reveling in the past's imperfections, temporalizing space, and reflecting on the passage of time, and the latter regressively seeking to metaphorically erase historical time and reinstate the "authentic" past in the present (2001, pp. 50, 44). And among those who theorize it as a stylized commodity, Linda Hutcheon (2000) and Elizabeth E. Guffey (2006) argue that some manifestations of nostalgia (what Hutcheon calls "postmodern nostalgia" and Guffey calls "retro") carry the potential for irony, thus undermining, in Hutcheon's words, "modernist assertions of originality, authenticity, and the burden of the past" (2000, p. 206). As even these few examples betray, nostalgia's definitions are vast, contested, and often contradictory, and the pluralization of its potential meanings must be acknowledged when considering its relationship to mediation. Visual cultures at once recirculate and question nostalgic moods, manufacture and ironize commodified nostalgias, and produce and poke fun at nostalgia for their own "classic" outputs and outdated technologies.

To address the questions and issues raised above, this book is divided into four parts. Parts I and II deal with the depiction of history and memory within visual media, the first focusing on their representation in period screen fiction and the second on their negotiation through non-fiction media. Both Parts I and II explore questions of period and historical representation by examining particular subjects: Part I is specifically concerned with contemporary films and television programs that retrospectively depict the mid–20th century, while Part II considers the depiction and negotiation of feminist histories and memories in factual media. The focused nature of these parts enables the essays to work cohesively alongside one another, highlighting various facets of each debate. Parts III and IV are less concerned with how the past is *portrayed* in media than with how the media themselves *become* objects and sites of history, memory and nostalgia, and how these are recycled to meet present demands. Part III considers this question in the context of contemporary cinematic style, exploring the interplay between digitized societies marked by relentless media recycling, and the tendency in contemporary films toward citing old visual media and media technologies. Media reuse is also at issue in Part IV, but the focus is shifted away from questions of style toward how the media and their archival remnants act as memory capsules to be repurposed for present-day uses, whether in the media or elsewhere.

Together, the four parts work to explore the multiple junctures between history, memory, nostalgia, and the media, whether fiction or non-fiction, and whether acting as a conveyor or a carrier of pasts.

Part I focuses on recently-produced historical and period screen fictions that retrospectively depict the 1940s, 1950s, and 1960s in the United States and Britain. In historical terms, these mid-century decades are acknowledged as periods on the cusp of old and new, marked by oscillations between conservatism and intense social transformation. Simultaneously, the authors recognize each decade's sustained cultural significance as an abstract construct shaped by popular remediations and recirculations. The three essays in Part I consider how period fiction media can act as platforms for renegotiating these pre-conceived decade paradigms, whether in the form of critically intervening in them or of bestowing upon them new meaning that serves the interests of present-day viewers.

Christine Sprengler considers the role of modern art in three 1950s-set American films: *Pleasantville* (Gary Ross, 1998), *Far from Heaven* (Todd Haynes, 2002), and *Mona Lisa Smile* (Mike Newell, 2003). Each film, she suggests, self-consciously draws from what she calls a "retromediated aesthetic" of the Fifties that originates from postwar television and has been recirculated in cinema, raising questions regarding the historical "real" and our mediated access to the past. Sprengler suggests that modern art is aligned with progressiveness in these films, acting as a catalyst to break free from the films' artificial stylization into social awakening.

Debarchana Baruah examines how nostalgia and memory work in and around AMC's 1960s-set television serial *Mad Men* (AMC, 2007–15). She considers the part that the period fiction series plays in both refiguring mediated memories of the Sixties and generating new memories, focusing first on *Mad Men*'s self-reflexive depiction of nostalgic processes and use of intertextual references, and next on the structures of memory embedded in its serial form.

Cat Mahoney backtracks to 1940s Britain and explores representations of the Women's Land Army in three British television series: *Backs to the Land* (Anglia, 1977), *Land Girls* (BBC, 2004) and *Foyle's War* (ITV, 2009). Mahoney considers the space offered by television for re-examining and representing the Forties, a period of considerable social change and shifting gender roles in British history. The programs are discussed in the context of a shift towards re-traditionalization of gender roles in fictional television, as well as towards a wider post-feminist media climate.

Part II explores relationships between history and memory in non-fiction media, with each essay taking the mediation of feminism as an example. The authors reveal the complex and uneven temporalities at play in the "storying" of gender politics and the feminist movement(s). The three essays in this part attest to the ways in which non-fiction media texts are not simply documentary "evidence" of feminist histories; they point to the power relations that are inherent in the visualization and mediation of feminism. Visual culture can thus be understood as a site of intense contestation around the production of memory, marked by discursive struggles over what kinds of stories are told, in which media spaces, and about whom. Moreover, they point to the ways in which both memory and history are never finally made stable; as such, they also highlight the importance of feminist archives as cultural resources for the vital work of re-theorizing the gender politics of the past, present, and future.

Jilly Boyce Kay seeks to historicize debates around post-feminism by looking back to the little-remembered 1980s British television program *Watch the Woman* (Channel 4, 1985). She argues that the shift to post-feminist discourse in the 1990s cannot be understood as a clean "break" from a previously-untainted collectivist feminism; a reading of *Watch the Woman* in the temporal present reveals the protracted and uneven processes by which neoliberal logics have become "entangled" with feminism in popular discourse.

Claire Sedgwick examines the feminist magazines *Ms.* and *Spare Rib*, attests to the importance of archival research in complicating some of the dominant stories that are told about feminism. Sedgwick draws upon the work of Clare Hemmings (2011) to problematize the narratives that have taken hold about fundamental generational differences between the various "waves" of feminism. As such, she points to the importance of revisiting archival feminist texts to enrich our understanding not only of the recent feminist past, but also of the gender politics of the temporal present.

Kaitlynn Mendes focuses on the global anti-rape movement SlutWalk, detailing how feminist activists have strategically intervened into the production of memories of the movement. While mainstream news media worked up a reductive narrative of the protest movement, focusing on a few scantily clad white women and obscuring the diverse bodies and voices that actually took part in SlutWalks, feminists used the tools available to them through social media to produce what Mendes calls "counter-memories" of their movement. As such, Mendes' essay constitutes an important intervention into the gender politics of archives, charting some of the discursive struggles and power relations that are inherent in the production of "stories" about feminism.

Part III is concerned with shifts in the cultural exchange of memory and nostalgia due to innovations in digital technologies, eased accessibility and recyclability of old media, and the widening space occupied by new media in daily life. The three essays in this part focus on recent popular American and British films that reflect these changes in their expressions of so-called "retromania," cinephilia and techno-nostalgia. These have been widespread cultural phenomena in both the United States and the United Kingdom throughout the 2000s, and are partly understood as by-products of advanced globalization and digitized mediation. While problematic expressions of nostalgic yearning are discussed, the authors also highlight the benefits of recycling and repurposing the media's collectively remembered pasts and defunct technologies in new visual media, reflecting on how they facilitate storytelling, interaction, and shared reminiscence.

Caitlin Shaw examines the British film *Submarine* (Richard Ayoade, 2010) in the context of global "indie" youth culture. She suggests that the film's relatively wide appeal was in part due to its quirky, retro aesthetic: it evokes an un-periodized pastness drawn from disparate media sources, aligning it with other global indie outputs. Simultaneously, Shaw considers how the film's self-aware approach toward both its cited material and its own indie-ness prevents it from coming across as a prefabricated youth product. The film therefore effectively demonstrates visual media recycling's value beyond commodity, as a language for youths in the globalized, participatory present.

Marta Wąsik discusses techno-nostalgia, examining two American films that depict Super 8 DIY filmmaking: *Super 8* (J.J. Abrams, 2011) and *Frankenweenie* (Tim Burton, 2012). Wąsik considers how the now archaic 8 mm home movie format and the films-within-films produced with it—which appear in both Abrams' and Burton's productions—are simultaneously yearned for nostalgically and used to interrogate nostalgic yearning.

Laura Mee looks at the interplay between cinephilia, nostalgia, and memory in the documentary *Room 237* (Rodney Ascher, 2012), which chronicles unusual theories proposed by certain fans of Stanley Kubrick's *The Shining* (1980). Mee is not concerned with the theories but instead with the film's formal appropriation of cinematic footage and depiction of cinematic memory. Discussing how the film both elicits shared memories of cinema and ruminates on the tenuousness of cinematic meaning, Mee reads *Room 237* as an example of how old media can be repurposed to tell new stories.

Part IV considers junctures between memory, nostalgia and mediated spaces, objects and ephemera. The spaces discussed in these essays range from the home to the museum to widely-recognized city landscapes, while objects include photographs, postcards, and others. The ephemera in question for the authors herein constitute iconic archival television footage: collectively familiar mediated images of famous people and significant events. The authors explore intersections and interactions between these. For some essays in this part, at issue is how recycled archival media are repurposed as vessels for history, memory, and nostalgia in new spaces or to new ends. For others, in question is instead how the histories and memories that become attached to spaces, objects, and ephemera are recalled through mediation.

Rowan Aust and Amy Holdsworth discuss what they call the "cavity" left in the BBC's archive after British broadcaster Jimmy Savile was exposed as a pedophile in the months following his death. Footage of Savile, the formerly beloved host of the popular long-running series *Top of the Pops* (1964–2006), had, until the scandal, occupied an integral space in the BBC's archive of reusable material. Aust and Holdsworth examine how the BBC has refigured and expunged Savile from this material in the wake of the scandal, reflecting on the implications of this for public memory and both the public's and the BBC's senses of accountability.

Jo Whitehouse-Hart draws on her wider research project on television and film "favorites" and the ways in which these visual texts can function as aide-memoirs in the production of personal biographies. As such, a discussion of "favorites" inevitably tracks memories into the terrain of life stories, childhood, and the psychosexual realm of the family. Whitehouse-Hart argues for the value of psychoanalytical approaches as a way of complementing—rather than displacing—an emphasis on the social dimensions of memory, drawing on interview material in which film and television texts are evoked in memory, inextricably in negotiation with psychosexual development and biography. She suggests that television, in particular, has special value as a psychosocial resource for memory.

Vanessa Longden considers the role played by cultural memory in the interaction between viewer and subject in Cindy Sherman's *Untitled Film Stills* (1977–80). Longden argues that the recognition of cultural, social, and historical motifs within the images creates a state of misrecognition that leads viewers to falsely identify the stills with specific films or moments in time to which they, in fact, do not belong. Longden uses Sherman's fluid depiction of self and identity to interrogate fixed notions of feminine identity in media and cultural discourses.

Finally, Helen Wood and Tim O'Sullivan discuss the role played by television at the National Space Centre in Leicester, United Kingdom. In the Centre, memories of the moon landing and of space exploration are interconnected with memories both of television broadcasts and, by extension, to the materiality of the television set itself. Examining the museum's exhibits as well as testimonies from visitors who, at the museum's behest, have written their memories of the moon landing on postcards, Wood and O'Sullivan consider television's wider role in public place-making and in the production and reiteration of memory and nostalgia.

References

Boym, S. (2001) *The Future of Nostalgia*. New York: Basic Books.
Collie, H. (2013) "It's Just So Hard to Bring It to Mind": The Significance of "Wallpaper" in the Gendering of Television Memory Work. *Journal of European Television History and Culture* 1 (3), pp. 13–21.

10 Introduction

de Groot, J. (2008) *Consuming History: Historians and Heritage in Contemporary Popular Culture*. Abingdon: Routledge.
Grainge, P. (2000) Nostalgia and Style in Retro America: Moods, Modes and Media Recycling. *Journal of American and Comparative Cultures* 23 (1), pp. 27–34.
Guffey, E. E. (2006) *Retro: The Culture of Revival*. London: Reaktion.
Hemmings, C. (2011) *Why Stories Matter: The Political Grammar of Feminist Theory*. Durham: Duke University Press.
Holdsworth, A. (2011) *Television, Memory and Nostalgia*. London: Palgrave Macmillan.
Hoskins, A. (2001) New Memory: Mediating History. *Historical Journal of Film, Radio and Television* 21 (4), pp. 333–46.
Hutcheon, L. (2000) Irony, Nostalgia, and the Postmodern. In: Estor, A. and Vervliet, R. (eds.) *Methods for the Study of Literature as Cultural Memory*. Atlanta: Rodopi, pp. 189–207.
Jameson, F. (1991) *Postmodernism, or, the Cultural Logic of Late Capitalism*. Durham: Duke University Press.
Landsberg, A. (2003) Prosthetic Memory: The Ethics and Politics of Memory in an Age of Mass Culture. In: Grainge, P. (ed.) *Memory and Popular Film*. Manchester: Manchester University Press, pp. 144–61.
Neiger, M., Meyers, O., and Zandberg, E. (2011) Introduction. In: Neiger, M. et al. (eds.) *On Media Memory: Collective Memory in a New Media Age*. Basingstoke: Palgrave Macmillan, pp. 1–26.
Niemeyer, K. (ed.) (2014) *Media and Nostalgia: Yearning for the Past, Present and Future*. Basingstoke: Palgrave Macmillan.
O'Sullivan, T. (1991) Television Cultures and Memories of Viewing. In: Corner, J. (ed.) *Popular Television in Britain: Studies in Cultural History*. London: BFI, pp. 159–89.
Rosenstone, R. A. (1995) *Visions of the Past: The Challenge of Film to Our Idea of History*. Cambridge: Harvard University Press.
Silverstone, R. (1994) *Television and Everyday Life*. Abingdon: Routledge.
Spigel, L. (1992) *Make Room for TV: Television and the Family Ideal in Postwar America*. Chicago: University of Chicago Press.
van Dijck, J. (2007) *Mediated Memories in the Digital Age*. Stanford: Stanford University Press.
Wheatley, H. (2007) Introduction: Re-viewing Television Histories. In: Wheatley, H. (ed.) *Re-viewing Television History: Critical Issues in Television History*. London: I.B. Tauris.
White, H. (1996) The Modernist Event. In: Sobchack, V. (ed.) *The Persistence of History: Cinema, Television and the Modern Event*. London: Routledge, pp. 17–38.
Williams, R. (1974) *Television: Technology and Cultural Form*. London: Fontana.

PART I

Recent Historical and Period Fictions: Reframing the 20th Century

Modern Art
and Mediated Histories
Pleasantville, Mona Lisa Smile
and Far from Heaven

CHRISTINE SPRENGLER

In the opening scene of *Mona Lisa Smile* (Mike Newell, 2003), Katherine Watson (Julia Roberts) gazes at a slide of Pablo Picasso's *Les Demoiselles d'Avignon* (1907), backlit by the light of dusk through her train car window. She, the "bohemian from California," is en route to Wellesley to teach for the 1953–54 academic year. Katherine's first lecture is an unmitigated disaster. She begins her art history survey class with the Altamira cave painting *Wounded Bison* (12,000–11,000 BCE), only to discover that her students have already memorized the textbook. Shaken but undeterred, she invents a new syllabus structured by three questions: What is art? What makes it good or bad? And who decides? To provoke debate she shows Chaim Soutine's *Carcass of Beef* (1925), an image that elicits disgust from her students. Her colleagues too become increasingly alarmed by her willful disregard for the approved curriculum and issue the directive: "A little less modern art, Ms. Watson." During her performance review they challenge her doctoral thesis that "Picasso will do for the twentieth century what Michelangelo did for the Renaissance." With deep incredulity they ask: "So, these canvasses that they're turning out these days with paint dripped and splotched on them, they're as worthy of our attention as Michelangelo's Sistine Chapel?" Undaunted, she persists with her syllabus and ferries her reluctant class to see a new Jackson Pollock, a scene shot to instill as much awe in us as it does in them (Figure 1).

Eventually, by exposing her students to radical artistic experiments, Katherine starts to get through to them, modernizing their perception of art and, in the process, their views on gender, sexuality and, to a minimal extent,

Figure 1. *Mona Lisa Smile*, Julia Roberts, 2003 (© Columbia/courtesy Everett Collection).

class.[1] She awakens their critical faculties, preparing them for participation in the following decade's social movements. However, that which is touted as highly subversive is often not. One need only ask why Soutine and not Marcel Duchamp's *Fountain* (1917) if she—and the film—truly intended to challenge tradition? And why would her introduction of modern art into the Wellesley curriculum be regarded as so shockingly innovative when Alfred Barr did just that, at Wellesley, decades earlier in 1926? I also cannot help wonder why Pollock awakens in her students a feminist consciousness. The film's logic may indeed enable us to chart a path connecting action painting to feminism, but the route seems just a bit too circuitous.

Whereas art signifies cultural capital, something Wellesley students already possess, modern art signifies what they still lack—a kind of moral or ethical capital. Though defined by *Mona Lisa Smile* as an oversimplified monolith without regard for individual movements, artists, or art historical debates, modern art is invested with transformative potential and presented as the catalytic seed that sprouts the social movements of the 1960s. Indeed, this film suggests that an appreciation for modern art is aligned with advocating for equal rights, supporting the women's movement, civil rights, and gay liberation. This is not unique to *Mona Lisa Smile*, but a strategy employed in other films set in the 1950s or, more accurately, a mass-mediated vision of the decade. More specifically, we see this correlation between modernity in art and progressivism in social attitudes play out, albeit in different ways, both in *Pleasantville* (Gary Ross, 1998) and *Far from Heaven* (Todd Haynes, 2002).

Although *Mona Lisa Smile*, *Pleasantville* and *Far from Heaven* all mobilize modern art to similar ends, the latter two, by virtue of their central formal investments in the mass media of the 1950s, differ from the former in their mediation of art in some marked ways. As such, I will first consider the significance of *Pleasantville*'s and *Far from Heaven*'s aesthetic approaches to the postwar past as well as introduce concerns stemming from the representation of art in film. I will then ask what modern art contributes to the critical potential of films whose investment in cultural memory and history are posed through self-conscious representations of the postwar period.

The 1950s and the "Fifties," to maintain Daniel Marcus' (2004) distinction between the actual historical decade and its mythologized construct, have been productive and provocative across a wide swath of contexts.[2] Representations of this decade—its worlds, events, objects, and figures—first entered the American popular consciousness at the start of the 1970s. Since then, multiple and sometimes conflicting visions have proliferated throughout the nostalgia economy, entrenching a series of now-familiar tropes in television, advertising, and fashion. The popularity of the 1950s/Fifties has certainly waxed and waned during its nearly half-century history. It has emerged in some unexpected contexts and transformed repeatedly to suit cultural need and political will. Visions of the Fifties have adapted to reflect changes to our conceptions of history and cultural memory, changes often brought about by technological innovation in practices of representation and shifting expectations of the role of the past in the present.[3]

While the first wave of Fifties nostalgia, bolstered by films like *American Graffiti* (George Lucas, 1973), entrenched a series of visual tropes with the signifying power to elicit that decade with the curve of a tail fin or spin of a poodle skirt, during the 1980s, the Fifties became increasingly politicized, thanks to Ronald Reagan as president (and actor). It also became more diversified, as Michael Dwyer (2015) reveals in his study of the Fifties in 1970s and 1980s culture.[4] By the 1990s, the Fifties had been subjected to the full gamut of postmodern aesthetic forces from pastiche to parody to irony, which only served to complicate its relation to nostalgia and indeed our understanding of nostalgia itself. At this point, distinctive versions of the Fifties emerged, especially in film and advertising. We encounter a "lounge Fifties" in style magazines, club events and films like *Swingers* (Doug Liman, 1996). A "Leave-It-to-Beaveresque Fifties" prevails, often ironically in its recreation of suburban domesticity in advertising and remakes of 1950s fare. The "McCarthyite

Fifties" includes a group of films that seeks to reveal the conformism of the time: *Fellow Traveller* (Philip Saville, 1991), *Guilty by Suspicion* (Irwin Winkler, 1991) and *Citizen Cohn* (Frank Pierson, 1992). A "rockabilly Fifties" that exceeds the musical origins of the term by slipping into fashion, home décor, and everyday life through a recycling and repair ethic, has enjoyed multiple revivals since the 1990s. These visions of the 1950s are not mutually exclusive and inform, at times, the type at issue here: a "retromediated Fifties."[5]

I have previously discussed the existence of a metacinematic Fifties: a vision of the Fifties based principally on cinema from the 1950s (2011, p. 236). It is a type that strives to generate a deliberately archaic aesthetic, in other words, to look like a film would have looked during the 1950s.[6] By proposing a retromediated Fifties I hope to suggest a broadened scope of media mined, one that includes television and advertising. I also wish to foreground "retro" in this equation, for the set of associations it carries are relevant here. Retro, a term with multiple connotations, as Elizabeth E. Guffey (2006) reminds us, has evolved to describe a particular sort of relationship with the past. It speaks to a focus on the recent rather than distant past and does so in a way unconcerned with revering tradition. It is intent on keeping our consciousness located firmly in the present as we consume its representations. Retro is also about the media of the past, how they shaped the images of the times they captured and how these images continue to be mediated as they circulate through new contexts. As such, retro images make us aware of the nature of representation itself and the technologies upon which they depend for their deliberate archaism.

Retro can also lead to realizations beyond the simple acknowledgment that an image references the past. Guffey (2006) looks to Raphael Samuel (1996) and argues for retro's capacity to function as an "unofficial form of knowledge" (p. 17). That is, retro's irreverent adaptations and play with "historicist fantasy" still have something to teach us about cultural memory and the present. Similarly, for Philip Drake (2003), retro relies on a set of well-defined codes that function metonymically to produce a "structure of feeling" and is "less concerned with historical accuracy than with a playful deployment of codes that connote pastness" (p. 188). Drake admits a resemblance between his conception of retro and Fredric Jameson's "nostalgia film," but argues that the latter "describes the mode of engagement between film performance and audience" while the former describes the film texts themselves (p. 188). This insistence on the absence of a "claim for historical or archival truth" and tendency to preserve a distinction between retro and nostalgia also marks Dwyer's definition. For him, retro functions foremost as a representational practice dependent on a set of familiar cultural signifiers and one that can lead to nostalgia (Dwyer, 2015, p. 9). However, he too suggests that retro and nostalgia ought not be conflated. Although I'm less inclined to divorce the two, owing in part to my belief that nostalgia, as Grainge (2002) argues, can function as both a mood and aesthetic mode, I do want to preserve the (sometimes implicit) argument that retro is in fact productive, even ana-lytical. Specifically, I want to chart how a retromediated Fifties might engage questions of history and consider what happens when this representational approach contains another representational practice: (modern) painting.

Cinematic representations of the visual arts have garnered steady but not necessarily sustained attention since Lauro Venturi's 1953 essay that sought to classify films on art.[7] Since then, the scope of this research has broad-ened significantly, producing clear favorites with respect to individual films, artists, and theoretical concerns. For instance, film scholars and art historians alike have consistently pursued analyses of artist biopics from Vincent Min-nelli's *Lust for Life* (1955) to Julie Taymor's *Frida* (2002) to challenge, among other things, the myth of artistic (male) genius, artistic creativity, and the nature of representation itself.[8] Likewise, the aesthetic and historical rela-tionship between film and painting has been tracked and surveyed since the birth of the former, resulting in illuminating accounts of reciprocity, conflict, and collaboration. More recently, art institutions—galleries, museums, and art schools—have garnered attention as sites in which past and present collide and through which ideologies of taste are produced. Studies focused on the multifaceted uses of art in film and the diverse relationships cinematically generated between film and other art forms have done much to show us the effects (and affects) of intertextuality, intermediality, and the intermingling of histories of representation with representations of history.[9] Some of these will be called on in the pages that follow in order to complicate our under-standing of how modern art is mobilized in a retromediated world to engage questions about postwar America, the "real," and the role of images in the production of history.

Art, film, and representations of the 1950s/Fifties coincide in various ways in several film and television offerings not addressed here. Biopics, like James Ivory's *Surviving Picasso* (1996), Ed Harris' *Pollock* (2002), Steven Shainberg's *Fur* (2006) about Diane Arbus, and Tim Burton's *Big Eyes* (2014) about Margaret Keane, set at least a portion of their narratives in the 1950s with their artist-figures against a carefully constructed *mise-en-scène* of that period. My concern here is not with films explicitly about art or artists at mid-century, but rather with films in which art plays a pivotal role in narra-tives about something else. Certain television programs also meet such cri-teria, like *Mad Men* (AMC, 2007–15), in which art functions as interior décor, including a preponderance of abstract paintings modeled on various 20th century movements.[10] At times, art becomes the subject of a scene, as in the *Mad Men* episode "The Gold Violin" (2008), which features a discussion of how employees ought to react to their boss' new Mark Rothko.[11] Yet, however rich these examples may be, *Pleasantville* and *Far from Heaven* present the best opportunity to consider modern art's critical and analytical function in otherwise heavily retromediated and overtly fictional realms.

Directed by Gary Ross, a former Clinton and Dukakis speechwriter, *Pleasantville* follows the adventures of two 1990s teenagers as they are unwittingly transported into a black and white 1950s television sitcom. Upon entering this fantasy world Jennifer becomes "Mary Sue" and her brother David, "Bud." Despite their acquisition of a pastel sweater set and a good dose of Brylcreem, respectively, both remain their 1990s selves with 1990s knowledge and (Democratic) values. Predictably, it doesn't take long for them to reject their seemingly utopian environment, to show at what cost such "perfection" is achieved, and to initiate a series of significant transformations affecting gender roles, the expression of sexuality and, implicitly, segregation. The realization of these changes is signaled by the introduction of color, beginning first with the appearance of a single red rose and concluding with the entire town bathed in lustrous, bright hues that evoke a (retromediated) Technicolor palette.[12] Eventually Mary Sue and Bud are celebrated as harbingers of progress for awakening in *Pleasantville's* inhabitants a 1960s social consciousness.[13]

A staunch Democrat, Ross embodies in his sitcom realm the neo-conservative mandates of the 1990s Republican platform, Bush Sr.'s own Fifties-inspired "kinder, gentler America," and thus participates quite directly in contemporary cultural politics. That is, in *Pleasantville*, a retromediated Fifties drawn from the already caricatured lives portrayed in 1950s domestic sitcoms positions this world as wholly unreal and fully fabricated by the political right. From the innocuous soundtrack to the stage-like quality of interior sets to the requisite "Hi honey, I'm home," *Pleasantville* recalls an amalgam of *Leave It to Beaver* (1957–63), *Father Knows Best* (1954–60), and others. It recreates the visual grammar of these series or, at least, what we think we remember from their various revivals and permutations. In *Pleasantville's* lampooning of the Fifties, Grainge (2003) sees not only a pointed response to a Republican sanctioned nostalgia, but also a rebuttal to *Forrest Gump's* (1994) portrayal of the 1960s as marred by an erosion of morals (p. 210). For him, both films are ultimately about the "memory and legacy of the sixties" and while *Forrest Gump* celebrates the Fifties and denigrates the Sixties, *Pleasantville* "plays reflexively with culture war discourse and its constituent politics of memory" (p. 213).

Indeed *Pleasantville* is very much about memory and its changes at the hand of advances in digital technologies of representation. To illustrate this claim, Grainge draws on the work of Andreas Huyssen, Vivian Sobchack, and Jim Collins. Although Huyssen argues that new media has eviscerated history, all three also recognize the ways in which active and reflective historical subjects obsessed with the past have emerged along with new stores of easily accessible memories (Grainge, 2003, p. 204). Such memories, as Grainge—and *Pleasantville*—remind us, are, however, always already mediated. They have been captured on or created for film and television, re-represented, re-circulated, and sometimes redefined. *Pleasantville* suggests that the cultural signifiers of the Fifties we oft encounter, from fashion to furniture, cars to suburban planning designs, colloquialisms to rote domestic practices, are deeply entrenched not necessarily in history, but in media. In fact, so much in *Pleasantville* is a reference to something else. Media practices and cultural products compete with a mélange of allusions to and allegories of historical events, some connected to postwar America (e.g., McCarthyism), others not (e.g., Kristallnacht), continually asking us to trace their lineages and consider their significance in a text on memory. The film thus prompts us to question the extent to which these things are in fact "real" parts of our collective past, especially when juxtaposed with attitudes and practices we now know to have been written out of certain sanitized versions of postwar history and ones which continue to stain our present: racism and patriarchal oppression.

In this array of allusions to other "real" things, art plays an important role. The art directly referenced in *Pleasantville*, including music, literature, and painting, is very much real in the way most other things in the film are not. Indeed, the film goes to great lengths to exclude any direct indications of the outside world by avoiding mention of geography or history.[14] Most references remain at the level of allegory. However, Titian's *Venus of Urbino* (1538), Mark Twain's *Adventures of Huckleberry Finn* (1884), and Gene Vincent's "Be Bop a Lula" (1956), are initially the only things from our world that escape allegory.[15] These cultural objects, which form part of our reality, are often named, carrying with them significant histories (usually of controversy). As the town of *Pleasantville* adjusts to its own evolution, other recognizable texts and songs appear. Painting, however, is singled out to play a more complex role in the film. It exists in multiple forms and locations. It is the subject of debate and provokes impassioned action from supporters and opponents of its expressions. It is also an obsession for one of the key characters in the film.

Bud first introduces art to *Pleasantville* by bringing Bill (Jeff Daniels), the soda shop owner, a survey book of canonical works to nurture his desire to paint. Bill gasps and is rendered speechless as he flips the pages to reveal Masaccio's *Expulsion from Eden* (1425), J.M.W. Turner's *Rain, Steam and Speed—The Great Western Railway* (1844), and Paul Cézanne's *Apples and Oranges* (1899), to name a few. Though both men are unable to pronounce the artists' names—Titian becomes Tight-ee-an—this doesn't seem to matter. Ross' stage directions for this sequence betray his own investment in the art shown. Consider his directions for the *Venus of Urbino*: "Soft, fleshy, in a rich, golden light. She is utterly real and entirely nude. The folds of her flesh almost seem to glow. Faintly, almost imperceptibly, the sound of a rich aria begins to underscore the images. It's so faint you can't be sure you even hear it at all ... like you're hearing it with your eyes" (Ross, 1998, no pagination). Ross' own delight in the sumptuousness of form and desire to exploit its synesthetic potential inform both the framing and identification strategies employed in this sequence. After considering the Masaccio and a Rembrandt self-portrait, Bill turns the book slightly to accommodate the landscape orientation of the Titian, but not far enough, leaving it at a severe angle. The book remains in this position as Bill flips through the remainder of the images, encouraging us to tilt our head and keep it there, generating a kinesthetic response and thus perhaps a kind of somatic identification with Bill.

Yet, despite the awe and reverence we are expected to feel for the art, no one picture remains on screen long enough to properly consider it. Masaccio—responsible for signifying Bill's own rebirth and consciousness—is granted two seconds of screen time, Turner only three, broken into two segments. The inspiration for Bill's cubist Santa is granted the most screen time of six seconds, but 4.5 of those have Bill's head superimposed over it. Consequently, art never remains still. Its inherent stillness is effaced for fear that it, rather than Bill's reverie, becomes the subject of this scene. As Susan Felleman (2006) cautions, "art threatens the seductive flow of the fictional world within the film with a spasm of viewer self-consciousness" (p. 3). It is a moment of stillness in images that otherwise move; it is an image governed by specific modes of viewing and engagement distinct from the type of spectatorship conditioned by the cinematic apparatus. Facilitating reflexivity might seem consistent with *Pleasantville*'s attempt to unravel a particular kind of mass-mediated representation of the Fifties. But here art's potential to facilitate such a thing is not fully realized. Although these paintings speak their own history to the knowledgeable viewer, they remain part of a fluid progression of images that denies their fetishization. That is, while Ross intends for their cultural and historical significance to inform *Pleasantville*'s narrative trajectory, a desire for narrative continuity wins out and the works selected never remain still long enough to think about them as discrete images.

There are two types of art in *Pleasantville* and both are significant. There are the "real" canonical images of Western art presented in the art book.[16] They span several centuries of painting's history, foregrounding works of early modernism and ending with examples that generously predate the film's era. Together, they inspire the second form of art: Bill's "modern" paintings and ones that belong only to the diegesis. However, the consumption of these two different types of art results in two very different narrative consequences: seeing canonical works initiates a personal awakening while seeing Bill's modern paintings initiates violent riots that pit the town's conservatives against the progressives. However, Bill's "progressive" or "modern" art is in many ways an achievement of a much earlier art historical era, while forms of art produced during the actual 1960s are derided by the film. In this way, *Pleasantville* shares much with *Mona Lisa Smile* in its effacement of art's actual history.

Once Bill discovers the joy of painting he does so furiously and without pause. A late-night visit from Betty (Joan Allen) brings him his muse and the two begin an affair. He first paints her portrait (Figure 2) and then a life size nude (inspired by Titian's *Venus of Urbino*) on the front window of his shop. This appalls *Pleasantville*'s conservatives, who are horrified by this vulgar representation of a "fallen" woman. Bill's Venus, and the public response, might remind us of Éduoard Manet's *Olympia* (1863). Like *Olympia*, the reclining and "fallen" Betty stares directly and defiantly at the viewer, a rejection of artistic convention that stirred controversy in the 19th century. In fact, Betty's face—her gaze that confronts the horrified townspeople—is the first target smashed by the angry mob. Thus, Bill's heroic defiance of convention was accomplished nearly a century and a half ago. To further confirm the film's conservative stance on art, one need only consider its treatment of an "artwork" accidentally created by Bill and Bud that might well have found a place among the "junk" sculptures of the Assemblagists of the late 1950s and early 1960s.[17]

Figure 2. *Pleasantville,* Joan Allen, Jeff Daniels, 1998 (© New Line/The Kobal Collection/Nelson, Ralph Jr/Art Resource).

Following the riots, the progressives collaborate to fix the damage to Bill's soda shop by piling sections of an old white picket fence and other debris over an opening. Bud joins Bill outside and the two stand silently for a moment, admiring their repairs. Bud then jokingly comments: "This is good, just do it?" The two men share a laugh at the prospect of this being art. Clearly, this is stretching the limits of what art ought to be. For Bill, art is representational, a personal expression of his desires, and, unfailingly, as colorful as possible. While Bill's "modern" art functions as one of the key catalysts that brings to *Pleasantville* an awareness of various social concerns, that actual art of the 1960s has no place in this newly progressive world. Indeed, Bill's first overtly political use of art also alludes to practices of a much earlier time. Dismayed by the new mayoral code of conduct restricting paint colors to black, white and grey, he creates a colorful mural for the outside wall of the police station to commemorate the town's struggles: the book burning, lover's lane, rock and roll, etc. The style, subject, and act itself recalls the political murals of the early 20th century, in particular those by Diego Rivera. Thus, yet again, Bill's artistic evolution celebrates the achievements of a much earlier era.

Pleasantville's collection of different types of art generates what Brigitte Peucker calls "intermedial layering." For her, "intermedial layering" makes us aware of the ontological differences between media in a way that "produce[s] an accumulation of textualities that aspires to the status of things" (Peucker, 2007, pp. 14–15). In other words, it reveals differences between representational practices and the distinctiveness of their materiality. We are prompted to acknowledge not only what painting, film, or sculpture conveys, but also how each makes "contact with the real" (ibid., 2007, p. 26).[18] The "real" for Peucker is multifaceted, grounded in theorizations by Kracauer, Bazin, Foster and others. Her interest is not in historically shaped "realisms," documentary images, or claims about the inherent unrepresentability of the real (ibid., 2007, p. 1). Instead, she focuses on film's indexicality, how "the film image itself is both material and referential, and the myriad ways in which the real is suggested on film" (ibid., 2007, pp. 1–2). In this way, art provides its own contact with history in a way that plays off other strategies of historical engagement adopted by films like *Pleasantville*. That is, while the retromediated Fifties constructed through the domestic sitcom world prompts one way to think about the generation, preservation, and circulation of memory, art offers another through recourse to its materiality. It is through this quality, and our acknowledgment that it exists in history (and as history) that we are encouraged to think about the past, the modes of its representation, and our access to it.

Although we know canonical works to be material components of history, the film does much to endow Bill's works with the same status by giving them the capacity to initiate change and memorialize its effects, and through the selection of material substrates on which his images appear. In other words, the realness/thingness of Bill's art is emphasized in several ways. First, his initial encounter with art in a book—and thus a set of representations twice removed from its referents—is contrasted with the transformation of his soda shop into an art studio where the tools to make art (paint, brushes, canvasses) remind us of the process by which images are physically created. Second, the material substrates of his paintings are called out in several scenes. His Betty as Venus is painted on glass, a vulnerable surface easily shattered by the reactionary mob. The slow-motion destruction of this image foregrounds its materiality by focusing our attention on the shards that fly through the air. Bill's response to next paint on the brick wall of the police station speaks of his desire for his work to acquire permanence. In this case, the painted image is a record of the town's history, a mural that bears historical witness and stands testament to events that changed life in *Pleasantville*.

Peucker's claims about film's indexicality lead us to one final consideration about *Pleasantville*'s engagement with history and the real, this time prompted by its general aesthetic appearance. The cinematographic look mobilized in *Pleasantville* demands classification as overtly artificial, as "not real" by virtue of its entrenchment in the visual language of postwar television and its marked distance from the cinematic "realisms" that have helped shape our expectations of mediated realities. However, it is "real" insofar as it registers the aesthetics of a particular type and genre of entertainment media— televised domestic sitcoms—from a distinct period. In this way, it gives us a type of access to a real historical past.[19] And while a primarily aesthetic recreation does not lay claim to historical truth as we might conventionally understand it (if we are first even willing to admit the possibility of such a thing), it enables us to think about what information and knowledge can be gleaned from an aesthetic strategy. In *Pleasantville*, this may not extend much beyond acknowledging the affective and analytical force of certain cinematographic strategies or the pastness of black and white and its complex set of ideological meanings that range from nostalgia to tradition to history to authenticity.[20] However, through *Far from Heaven*'s precisely calibrated Sirkian palette, one that makes use of color in self-conscious and sometimes decidedly artificial ways, even that which is ostensibly fake points to things that are substantively "real," including the significance of such past practices and the emotional truths that find grounding in historical circumstances. Or, as Geoffrey O'Brien (2002) puts it, *Far from Heaven*'s "path of conscious artifice leads toward a tragic sense of reality" (p. 152).

Set in 1957, *Far from Heaven* stars Julianne Moore as Cathy Whitaker, a suburban housewife who becomes attracted to her black gardener, Raymond Deagan (Dennis Haysbert), and whose husband Frank (Dennis Quaid) initiates an affair with a younger man. Written and directed by Todd Haynes, *Far from*

Heaven pays tribute to the films and film style of Douglas Sirk, director of *Magnificent Obsession* (1954), *All That Heaven Allows* (1955), and *Imitation of Life* (1959). Initially dismissed as a purveyor of the most excessive brand of Hollywood melodrama, Sirk was eventually outed in the pages of *Cahiers du Cinéma* as a great ironist and astute critic of postwar America. His critiques were often effected visually, as a way to subvert the Production Code but also to channel his fascination with the image. In his 1950s films, he transformed the surface of the screen into a visual spectacle of garish and complimentary color in order to unsettle the audience, to facilitate critical distance, and to suggest that something might be a little off in the worlds he represented. Yet, *Far from Heaven*, as an offering of 21st century film culture, could and did explicitly address the once closely regulated triumvirate of sexuality, race, and gender. Production Code era films could only ever surreptitiously hint at homosexuality, interracial relationships, and sex or at the possibility that a desire to break with rigidly prescribed gender roles was healthy and acceptable. *Far from Heaven* foregrounds and narrativizes what Sirk could not, but does so using Sirk's distinct palette that confirms for the spectator that what Haynes offers is, at heart, a Fifties melodrama.

In fact, Haynes claimed he was not interested in the actual 1950s but only with Sirk's cinematic vision of America at mid-century. He found his "Hartford, Connecticut" setting in Patterson, New Jersey, because, to him, the old downtown core looked like a Hollywood sound stage. He aimed to make locations resemble sets and to create what he called a "hermetically sealed fictional realm" (Haynes, 2002, no pagination). This he certainly managed to achieve. Like *Pleasantville*, *Far from Heaven* makes virtually no reference to the historical 1950s, to any political reality or event, to popular media or personalities. However, there are two exceptions to this almost wholesale exclusion when we recognize something in Cathy's world that also belongs to our own: Eisenhower and modern art. Both are significant. Whereas Eisenhower functions synechdocally for conservative America, modern art, featured in an exhibition staged at the Hartford Cultural Center, is aligned with the impulses of the 1960s social movements.

The look of the "Modern Art Show" was precisely crafted according to Haynes' detailed color charts, ones signaling a clash of complementary cool and warm tones to inform the mood of the scene. At first glance, a distinct coolness permeates the gallery space, achieved in part with bluish grey walls, blue streams of light, dark suits worn by men and various shades of dark, dull greens worn by virtually all women in the scene. Cathy, too, is dressed in dark green but, as will become significant later, her outfit boasts goldenrod-colored trim and buttons on its jacket and goldenrod pleats nestled in its skirt. Initially she appears to fit in, to belong to Hartford's bourgeois social set. However, traces of this warm hue hint at an underlying difference.

Near the beginning of the scene, a tracking shot crosses the room to show visitors looking at a series of green and blue abstract artworks. The camera comes to a rest on Cathy engrossed in a painting composed of red and orange patches. The flash of a camera and Mrs. Leacock's observation, spoken as a newspaper headline, interrupts her rapt attention: "Wife of Hartford executive caught communing with Picasso?"[21] This reinforces, yet again, Cathy's status as image, and one among many in this particular scene. It also sets up the appearance of Raymond, announced through the first substantial intrusion of warm color. As Cathy turns to face Mrs. Leacock, color cues us to notice Raymond and Sarah, his daughter. They are bathed in a diagonal band of orange-red light streaming in through the stained glass window. Once they catch Cathy's eye, she excuses herself, walks toward them and directly into the warm, red light. As she does, the goldenrod sections of her dress glow orange, outshining the dull dark green that initially signaled her connection to the other visitors. In the presence of Raymond and Sarah—who also wears the same color trim on her hat and collar—Cathy's tentative signifiers of difference are illuminated (Figure 3). That Raymond brings out what is purportedly her "true" and warm inner essence is confirmed by the painting behind them. Positioned centrally in the frame and flanked by Cathy and Raymond, this painting functions as a visual analogue for the staging: the taller black figure clearly mirrors Raymond while the shorter red figure functions as a substitute for Cathy.[22]

In some ways this image suggests a type of *tableau vivant*, if we are to accept Peucker's (2007) plea to consider this practice in an expanded sense and beyond the simple staging of well-known paintings by actors (p. 31). At this moment, through Cathy and Raymond's positioning and stillness while in conversation, they "perform" the painting that hangs behind them. It is a moment of intermedial intensity as Peucker suggests is the province of *tableaux*, drawing attention to art, registers of stillness and time in both art and film, and Raymond and Cathy as representations, both cinematic and historic insofar as they stand in for the often "tragic realities" of American postwar interracial relationships. In this way, "[t]ableaux in their different permutations exemplify the merger of representation with reality with which we are concerned here insofar as they represent the 'real' body as an arrested image in a variety of scenarios" (ibid., 2007, p. 14). But as much as this moment reminds us of Cathy and Raymond as representations, it paradoxically also invests them with materiality and a heightened degree of "realness." This is the product of the *tableau* and painting inhabiting the same space and the comparison this allows between an image that is expressionistic and framed for an art show, and the physical, living bodies that stand before it. One result of this twist on the conventional *tableau vivant* is a heightening of what Steven Jacobs (2011) calls their "mysterious density" and capacity to

Figure 3. *Far From Heaven*, Julianne Moore, Dennis Haysbert, Jordan Purer, 2002 (© Killer Films/The Kobal Collection/Genser Abbot/Art Resource).

"create blockages in the flow of a narrative film that result in a kind of enigma" (p. 95). And indeed it is through this oscillation between representation and the real that the histories represented by Cathy and Raymond and by modern art itself flood in. The painting here is to be read as progressive, not only in formal terms, but also because of what it represents—an interracial relationship. But in its uncertain temporal relation to Cathy and Raymond's reality, the viewer is left to wonder if it commemorates that moment of intimacy or prefigures their future. Does it freeze a moment about to be awakened into action by a narrative arc that resolves with a "happily ever after" ending? Or does it document the height of their closeness and suspend in time one possible future that will sadly never come to be?

Whereas in this shot, art visually reinforces the narrative, in the next shot, art becomes the subject of the narrative in a way that foregrounds the potential for a non-representational visual language to provoke deeply felt emotional responses. Following a short sequence outside the gallery, Cathy and Raymond immerse themselves in a Miró and in conversation about its emotional hold on them. Cathy says of this "Mira" (as she falters, recalling Bill's mispronunciation in *Pleasantville*), "I don't know why, but I just adore it, the feeling it gives." To this Raymond replies as the camera scans the painting:

"No, no, actually it confirms something I've always wondered about modern art, abstract art. That perhaps it's just picking up where religious art left off, somehow trying to show you divinity. The modern artist just pares it down to the basic elements of shape and color. But when you look at that Miró, you feel it just the same." Their reverie is rudely interrupted by a loud cackle. The scene abruptly cuts to an elderly woman commenting to Eleanor: "To tell the truth, I've always preferred the work of the Masters. Rembrandt, Michelangelo." "Master," of course, has a double meaning here, evoking the history of slavery and the racism that permeates Hartford's still segregated society. It speaks to a binary that separates white and black, conservative and progressive and, in the realm of art, representational and abstract.[23]

Though the film's visual pastness distances the art show patrons' racism from the present, certain strategies encourage an awareness of the contemporary social and cultural lenses through which we interpret the action on the screen and evaluate the bigotry of Haynes' Hartford against that which persists today. What maintains our consciousness of the present is Raymond's assessment of modern art. His comments are as relevant to what we see as they are to what he sees. In other words, Raymond's observations on the capacity for abstract forms and colors to elicit deeply felt emotion seem as much directed toward the various *mise-en-scènes* he and Cathy inhabit as they do to the Miró. In this scene especially, the clash of warm and cool colors oppose passion and compassion to malice and callousness, and help to articulate the resolve with which Raymond and Cathy seek comfort in each other in the face of social prejudice. Color, costume, art, and light collaborate to elicit both sympathy and empathy for them.

A strong emotional response is not the only thing that abstract forms evoke. Visual signifiers, practices, and codes can be entrusted with several functions simultaneously, and this complexity does not necessarily compromise the force of the meanings or sentiments they generate. The use of Miró is a testament to this. Although the specific painting featured here is, as Celeste-Marie Bernier (2007) reminds us, a response to the traumas of war, appealing to Miró more generally speaks to Cathy and Raymond's relationship (p. 124). Miró was not a formal member of the Surrealists, but his paintings mobilized sexual symbolism in an effort to delve into the fantasies of the unconscious, prompting André Breton to proclaim that he might be "the most Surrealist of us all" (Breton cited in Matthews, 1991, p. 152). Miró's link to Surrealism and thus to sex, fantasy, and unconscious desires is highly relevant to the palpable sexual tension between Cathy and Raymond and to their practice of displacing their passion for each other onto art. Miró's abstract composition does more than evoke their passions or communicate the affective power that non-representational codes might yield. It also reminds us that color and form can function as the source of particular, historically specific meanings that enrich a scene conceptually, offering not just visual, but analytical pleasures.

Far from Heaven's retromediated Fifties certainly qualifies it as a paradigmatic postmodern nostalgia film. But it also shows why indulging in visual spectacle and obsolete, non-representational media codes does not preclude a critical exploration of the past and present or means by which we access and understand history. In fact, *Far from Heaven* does more than simply reveal how both tendencies might coexist. The very same visual elements that indulge in the pastness of cinema are also complicit in the film's penetrating critique of how racism, homophobia, and patriarchal oppressions permeate the fabric of everyday life, structuring the relationships between ordinary people in postwar and present-day America. Visual spectacles fashioned by vibrant color palettes, elaborate set designs and extravagant dresses are not set in opposition to a narrative critique of the 1950s or the Fifties. Their role in the film is far more complex and one that acknowledges the postwar discourses in which they were implicated and how, during the 1950s, they could very well have been mobilized to challenge their authorized role in the expression of conspicuous consumption. As such, and as Lynne Joyrich (2004) argues, *Far from Heaven* "thinks through the media, making media forms not only objects of analysis but modes of analysis, mediums of thought and reflection themselves" (p. 191).

Given the persistence of the present enabled by the film's retromediated Fifties, the histories told visually through costume and color also encourage us to evaluate our contemporary moment against Haynes' Hartford. *Far from Heaven* does not mobilize the Fifties to show how far we have come, to tell us not to worry because the 1960s are just around the corner. On the contrary, its deeply unhappy ending betrays a pessimistic view of the present in which social conventions, pressures, and prejudices continue to marginalize and oppress. Cathy, Raymond, and Frank may be trapped in a hermetically sealed fictional realm, but it seems we might just be trapped there with them.

As are David and Jennifer too. And for all of us, art shows us the way out. In *Pleasantville* and *Far from Heaven*, modern and abstract art align with an awakening social consciousness that aids in an escape from the Fifties while simultaneously reminding us of its constructedness. The power of form is only heightened by its situation in a retromediated aesthetic—one drawn from postwar television, the other Sirkian cinema. And although each palette reads as overtly artificial in its own way, it is in part at the behest of such an aesthetic that we confront the "real," questions about our access to the past through representations, and our relationship to history with a self-consciously critical gaze. The progressiveness inherent in the "modern" of modern art may at times oversimplify and homogenize its myriad strands, overestimate what it achieved, and miscalculate when it did so. But art in these films nevertheless functions as a catalyst for change, consciousness, and collective action. These films remind us what art can do and what film as art can reveal about cultural memory and its mediations, images, and their circulations. While modern art purports to look forward and retromedia backward, the complex temporalities each engages—separately and together— keep our sights set on how the past is constructed, used, and remembered.

NOTES

1. Race, as an issue, is conspicuously absent in this film.

2. Others who preserve this distinction include Michael Dwyer (2015) and Mary Caputi (2005). Caputi aligns those who believe in the 1950s as a knowable, historical entity with right leaning politics while those who prefer to characterize that era as "the Fifties," a mythological construct, with left leaning tendencies. See especially Chapter 1, "The 'Fifties,' an American Metaphor." I have argued elsewhere (2009) that this distinction between the 1950s and Fifties is not always or necessarily a tidy one but rather should be seen as a dialogical and reciprocal relationship that has been nurtured since the start of the 1950s in popular and political cultures.

3. As Mary Caputi (2005) points out, the 1950s continue to "bristle with an array of ideological connotations, a swirl of aesthetic resonances, a battery of moral implications so highly charged and emotionally laden that any mention of the decade in the current context far exceeds literal, historical references" (p. 1).

4. Dwyer considers the Fifties' emergence in expected sites like film, but also its less well-known and analyzed incarnations in exercise programs, chain restaurants, music videos, video games, and popular fiction.

5. Nor is this list exhaustive or definitive. These types continually evolve and change over the course of their own specific histories.

6. For an extended discussion of deliberate archaism, see Le Sueur (1977). In short, the term describes the practice of creating new images to resemble older ones by mimicking the aesthetics of old media technologies (e.g., black and white, sepia, Technicolor, etc.).

7. Venturi offers four categories: (1) films for which prop art was created; (2) films that addressed the narrative content of art; (3) films about the historical and technical aspects of art; and (4) films that mobilized specific artworks as narrative catalysts. As we shall soon see, all four categories define *Pleasantville*.

8. See, for example, Pollock (2000), Nead (1995) and Olsin Lent (2007).

9. Some of the earlier studies include Hayward (1988), Walker (1993), Dalle Vacché (1996), and Sykora (2003).

10. Although *Mad Men* begins in 1959, a Fiftiesness persists for the first several seasons thanks in large part to Don Draper's (Jon Hamm) cultural and personal entrenchment in the 1950s.

11. This scene involves Ken Cosgrove (Aaron Staton) describing Bert Cooper's (Robert Morse) Rothko and modern art's power in a way that recalls a pivotal scene featuring a Miró in *Far from Heaven*, a scene that I will consider shortly.

12. In some ways this suggests an aesthetic shift from television to film, even if this is unlikely to have been Ross' intention. And with this shift, we see a move from a heavily regulated medium to one that, even under Production Code conditions, arguably allowed for more moments of subversion than television.

13. In fact, the film ends with Fiona Apple's 1998 cover of The Beatles 1969 song, "Across the Universe." As such the 1960s and film's present converge at the very end.

14. The outside world only comes into *Pleasantville* at the very end, after everything has been colorized. Only then does a bus stop appear suggesting an elsewhere as well as footage on televisions featuring historic landmarks like the Sphinx, the pyramids at Giza, and the Eiffel Tower.

15. *Leave It to Beaver* also appears on the television set, but only in a quick flash and is not identified or acknowledged by the characters.

16. While the art works may be "real," the art book *The World of Art* by Edward Bissell was a prop created for the film.

17. In fact, assemblage and the use of found objects in a manner that resonates with Bill and Bud's "repairs" date back to the early 20th century and includes practitioners like Picasso, otherwise revered by Bill.

18. This is also Felleman's (2014) concern, namely the role that original artworks as authentic objects with provenance play in a film.

19. Of course *Pleasantville* used a complex digital process to create its black and white palette and thus the film's aesthetic is not a perfect recreation of the look of postwar American television.

20. See, for example, Grainge's (2002) account of the significance of black and white in contemporary popular culture.

21. Incidentally, the stage direction called for Picasso's *Weeping Woman* (1937), a work that mirrors the color palette for this scene (Haynes, 2002, no pagination). The blue of the central area of the composition is precisely the shade on the walls of the gallery and the deeper blue, red and yellow are a match to the colors of light streaming in through the windows. Unfortunately, Picasso never made the final cut. It is left to the red and orange abstract composition situated behind Cathy to foreshadow the warmth to come.

22. Dialogue early on in the film informs us that Cathy's friends used to call her "Red" in college, not only because of her red hair, but also because of her political leanings.

23. The relationship between the film's cinematographic palette and the abstract art works featured has been the subject of some debate. Amelia de Falco (2004) suggests that there is a strong distinction between Miró's paring down of color and shape, as Raymond explains, and the film's own excessive use of color (p. 33). Bernier (2007) disagrees and reminds us that many "modern and abstract artists frequently relied upon an explosion of 'excessive' color and forms" (p. 127). As such, Haynes is simply replicating the strategies of abstractionists. Bernier also observes that Haynes himself has long been dissatisfied with realism in film and representation in art. For him, both are guilty of "conservative leanings" and "reinscribing normative values and ideologically dominant discourses of oppression in terms of gender, race and sexuality" (p. 125).

References

Bernier, C-M. (2007) "Beyond the Surface of Things": Race, Representation and the Fine Arts in Far from Heaven. In: Morrison, J. (ed.) *The Cinema of Todd Haynes: All That Heaven Allows*. London: Wallflower, pp. 122–31.

Caputi, M. (2005) *A Kinder, Gentler America: Melancholia and the Mythical 1950s*. Minneapolis: University of Minnesota Press.

Dalle Vacche, A. (1996) *Cinema and Painting: How Art Is Used in Film*. Austin: University of Texas Press.

De Falco, A. (2004) A Double-Edged Longing: Nostalgia, Melodrama, and Todd Haynes's Far from Heaven. *Iowa Journal of Cultural Studies* 5 (1), pp. 26–40.

Drake, P. (2003) "Mortgaged to Music": New Retro Movies in 1990s Hollywood Cinema. In: Grainge, P. (ed.) *Memory and Popular Film*. Manchester: Manchester University Press, pp. 183–201.

Dwyer, M. (2015) *Back to the Fifties: Nostalgia, Hollywood Film, and Popular Music of the Seventies and Eighties*. New York: Oxford University Press.

Far from Heaven. (2002) [Film] Directed by Todd Haynes. USA: Killer Films.

Felleman, S. (2006) *Art in the Cinematic Imagination*. Austin: University of Texas Press.

_____. (2014) *Real Objects in Unreal Situations: Modern Art in Fiction Films*. Wilmington, NC: Intellect Books.

Fiona, Apple. (1998) [CD] *Across the Universe*. USA: New Line Records.

Grainge, P. (2002) *Monochrome Memories: Nostalgia and Style in Retro America*. Westport: Praeger.

_____. (2003) Colouring the Past: "Pleasantville" and the Textuality of Media Memory. In: Grainge, P. (ed.) *Memory and Popular Film*. Manchester: Manchester University Press, pp. 202–19.

Guffey, E. E. (2006) *Retro: The Culture of Revival*. London: Reaktion.

Haynes, T. (2002) [DVD] *Far from Heaven Director's Commentary*. USA: Killer Films.

Hayward, P. (ed.) (1988) *Picture This: Media Representations of Visual Arts and Artists*. London: John Libbey.

Jacobs, S. (2011) *Framing Pictures: Film and the Visual Arts*. Edinburgh: Edinburgh University Press.

Joyrich, L. (2004) Written on the Screen: Mediation and Immersion in Far from Heaven. *Camera Obscura* 19 (3), pp. 186–219.

Le Sueur, M. (1977) Theory Number Five: Anatomy of Nostalgia Films: Heritage and Methods. *Journal of Popular Film* 6 (2), pp. 187–97.

Mad Men. (2008) [TV] "The Gold Violin." Series 2, Episode 7. American Movie Classics, September 7.

Marcus, D. (2004) *Happy Days and Wonder Years: The Fifties and the Sixties in Contemporary Cultural Politics*. New Brunswick: Rutgers University Press.

Matthews, J.H. (1991) *The Surrealist Mind*. Selingrove: Susquehanna University Press.

Mona Lisa Smile. (2002) [Film] Directed by Mike Newell. USA: Revolution Studios.

Nead, L. (1995) Seductive Canvases: Visual Mythologies of the Artist and Artistic Creativity. *Oxford Art Journal* 18 (2), pp. 59–69.

O'Brien, G. (2002) Past Perfect. Todd Haynes' Far from Heaven—Interview. *Artforum* 41 (3), pp. 152–57.

Olsin Lent, T. (2007) Life as Art, Art as Life: Dramatizing the Life and Work of Frida Kahlo. *Journal of Popular Film and Television* 35 (2): pp. 68–76.

Peucker, B. (2007) *The Material Image, Art and the Real in Film*. Stanford: Stanford University Press.

Pleasantville. (1998) [Film] Directed by Gary Ross. USA: New Line Cinema.

Pollock, G. (2000) Crows, Blossoms and Lust for Death: Cinema and the Myth of van Gogh the Modern Artist. In: Florence, P. (ed.) *Looking Back to the Future: Essays on Art, Life and Death*. London: Routledge.

Ross, G. (1998) [DVD] *Pleasantville Director's Commentary*. USA: New Line Cinema.

Samuel, R. (1996) *Theatres of Memory: Past and Present in Contemporary Culture*. London: Verso.

Sprengler, C. (2009) *Screening Nostalgia: Populuxe Props and Technicolor Aesthetics in Contemporary American Film*. Oxford: Berghahn Books.

_____. (2011) Complicating Camelot: Nostalgia and Deliberate Archaism in Mad Men.

In: Stoddart, S. F. (ed.) *Analyzing Mad Men: Critical Essays on the Television Series*. Jefferson, NC: McFarland, pp. 234–52.

Sykora, K. (2003) *As You Desire Me: Das Bildnis in Film*. Cologne: König.

Venturi, L. (1953). Films on Art: An Attempt at Classification. *Quarterly of Film, Radio, and Television* 7 (4), pp. 385–91.

Walker, J. A. (1993) *Art and Artists on Screen*. Manchester: Manchester University Press.

Mad Men and Memory
Nostalgia, Intertextuality and Seriality in 21st Century Retro Television

Debarchana Baruah

Television is an evocative reference point in domestic spaces and daily lives. Watching a serial television program in an intimate setting on a prolonged routine basis tends to encourage an emotional connection and identification with its characters and, in turn, the formation of televisual memory. The long-running AMC television series *Mad Men* (2007–15), set in 1960s New York, lends itself to this process, creating memories in the present for both the text and the context in which it is viewed. In addition, it evokes 1960s televisual memory through its sets, narrative, and intertextualities, demonstrating retro's dual process of memory-making. *Mad Men* entwines these threads of televisual memory, interweaving the period television iconography and archival footage that form part of collective memory with the everyday personal memories formed by experiencing and interacting with its mediations of the former. In doing so, it creatively weds together memories old and new, cultural and personal; it creates a unique montage of televisual impressions tied together by continuities and dissonance and draws attention to the processes of mediation, selection, and sequencing of cultural memories.

Mad Men can be read as an example of contemporary American "retro," layering intertextual references from "high" and "low" 1960s culture and recalling 1960s cinema and television in its cinematography and stylized sets. Elizabeth E. Guffey traces retro's evolution from 1970s France, in which "*la mode rétro*" referred to art and cinema that resisted standardized narratives of World War II history and repackaged the past in a stylized and detached manner, to its eventual incorporation into American popular culture, where it served "as a shorthand for a period style situated in the immediate postwar years" (Guffey, 2006, pp. 9–10). Over time, the idea of retro has diversified to describe music genres, television, cinema, advertising, visual arts, architecture, design, and fashion, and, as Guffey argues, its temporal focus has broadened to include pasts so recent that they "might seem to have slipped out of sight only yesterday" (p. 17). Guffey suggests that while retro is often thought of as a form of nostalgia, its chief characteristic—its "ironic stance" (p. 20)—distinguishes it from the earnestness of nostalgia. Yet, the interrelations between retro and nostalgia are evolving and dynamic. Particularly relevant to the ideas presented in this essay is Svetlana Boym's (2001) recognition that nostalgic desires are situated at "the very core of modern condition" (p. xvi), and she acknowledges two distinctive forms of nostalgia—restorative and reflective—based on how "one's relationship to the past" is characterized (p. 41). She argues that the former "protects the absolute truth" while the latter "calls it into doubt" (p. xviii). When considered alongside reflective nostalgia, retro cannot be defined in direct opposition to nostalgia, as Guffey suggests it was in the '70s. As nostalgia increasingly accommodates critical stances, retro must be thought to work in conjunction with it.

In this essay, I outline three distinct ways in which *Mad Men* engages with memory. First, it does so textually, evoking memories of the 1960s through its narrative. It is self-conscious and reflectively nostalgic; it recalls but does not idolize. Second, it engages with memory intertextually, invoking the era's cultural artifacts in novel ways that add layers of emotion and interpretation. And third, because of its serial format and long run, *Mad Men* engages with processes of televisual memory, forming its own internal network of new memories in the present. Its mode of representation is definitively retro, maintaining detachment from the standardized iconography of the decade and seeking to challenge its audience's encyclopedic knowledge of history. In this process, the series shifts the focus to an alternative selection of memorable events borrowed from iconic ad campaigns, music, and movies from the '60s. *Mad Men*'s thoughtful integration of old memories and participation in producing new ones, I suggest, have developed new contexts of appreciation for its contemporary audience, facilitating a small memory boom in the present for the 1960s.

The Place That Cannot Be: Dislocation and Yearning in Mad Men

Mad Men follows the lives of wealthy, white advertising executives working at Sterling Cooper, a fictional Madison Avenue agency, throughout the 1960s. Most of these are men who, unhappy in their suburban domestic lives, aim to find meaning through their work, while the series' female characters are comprised of the male executives' bored housewives and of single women who work as secretaries. The agency's white, male elite is modeled on the WASP archetype who resists changes in structures of privilege. They choose to uphold '50s-style conservatism while disregarding the cultural and civil rights movements that are known to have marked the '60s. This unique focal point allows the series to represent and explore the continued preservation of the status quo in insulated pockets of white, upper-class America, conflicting with and challenging narratives of change popularly associated with the '60s. The era remains an insistent presence in the American imagination: it is seen as the cradle of many progressive movements, such as the countercultural movement, the feminist movement, the civil rights movement, the anti–Vietnam War movement, the environmental movement, and the gay rights movement. *Mad Men*, by upholding a contrasting image of conservatism and non-change, reminds viewers of the multiplicities of experience in the 1960s and interrogates the efficacy of these progressive projects.

There is room, among the privileged white enclaves wherein the series' story unfolds, for critical engagement with traditionally gendered institutions and with the subordination of women which happens irrespective of their class position or marital status. The sexism experienced by, and the familial pressures placed on, single (white) women living in places like Manhattan form an important theme, while marriage is shown to provide no refuge. By questioning the sanctity of institutions like marriage and family within a white, mid-century world of privilege, *Mad Men* questions the possibility of finding a sanctuary no matter how far one travels into the past. Still, the series' engagement with the past speaks to the decade's continued symbolic power over the present.

Processes of memory and nostalgia are explored directly in *Mad Men*'s narrative, where characters' yearnings for return are highlighted and often destabilized. This is notable from the first season; in the sixth episode, for instance, Sterling Cooper's creative head Donald Draper (Jon Hamm) approaches Jewish client Rachel Menken (Maggie Siff) in an effort to understand what Israel means to Jewish Americans, hoping for some insight to assist in the agency's ad campaign for Israel Tourism. Menken confesses that she feels closer to her American identity than her Jewish heritage, but explains reluctantly that although Jews have long lived in exile, they value the existence of Israel as a haven. When Draper asks, "Why aren't you [in Israel]?" Menken replies that her life is in New York, adding: "I'll visit but I don't have to live there." She stresses that Israel is more of an idea than a real place for her, and when Draper mentions utopia, she explains that "utopia" had two meanings for the Greeks: "*Eu-topos*, meaning the good place, and *ou-topos*, meaning the place that cannot be" ("Babylon," 2007).

Menken's relationship with Israel functions as a metaphor for contemporary Americans' ambivalent relationship to the early 1960s: as an idealized fantasy, the era at once sustains influence over contemporary American consciousness and is ultimately impossible. The metaphor extends beyond the sequence described above: thematically, dislocation lies at the heart of the series, epitomized by the falling man in the show's title sequence. Characters, in particular, are often displaced. Apart from Menken, these include those more attuned to 1950s values and customs, whether too old to be absorbed or too unwavering to adapt, who find it hard to cope with the rapid changes that mark the new decade. Reflective nostalgia as theorized by Boym often underpins the show's depiction of fractured and dislocated lives; Menken, for example, claims that despite the relevance of Israel for Jewish Americans, she can reconcile her hyphenated identity and negotiate a space between longing and belonging.

To a great extent, the narrative of *Mad Men* focuses on the negotiation of its central characters' longing for past modes of existence and on their eventual need to accept belonging in spaces that differ from what they expected. In a scene in Season 7's "The Strategy" (2014), the three central protagonists of *Mad Men* sit together and enjoy a meal at Burger Chef, reflectively enacting the negotiation between dislocation and yearning and the process of finding a space in between. Draper, Peggy Olson (Elisabeth Moss) and Pete Campbell (Vincent Kartheiser), colleagues at Sterling Cooper, share their awareness of alienation from familial relationships, forming an ersatz family at the Burger Chef table. They discuss archaic notions of the familial dining experience, changes in the traditional composition of the family, and the consideration of a new equation, even though temporary, which enables them to experience the familial warmth that they yearn. Their consolatory understanding of the impossibility of a return to traditional American family structures reassures them in their dislocation. Acknowledgment of ruptures inform a mediation of nostalgic yearning, creating a space which hints at the possibility of belonging.

Occasionally, the typically implicit relationship between dislocation and nostalgia is made explicit. This is true in the first season's final episode, "The Wheel" (2007), which thematically expands on an advertising pitch Draper makes for Kodak. In the pitch, Draper defines nostalgia, calling it "delicate but potent." He describes it as an emotional connection with "home," a transhistorical space that is reassuring and unchanging and where one always belongs, and compares it to a carousel, a carrier that transports us to pasts composed of postcard memories. He comments that nostalgia "takes us to a place where we ache to go again, […] where we know we are loved." The speech, suffused with restorative nostalgia, is accompanied by a slide show filled with compelling images from his own family moments. Moved by Draper's eloquence and artistry, the Kodak clients cancel their meetings with competing agencies.

Yet, Draper's restoratively nostalgic rhetoric contrasts his reality: he has had numerous affairs, of which his wife Betty Hofstadt (January Jones) is aware. The pair have grown distant and Betty has sought psychiatric help. Still, on Draper's train ride home after the pitch, energized by nostalgically revisiting his seemingly happier past and temporarily persuaded by his own rhetoric, he imagines reaching home just in time to accompany his wife and children to her parents' home for Thanksgiving. However, he arrives to find the house empty, undercutting the promise of homecoming. The scene fades and Bob Dylan's "Don't Think Twice, It's All Right" (1963) plays as the credits roll. The widely recognizable song is itself nostalgic for viewers, evoking the sentimentality in Draper's pitch. Yet, if nostalgia is the axis of this episode, the song's opening line is a gesture to the irreversibility of past events that must be taken in stride.

Intertextuality and New Media: Appropriation, Adaptation and Online Participation

The use of "Don't Think Twice, It's All Right" exemplifies the thematic and tonal value of intertextuality to contemporary retro productions. *Mad Men* draws from a wealth of 1960s cultural texts, most prominently pop music, film, and television. These references chart a new way of experiencing the '60s as refracted through a contemporary television program. Pop music plays an essential role in *Mad Men*; although it is primarily used to ground the viewer in a place and time, it also contributes a further dimension of comprehension. On this point Tim Anderson has noted, with reference to *Mad Men*'s use of songs to conclude each episode, that they bring "a tone that provides one final critical dimension to the episode: Punctus contra punctum: the structure to shake out nascent meanings and allowing them to come to fruition" (2011, pp. 80–81). This sometimes manifests as an emphasis on the episode's themes, as a continuation of an ongoing dialogue, or as a counterpoint to the on-screen narrative. As suggested previously, the Bob Dylan song in "The Wheel" foreshadows the impending separation of the Drapers; there is an air of its inevitability given Draper's long absences and the breakdown in communication between him and his wife, and the lyrics confirm this, justifying their eventual parting. In "The Strategy," Draper and his former secretary Peggy Olson admit their mutual regret in not sustaining meaningful relationships. At this point, Frank Sinatra's "My Way" (1969) begins to play on the radio, and Draper and Olson share a slow, reassuring dance to the song. Its refrain speaks to Olson's isolation and struggle as a woman copywriter in a gendered work environment. As such, it acts as a continuation of the dialogue preceding it, offering the final word.

The selection of songs used in *Mad Men* is carefully meditated. The songs often highlight themes that underpin a particular episode or those that recur throughout the series' narrative. For example, in the episode "Shoot" (2007), the Bobby Helms single "My Special Angel" (1957) is used as a counterpoint to the onscreen image of Betty Draper shooting her neighbor's pigeons. The contrast between the sentimental lyrics and Betty's act of frustration foregrounds the schism between the identity she wants to assert throughout the episode—"I did do some modeling, you know"—and the expectation of motherhood imposed on her from the outside to be "[b]eautiful, and kind, and filled with love like an angel." By setting up contrasting images of motherhood, the episode demystifies the angelic mother myth, and the song at the end works to tie together these threads. The aural cue, although at odds with the onscreen image, supplements the narrative agenda. The dissonance between the visual and the aural stimuli provokes the audience's attention to the composition of the scene, and heightens the underlying theme of Betty's conflicting existence, which was stressed in the episode. The use of "My Special Angel," now widely forgotten, also exhibits retro television's ability to revive music and reframe it according to contemporary concerns. Many songs by Bob Dylan and Frank Sinatra continue to exert cultural influence and therefore belong to the present as much as they do to the past, but Helms' song resonates primarily as a '50s relic. While its use lends period specificity, as it would likely have been played regularly on the radio in the early 1960s, its status as a '50s hit also serves to further associate Betty Draper with '50s tastes and practices. The romantic ballad thus finds a new context for appreciation; *Mad Men* adds a new layer of interpretive possibility to the song at the very instance that it is revived.

Mad Men also features several cinematic references. These citations provide the opportunity to draw on and explore subjects and themes often central to 1960s cinema while simultaneously drawing attention to rifts in cinematic nostalgia. The easy solutions presented in the cited film representations of these subjects and themes are complicated by *Mad Men*'s more nuanced treatments, thus altering contemporary viewers' reception of its references. As such, these intertextualities transform cultural memories of the '60s, broadening the horizons of collectively remembered texts and their contexts. For example, Billy Wilder's *The Apartment* (1960) is invoked in an episode from the first season that deals with anxieties felt by single working women in the 1960s ("Long Weekend," 2007). Office manager Joan Holloway (Christina Hendricks) references *The Apartment* to her boss and lover, Roger Sterling (John Slattery), noting the similarities between her own life and that of the film's central female character, elevator operator Fran (Shirley MacLaine), who is also in a relationship with her boss. Joan explains that Fran attempts suicide after discovering that she is but one among many of her boss' casual affairs and that he does not intend to divorce his wife.

Joan's reference to *The Apartment* is significant; although the film depicts the pressures faced by single working women, it ultimately opts for a romantic resolution, thus neutralizing those stresses by making them appear easily surmountable. *Mad Men*, by comparison, frequently stresses the everyday humiliation faced by single working women. Later in the same episode, when Sterling has a heart attack, founding partner Bertram Cooper (Robert Morse) calls Joan to the office to send telegrams to clients, ensuring them that business will continue as usual. While leaving the office late at night, they get into the elevator and Cooper asks Joan to operate it. At that moment, Joan *becomes* Fran. A few episodes later, Joan, having evidently taken note, ends her affair with Sterling and attempts to settle down by getting engaged to a young medical student.

The Apartment also provides an influence for *Mad Men*'s office set designs. Jeremy G. Butler suggests that the Sterling Cooper set's "most striking element [...] is its ceiling—an oppressive grid of fluorescent lights," and notes its indebtedness to *The Apartment* director Billy Wilder's visual designs, which also recognize "this lighting fixture's oppressiveness" (2011, pp. 60–61). Indeed, in its set design and cinematography the series draws heavily on 1960s cinema and television, and in this regard, *Mad Men*'s location on AMC introduces an interesting paratext to its expectations and reception. Originally known as American Movie Classics, AMC is a site of televisual memory and a place of remembrance, circulating old American classics, and, as such, it creates an expectation of cinematic continuities for its audience. In the early 2000s, AMC embarked on a rebranding strategy, expanding its repertoire to include original "quality" programming that aimed to be both cinematically on a par with and complementary to its exhaustive library of classic American films (Edgerton, 2011, p. 8). *Mad Men* benefits from sharing network space with AMC's oeuvre and delivers on the expectation of cinematic continuity. Its title sequence is a nod to the opening sequence of *North by Northwest* (Hitchcock, 1959) which was designed by Saul Bass, as well as the falling man poster of *Vertigo* (Hitchcock, 1958). Evidencing the extent to which the *Mad Men* viewing experience is intertwined with cinematic nostalgia, the exhibition "Mathew Weiner's *Mad Men*" (Museum of the Moving Image, New York, March 14–April 26, 2015) featured screenings of ten films—including *North by Northwest* and *Vertigo*—that influenced the show. The series of film screenings, entitled "Required Viewing: *Mad Men*'s Movie Influences," was curated by Weiner, who wrote descriptions for each of the films on the museum's website ("Exhibition," 2015).

Curated lists like Weiner's also have the capacity to create new networks for the circulation of memories of the 1960s, and online responses to *Mad Men* suggest that these circuits have contributed to a small '60s memory boom among its audience. Many contemporary viewers who are active in online forums confess to researching intertextual references to fully decode the episodes' conveyed messages. For example, a *Mad Men* viewer, who goes by the username "60'schild," writes of *The Apartment* on the AMC *Mad Men* talk forum: "If it wasn't for *Mad Men*, and the people who write on this Forum, I wouldn't have watched [*The Apartment*]. It has now become one of my favorite early '60s flicks" (60'schild, 2010). The viewer's comment reveals how *Mad Men*'s references do more than provide additional layers of textual meaning, also encouraging its audience to seek out extratextual knowledge. Citation validates *Mad Men*'s position as a quality cultural product suited for a niche audience with cultural capital, and online activity suggests that both critics and fans consider a model *Mad Men* viewer to be one who can recognize its cultural and historical references. Even so, contextual information is made readily available online by critics and commentators, with weekly recaps and review articles published by television critics after each episode. Most of them include lists of references, such as those published by television critics in *The Guardian Online*'s "Mad Men: Notes from the Break Room" (Dean, 2010). Articles also often provide links to short *YouTube* clips.

The online platforms described above, which enable and invite participatory viewing practices, are characteristic of contemporary "quality" television serials. In these online contexts, episodes in which significant events occur take on certain qualities of factual televised events, encouraging viewers to ask one another what they did after watching, where they were when they watched, and other questions related to memories of mediation. For *Mad Men*, these shared memories contain two layers: the memory of the episode itself and the newly mediated memory of its 1960s reference. This was notable after the death of Bertram Cooper in Season 7, a fictional "event" that triggered the publication of several online articles, blogs, and fan-produced videos commemorating the character on *YouTube*. In the process, memories of the character became intertwined with memories of actor Robert Morse, whose presence in the series is itself an intertextual citation: Morse's performance as J. Pierrepont Finch in the stage and onscreen productions of *How to Succeed in Business Without Really Trying* (Burrows, 1961; Swift, 1967) inextricably ties him to cultural memories of the 1960s. "Waterloo" (2014), the episode in which Cooper dies, features an imagined song and dance sequence in which Morse performs "The Best Things in Life Are Free" (Brown, DeSylva and Henderson, 1927), self-consciously drawing on viewers' memories of Morse's 1960s musical comedy fame. The episode motivated viewers to share not just their memories of viewing the program, but also of Robert Morse's 1960s performances, with critics such as *The Moderate Voice* editor-in-chief Joe Gandelman (2014) calling attention to Morse's former fame and several fans uploading clips from previous Morse films to *YouTube*.

The above example indicates how *Mad Men*'s intertextualities stir the desire to revisit the past by pointing to continuities and relevance; Robert Morse's final song and dance sequence reminds viewers of the continued exchanges between the 1960s and contemporary popular culture. However, in interviews with the series' producers and crew, the value of intertextuality is never located in its potential to restore a point of origin in cultural history; instead, it is located in the opportunities it affords to appropriate, adapt, and repackage 1960s texts in exciting and challenging ways. For instance, cinematographer Phil Abraham points out, "Movies [of the '60s] were an influence, but we didn't say, 'Let's make *The Apartment*'" (Feld, Oppenheimer and Stasukevich, 2008). Similarly, Steve Fuller explains of *Mad Men*'s title sequence, which he co-created, that it is "a kind of an update of Saul Bass" (Landekic, 2011). The word "update" is significant here: technological advances in cinematography, styling and graphics play an important role in the series' transformations. In the case of the title sequence, its After Effects 3D graphics at once echo Bass' work, evoking nostalgia for 1960s cinema, and render it novel and contemporary. By technologically updating its intertextual references, *Mad Men* both highlights continuities with 1960s popular culture and reimagines contemporary contexts for its reception, validating its persistence in American culture. Simultaneously, new technologies aid in the dispersal of this new hybrid content via video-streaming and other online platforms, sustaining the memory boom initiated by the televisual text.

Generating New Memories: Television Seriality and Nostalgia for Mad Men

As *Mad Men* textually explores states of dislocation and yearning and intertextually engages with contemporary practices of nostalgia and recollection, a third process of memory emerges: the series begins to refer to its own internal networks of serial memory. *Mad Men*'s complex narration, serial format, and long run, featuring seven seasons and 92 episodes in total, encourages sustained engagement in its narrative and an intimate connection to its characters. As the narrative progresses, the series contains increasing references to its earlier episodes, embedding its own, new, televisual memories into the text. For viewers, these memories which the show increasingly invokes are simultaneously of both the events in the narrative (the text) and of the contexts in which they viewed *Mad Men* over time. Nostalgia, in this respect, is distinct from nostalgia generated for the '60s and the intertextual references in the text; the nostalgia here is within and for *Mad Men*. In the following section I use two examples from the text to show how *Mad Men* evokes nostalgia for its early episodes through mnemonic devices of serialized television to achieve identification and narrative depth. This resonates with viewers' memories for the long periods in their everyday life spent with the characters. The show's amalgamation of textual and contextual serial memory speaks to the interactive nature of contemporary memory processes in relation to television viewing practices. The examples elucidate a consistent posture of the series towards nostalgia; there is a correspondence between the relationship of the series to the '60s and the relationship that it has with its own diegetic past.

In Season 4's "Waldorf Stories" (2010), Draper returns to the office on a high after celebrating the win of a Clio Award, and offers a drunk and unprepared pitch for Life Cereal. In the sequence, he delivers fragments of his earlier Kodak pitch, evidently trying to recreate its spell: "Look, there are sweeter cereals than this, but I kept thinking about, you know, nostalgia. How you remember something in the past, and it feels good, but it's a little bit painful, like when you were a kid" (2010). The clients are not impressed this time with Draper's appeals to nostalgia, and in a desperate attempt to maintain the client, he lifts ideas from the work of a mediocre copywriter that he had earlier regarded with contempt; the clients settle on the copywriter's "Life: the cure for the common breakfast." By alluding to Draper's successful Kodak pitch, the series calls on its audience's televisual memory to highlight Draper's debasement. Increasingly, viewers' assumed memories of characters' pasts inform *Mad Men*'s depictions of their present situations.

In addition, the audience's memory is refreshed from time to time by mirrored storylines which subtly pay homage to earlier episodes. Serial memory thrives on episodes which share thematic similarities or make indirect allusions to previous episodes because comparing the past and the present is a device central to the function of memorizing. *Mad Men* enables this process by introducing episodes that recall earlier ones in theme and composition, provoking viewers to take stock of events within its diegetic universe. These become more frequent and explicit in Season 7, the program's final season. They include repeated patterns; for instance, a coup in its seventh episode, "Waterloo," alludes to a similar coup in Season 3's "Shut the Door. Have a Seat" (2009). Other Season 7 episodes recall previous episodes thematically; "The Strategy," for example, pays homage to Season 4's "The Suitcase" (2010). Both are organized around a similar temporal marker, Peggy Olson's birthday, which calls for an occasion to compare and review Olson's growth and her relationship to the other central protagonist, Draper. "The Strategy" acts as a point of culmination, reflecting on the repercussions of Olson's choice to value work over family in the earlier "The Suitcase." Viewers who have witnessed Olson's growth as a professional in the time since can participate in validating this choice despite her own anxieties about it. By offering audiences comparable episodes in which events repeat (birthdays, coups) and by presenting circumstances in which previous decisions made by characters are validated, *Mad Men* establishes character consistency, thus encouraging immersion and a sense of identification. These occasions particularly draw attention to the passage of time, the growth of characters, and the deepening of their interpersonal relationships.

The extent to which this engagement with the mechanics of memorizing was contemplated in *Mad Men*'s production is clear in a comment made by Mathew Weiner on the relationship between memory and long-running serial television. He notes that

> part of my intention when I pitched the show, even before I talked to anybody, was wouldn't it be amazing to do ten or 12 years of these people's lives, have the actors age that amount. And you will immediately, no matter how many bad things happen that first season, you see Peggy and you have nostalgia for her first day at work because you knew her then—there's just that process of the human mind, just because it's in the past [Poniewozik, 2014].

Here, Weiner recognizes how the passage of time is crucial for serial television, arguing that it enables mediated intimacy and even nostalgia for the characters. This nostalgia is arguably reinforced by nostalgia for the experience of watching *Mad Men*; it is a result of the interaction between the televisual text and the context in which the text is viewed. Experiential memory of watching a long-running serial is coextensive with televisual memory, and these multiplicities of remembrance point to the porous and assimilative nature of contemporary memory, which integrates divergent strands—televisual and contextual, immediate and cultural.

Because of its breadth, serialized television provides the opportunity for a retro production to rework its own representation of the past. In addition to *Mad Men*'s long run (2007–15), the time frame of the narrative is spread over a decade (March 1960–November 1970), and this temporal stretch allows character engagement to be both intense (a particular event or personal crisis can be concentrated upon in one or more consecutive episodes) and expansive (repercussions of actions and choices can be explored over an entire decade). *Mad Men*'s circular structure—a byproduct of its hybridization of the series and the serial by combining episodic closures with continuous plot development—facilitates returns to previous events while denying absolute closures. Furthermore, commonplace, day-to-day experiences often constitute the basis of serialized narratives and, as such, *Mad Men* naturally moves beyond depictions of historical events and popular cultural memories towards an exploration of the everyday. In these ways, the show's structure both suits and enables its posture of reflective nostalgia. For instance, even if Joan's story is mapped upon Fran's "happily ever after" from *The Apartment*, Joan's trajectory continues in the serial beyond that apparent closure to open up again to the possibility of another struggle. *Mad Men*'s seriality keeps the process of negotiation with history and cultural memories open and dynamic, and in so doing broadly implies that reprising historic periods always involves a process of meaning-making that shifts in accordance with present needs.

Conclusion

Contexts of television viewing have changed substantially in recent years, with televisual texts now available in multiple formats. DVD box sets and streaming platforms like Netflix have transformed the traditional parameters that define television texts, making it possible for viewers to regulate how much of the text is consumed in one sitting, to pause the narration at any point to interact with the content, and so forth. *Mad Men*'s unique approach to depicting the past resonates with these autonomous and interactive television viewing practices. The series negotiates interactions between the past and the present without favoring one over the other. It acknowledges the need to revisit the past; yet, when Menken claims, "I'll visit," what is implied is that she will visit *when she wants to.* *Mad Men*'s intertextualities work similarly: they are heterogeneous, derived from both high and low cultures, and ultimately serve the series' present needs. These references are not trivialized; their significances are acknowledged in the intelligent and creative ways by which they are incorporated into the televisual text. Still, the series emphasizes the capacity of the contemporary, whether in the form of ideas, of technologies, or otherwise, to transform the cultural memories that it reintroduces to present-day consciousness. It also encourages viewers to become invested in its appropriated fragments of 1960s popular culture, to participate in online discussions around them, and to derive pleasure from seeing them recalled in novel ways.

Contemporary memory is inundated by sites and cultures of memory (Huyssen, 2003); our intensely connected environment makes the transference of memories easy and accessible. New technologies for storing memories have given rise to new cultures of memorizing in a present marked by its capacity to accommodate various interpretations of history and uses of cultural memories. Retro productions are symptomatic of this climate of memorizing. The proliferation of memory cultures and the consequent diversity of narratives of the past has complicated neat closures and nostalgia for *one* particular interpretation of history. The expansion of nostalgia discourse to include reflective and critical stances evinces our overall acclimation to this environment. History is no longer sacred; it is shared. It is not reverence for intertextual references, but instead the manner in which they are creatively woven into contemporary narratives that holds our attention. If, as Boym argues, nostalgia is at the core of our modern existence, the majority of us become every day all the more reflectively nostalgic. This might explain the popularity of retro television and cinema: we are ever-more enthusiastic to see historical periods uniquely and unconventionally re-enacted.

Retro is invested in contemplating the past, albeit with new perspectives or through novel appropriations of the old. While its authenticity rests in the *mise-en-scène*, its goal is adaptation. Retro's emphasis is always on the present, forming a continuum between two networks of memory: memories of the past's cultural artifacts and the new memories that are created daily. Instead of approaching the American '60s as a monolith to be preserved, *Mad Men* engages with the era interactively. It provides a space for multiple registers of language, form, and cinematic vocabulary to co-exist, equalizing and subsuming in its flow its various centers of cultural influence. By revisiting the 1960s in a way that is intertextual, idiosyncratic, and imperfect, *Mad Men* highlights contradictions in notions of historical authenticity and offers up the 1960s in a way that is suited to its contemporary audience's constant interactions and participation with the past.

REFERENCES

60'schild. (2010) Another Critical Mistake from the Writers of MM Found. February 20. Message posted to http://www.amc.com/shows/mad-men/talk/forum/2010/02/another-critica.php. (Accessed December 2, 2015).

Anderson, T. (2011) Uneasy Listening: Music, Sound and Criticizing Camelot in Mad Men. In: Edgerton, G. R. (ed.). *Mad Men: Dream Come True TV*. New York: I.B. Tauris, pp. 72–85.

Anonymous. (2015) Exhibition: Matthew Weiner's *Mad Men*. *Museum of the Modern Image*, 2015. http://www.movingimage.us/exhibitions/2015/03/14/detail/matthew-weiners-mad-men/. (Accessed May 7, 2015).

The Apartment. (1960) [Film] Directed by Billy Wilder. USA: United Artists.

Boym, S. (2001) *The Future of Nostalgia*. New York: Basic Books.

Brown, L. and DeSylva, B.G. (Lyrics); Henderson, R. (Music) (1927) [Song] The Best Things in Life Are Free for *Good News* [Musical]. New York: Broadway.

Burrows, Abe (1961) [Musical] *How to Succeed in Business Without Really Trying*. New York: Broadway.

Butler, J. (2011) "Smoke Gets in Your Eyes": Historicizing Visual Style in Mad Men. In: Edgerton, G. R. (ed.). *Mad Men: Dream Come True TV*. New York: I.B. Tauris, pp. 55–72.

Dean, W. (2010) Mad Men: Season One, Episode 10. In: *Mad Men*: Notes from the Break Room. *The Guardian*, June 1. http://www.theguardian.com/tv-and-radio/tvandradioblog/2010/jun/01/mad-men-season-one-episode-10. (Accessed April 28, 2014).

Dylan, B. (1963) [Song] Don't Think Twice It's Alright. *The Freewheelin' Bob Dylan*. New York: Columbia Records.

Edgerton, G. R. (2011) The Selling of Mad Men: A Production History. In: Edgerton, G. R. (ed.) *Mad Men: Dream Come True TV*. New York: I.B. Tauris, pp. 3–24.

Feld, R., Oppenheimer J., and Stasukevich, I. (2008) Cinematographers from Three Top Series (*Mad Men*, *Desperate Housewives* and *Bones*) Reveal Their Secrets. *The American Society of Cinematographers*. https://www.theasc.com/ac_magazine/March2008/Television/page1.php. (Accessed October 19, 2014).

Gandelman, J. (2014) Mad Men's Pitch Perfect Bert Cooper Robert Morse Send-off (Videos). *The Moderate Voice,* May 26. http://themoderatevoice.com/195225/mad-mens-pitch-perfect-bert-cooper-robert-morse-send-off-videos/. (Accessed January 15, 2015).

Guffey, E. E. (2006) *Retro: The Culture of Revival.* London: Reaktion Books.

Helms, B. (1957) [Song] My Special Angel. *Bobby Helms Sings to My Special Angel.* New York: Decca Records.

How to Succeed in Business Without Really Trying. (1967) [Film] Directed by David Swift. USA: United Artists.

Huyssen, A. (2003) *Present Pasts: Urban Palimpsests and the Politics of Memory.* Stanford: Stanford University Press.

Landekic, L. (Writer) (2011) Mad Men (2007). *Art of the Title,* September 19. http://www.artofthetitle.com/title/mad-men/. (Accessed November 8, 2013).

Mad Men. (2007) [TV] Babylon. Directed by Bernstein, A. Written by Weiner, M., Jacquemetton, A., Jacquemetton, M. Los Angeles: AMC, August 23.

_____. (2007) [TV] Shoot. Directed by Feig, P. Written by Weiner, M. and Provenzano, C. Los Angeles: AMC, August 31.

_____. (2007) [TV] Long Weekend. Directed by Hunter, T. Written by Weiner, M., Bedard, B., Jacquemetton, A. and Jacquemetton, M. Los Angeles: AMC, September 27.

_____. (2007) [TV] The Wheel. Directed by Weiner, M. Written by Weiner, M. and Veith, R. Los Angeles: AMC, October 18.

_____. (2009) [TV] Shut the Door. Have a Seat. Directed by Weiner, M. Written by Weiner, M., Levy, E. and Kater, G. Los Angeles: AMC, November 8.

_____. (2010) [TV] Waldorf Stories. Directed by Weiner, M. Written by Weiner, M. and Johnson, B. Los Angeles: AMC, August 29.

_____. (2010) [TV] The Suitcase. Directed by Getzinger, J. Written by Weiner, M. Los Angeles: AMC, September 5.

_____. (2014) [TV] The Strategy. Directed by Abraham, P. Written by Weiner, M., Chellas, S. and Igla, J. Los Angeles: AMC, May 18.

_____. (2014) [TV] Waterloo. Directed by Weiner, M. Written by Weiner, M., Wray, C. and Igla, J. Los Angeles: AMC, May 25.

North by Northwest. (2002) [Film] Directed by Alfred Hitchcock. USA: Metro-Goldwyn-Mayer.

Poniewozik, J. (2014) Making History: A Q&A with Mad Men's Mathew Weiner. *Time,* March 27. http://time.com/37719/matthew-weiner-mad-men-q-a/. (Accessed April 1, 2014).

Sinatra, F. (1969) [Song] My Way. *My Way.* Los Angeles: Reprise Records.

Vertigo. (1958) [Film] Directed by Alfred Hitchcock. USA: Paramount Pictures.

The Women's Land Army Remembered on British Television

CAT MAHONEY

This essay will examine three British televisual representations of the Women's Land Army (WLA): *Land Girls* (BBC, 2009), an episode of *Foyle's War* (ITV, 2004), and *Backs to the Land* (Anglia/ITV, 1977). It will consider the roles these three series play in perpetuating dominant discourses surrounding British women's war work and the re-negotiation of gender roles after the Second World War. In its close, critical reading of the texts, the essay will examine their portrayals of gender, class, patriotism, and sexuality, and the ways in which they feed in to a wider conceptualization of British femininity at a moment of national crisis—as well as the long reaching consequences of this crisis. Falling into different genres of television—a female ensemble drama (FED), a detective series, and a situation comedy, respectively—each of the three series analyzed offers a different space for telling women's history, as well as shaping and perpetuating myths of women's participation in the Second World War. Drawing on recent feminist television scholarship, the essay will locate these representations within a wider televisual trend towards re-traditionalization in a "post-feminist" media climate (Ball, 2012). In the case of *Backs to the Land,* which had an earlier broadcast date that was arguably at the height of second wave feminism, it will discuss the series as a reaction to, and backlash against, this movement. It will also take this as an opportunity for comparison, considering the changes both in the representation of female liberation and the changing tone of representations of the Second World War in different, gendered historical contexts.

To achieve this, I will first give a brief overview of the programs to be considered and their relevance to the scholarship, before moving to provide a short, contextualizing historical overview of the importance of the WLA. Each program will then be studied in detail, analyzing the themes, narratives, and characters, and their representation of historic gender roles and female participation in the national war effort. Through this discussion, the importance of these televisual representations of the WLA to discourses surrounding women's war work and the changing role of women in British society will be scrutinized, as well as the wider debate of the use of history as a lens through which to view and assess the present.

As Roland Barthes (2013) suggests, the "facts" or bases of cultural myths are endowed with a secondary significance by the process of myth making, becoming part of a "second-order semiological system" (ibid., p. 223). Events and images from the past are repurposed and deployed in the present as vessels, emptied of their original meaning and re-filled with a "truth" significant to the needs of the present moment. Therefore, as this essay will suggest, to understand the relevance of the myth of the Land Girl, it is often more important to understand the cultural significance attached to the image in the moment of its production, than the "reality" (throughout this essay I use this word, with all of its associated problems, for want of a better one) from which it was taken. The myth of the Land Girl calls up ideas of patriotism, self-sacrifice, hard physical labor, and, beyond this, an unquestioning willingness to serve the British state and contribute to the war effort. Just as in Barthes' example of *Paris-Match* magazine utilizing the image of a young black soldier saluting the Tricolore as an answer to criticisms of French imperialism, the image of the Land Girl is removed from its actual history and repurposed by the three television series explored here.

Production Context

Aired in 2009 to coincide with the 70th anniversary of the outbreak of the Second World War, *Land Girls* was the first time BBC Daytime had commissioned a period drama (BBC Press Pack, 2015). The first series formed part of a "unique week of programming" which aimed to commemorate and celebrate "everyday heroes on the Home Front" and was broadcast on five consecutive days beginning on Monday, September 7, 2009 (ibid.). Created by Roland Moore, the series was less a depiction of the roles and duties of the Land Girls, and more an exploration of the ways in which service in the Women's Land Army affected and changed the lives of its members. In an interview, Becci Gemmell (who plays Land Girl Joyce Fisher) explained: "We could have made something very gritty, but really this series is about people's lives. It had wide appeal because it picks up on the hope and camaraderie and on people from all walks of life pulling together" (BBC Press Office, n.d.).

The series was broadcast alongside *The Week We Went to War* (BBC1, September 7–14, 2009), which was presented by Katherine Jenkins and Michael Aspel, and focused on everyday experiences of ordinary people living on the Home Front during the Second World War. This placed *Land Girls* in a context of personal and previously untold stories, outside of dominant public narratives. *Land Girls* was awarded "Best Daytime Program" at the 2010 Broadcast awards and has been praised as an intelligent drama series, aimed at a more discerning audience and benefitting from "creative inspiration [which] comes from loftier places than the usual pedestrian off-peak drama" (Warren, 2010).

Backs to the Land was broadcast by Anglia Television in 1977. It was the first situation comedy commissioned by Anglia, and featured the exploits of three city girls sent to work on the Whitlow farm. Created in the wake of the success of *Dad's Army* (BBC, 1968) the series reflected Anglia's firm regional roots in the East of England, making "extensive use of the region's countryside with location filming taking place in a Norfolk village and its local pub, church and community hall" (Teletronic, n.d.). As a sitcom, *Backs to the Land* differs considerably from the other two series discussed in this essay and offers a very different space for telling history, and this difference is taken up and explored later in the essay.

With each series comprising three or four two-hour-long film-style episodes, *Foyle's War* (ITV, 2002) is the most structurally distinctive series considered in this essay. Evoking the style of well-established British detective series, such as *Morse* (ITV, 1987) and *Taggart* (STV/UTV/ITV, 1983)—the former being that which *Foyle's War* was actually commissioned to replace—the series contrasts with recent trends towards a grittier, darker tone exemplified by series such as *The Killing* (DR1, 2007), and relies on a "traditional, romantic, individualistic, and typically English" construction of the police detective in its leading character, Foyle, who drives the narrative (Cooke, 2001, p. 22). Each episode features a self-contained plot which, with the exception of some overarching storylines, is fully resolved at the end of each installment. Despite its enduring popularity, *Foyle's War* came to an end with its eighth series in January 2015. Series creator, Anthony Horowitz (2015), whose concern for authenticity resulted in ongoing collaboration with the Imperial War Museum over historical accuracy, implied that after 15 years on British television, the premise of the series was somewhat exhausted and there were few remaining stories tell (ITV Press Centre, 2015).

This essay focuses specifically on an episode from Series 3 entitled "They Fought in the Fields"; the analysis of *Foyle's War* is thus distinct from the other two texts considered in this essay in the sense that it examines a particular episode rather than a whole season. This episode has been selected for close textual analysis because of the ways that it depicts the physicality of the work undertaken by Land Girls, their active and vital role in wartime agriculture, and the anxiety this caused in relation to traditional concepts of gendered labor and skill. The various antagonistic relationships between all of the female characters in this episode also create interesting dynamics, both between women of different classes and women undertaking different kinds of war work. The episode goes some way towards challenging the idea that once initial differences were overcome, class boundaries were put aside for the duration of the war as everyone "did their bit," an idea which largely goes unquestioned in the other two series. As such, its representations provide a useful countervailing historical narrative, and the implications of this are examined in detail.

Historical Context

The creation of the first Women's Land Army stemmed from the desperate need to increase food production during the First World War after the enemy began a highly successful blockade of allied supply lines in 1915. This was compounded by the problems of a disastrous harvest in 1917, as well as the loss of horses and skilled farm labor to the armed forces. The resulting shortages meant that before the end of that year, with the population at 36 million, British food reserves could be expected to last no longer than three weeks. From a register, compiled in 1915, of "women willing to do industrial, agricultural and clerical work" (Thornton, 2002, p. 144) women were recruited to form the first Women's Land Army. By 1918, 23,000 girls had been recruited from 45,000 applicants (Powell and Westacott, 1997, p. 5). The first Women's Land Army was disbanded with the peace in 1919, but preparations were put in place to resurrect it in 1938 when war appeared to be once more inevitable. The second Women's Land Army was officially formed on 1st June 1939, and by the time war was declared in September, recruitment offices had opened up all over the country.

Gill Clarke has described the Women's Land Army as "one of the most conspicuous and memorable aspects" of the food production campaign in Britain during the Second World War (2008, p. 101). The formation of a recognizable visual culture surrounding the WLA was accepted, almost from its inception, as vital to promoting cohesion and a sense of community to what was otherwise a disparate body. Ann Kramer argues that the fragmented nature of the Women's Land Army, with small groups of girls serving on remote farms or living in hostels, rather than a single body of women operating from a common base, was detrimental to the formation of a community spirit (2001, Loc 1900). The Land Girls were intended to be a trained and mobile contingent of women who could be sent around the country wherever the need arose, with some girls banded together in gangs and stationed in hostels to be moved as required. The magazine *The Land Girl* was intended to create a channel of communication between members of the WLA and promote a positive image of the Land Girls themselves and their contribution to the war effort, as well as reducing feelings of isolation for individual Land Girls (for a discussion of this magazine, see The Women's Land Army, n.d.). The magazine began in 1940, as an unofficial publication for members of the WLA; however, after its popularity garnered sales of approximately 21,000 copies per week, the Ministry of Agriculture began to fund its publication. In an extract from April 1943, *The Land Girl* warned its members against complacency and reminded them that, despite "two out of every three meals" being produced at home, that still left "forty-seven million meals a day [...] to be brought in from overseas" (*Women at War,* n.d.).

Interestingly, as early as 1918 the *Landswoman,* the predecessor to *The Land Girl,* had begun to speculate as to the lasting effect women's service in the Land Army would have on women's future role in society. It suggested that "the Land Army may be the pioneer of a newer and a far higher civilization for the British Race" in which women would have a more active and equal role in society and enjoy much greater freedoms (Kramer, 2001, Loc 358). However, as part of the food production campaign the Women's Land Army was one of several initiatives which saw dramatically increased state intervention in food production and distribution. The various initiatives represented considerable intrusion by the state into the affairs of country farmers, who were noted for their conservatism and reluctance towards centralized agricultural change (Martin, 2000, p. 36). In many ways the Land Girl became a symbol of state interference in the countryside, one towards which farmers could direct their resistance and express their displeasure. The happy image of welcome and co-operation that was promoted by recruitment posters was not always the reality for girls reporting for training and duty on farms in the early years of the Second World War.

This brief historical contextualization illustrates the place and purpose of the WLA in wartime Britain, but also its significance to the lives of the women who became its members. While the purpose of this essay is not to scrutinize historical accuracy in the series in question, it is important to consider their relationship to historical "reality," to think through the ways in which it has been repurposed and redeployed for the politics of the present, and to consider them in relation to the gendered and classed politics of myth and memory.

Land Girls

With a cast dominated by women and a central group of female leading characters, *Land Girls* can be categorized as a female ensemble drama (FED).

Vicky Ball (2013, p. 245) describes FED as a specific and important form of "heroine television" (a concept first discussed by Charlotte Brunsdon, 1997), which came to be as a result of "television's attempt to construct and address a more pluralized sense of female identity in the wake of liberalizing movements and women's increased visibility in the public sphere" (Ball, 2013, p. 246). In spite of, and yet also in part because of, their status as secondary to more traditionally male-centered drama series, FED are a significant site for the construction of feminine identity on television. The marginalization of male characters allows a much wider scope for female narratives and creates a space in which "subaltern feminine identities that have been marginalized on television and in history more generally" (ibid.) can be represented and explored. Because of the dominance of male perspectives in television narratives, the secondary status of male characters within FED must usually be attended to and explained within the narrative. The setting of *Land Girls* during the Second World War creates plausible conditions for the absence of men, because of their service in the armed forces at this time. The absence of men legitimates a focus on female experiences of war and specifically on a body that is entirely female: the Women's Land Army.

It can therefore be argued that, unlike the other two texts considered in this essay, *Land Girls'* identity as a female ensemble drama offers what I have elsewhere referred to as a "simultaneously progressive, yet clearly delineated space for telling women's history" (Mahoney, 2015, no pagination). The removal of the standard male lead characters produces "central female protagonists to whom things can happen" (Brunsdon, 1987, p. 187). However, as Brunsdon notes, to be *acceptable* heroines, the women must also be seen to be "properly feminine" in that they are wives, sweethearts and mothers, confirming to the viewer that—crucially—"men have wanted them" (ibid.).

This positioning of women center stage, a space traditionally occupied by male characters, where their feelings, experiences, and reactions drive the narrative, could be seen to problematize the text's claim to realism as a "war story," a narrative category that has traditionally focused on normatively public, political, and military history. However, the foregrounding of emotional relationships and experiences and family issues in *Land Girls* creates a generic affiliation with women's drama that helps to construct an alternative sense of realism based on what Ball refers to as "generic and textual histories, rather than any direct relation to the real" (ibid., p. 187). Thus, despite the fact that women *did* take up such roles during the Second World War, the success of *Land Girls* as a representation of women's history, and as a women's drama series, lies more in its utilization of established generic traits, than its faithful recreation of the past. As a result, despite some lapses in historical accuracy, *Land Girls* successfully functions both as a space in which unfamiliar and sometimes transgressive stories can be told and as a recognizable prime time television drama. The cyclical nature and closed structure of serial television drama means that it requires resolution; thus, storylines which could be perceived as challenging to normative constructions of femininity are neutralized by the need for closure—and a "return" to normativity—at the end of each series.

An example of this narrative closing off subversive potential can be read through a character named Bea (Jo Woodcock), who primarily joined the WLA as a means of escaping her abusive father, and in the program sees her time away from home as an opportunity to chase new experiences. In the episode entitled "Secrets," Bea attempts to end an unwanted pregnancy by drinking alcohol distilled from carrots and placing herself in deliberately dangerous situations in the hope of bringing on a miscarriage. Within the narrative and reflecting the attitudes of the time, a great deal of shame and humiliation is attached to being an unwed mother. Faced with being forced to leave the WLA—as a woman falling pregnant would have been in reality—and choosing to attempt to end the pregnancy instead, Bea's rejection of the "natural" state of motherhood could be seen as transgressive and even deviant. However, this "problematic" storyline in which normative femininity is temporarily disrupted is ultimately resolved with Bea's marriage to farmhand Billy (Liam Boyle) ("Destinies," 2009). Even though Billy is not the baby's father, the marriage allows her to keep her baby, protects her from shame, and means that she can remain on the farm. However, this also repositions her in the more traditional role of wife and mother; her time as a liberated young woman with the space and freedom to explore her sexuality is cut short.

This narrative repositioning of women back into more readily acceptable "feminine" roles perpetuates and "relies on universal, essentialist conceptions of gender which naturalize and reinforce the relationship between women and 'the feminine'" (Ball, 2013, p. 252). Therefore, although a space *is* offered for the representation and exploration of fluid and transgressive femininities, it is curtailed by the need for narrative closure, which requires the female characters to be relocated back into traditional gender roles (Mahoney, 2015).

As a result of the ultimately conservative nature of its narrative structure, *Land Girls* is able to represent the WLA as a liberating space, in which women can achieve temporary transcendence of traditional gender roles for the duration of their service. For a character called Annie (Christine Bottomley), the WLA offers the chance to escape both an abusive father and a hasty and unhappy marriage. In joining the Women's Land Army, Annie discovers a space in which she can be free of her father without dependence on her husband. In the episode "Secrets," Annie's choice to place herself in this new context, defined not by men, but by the women around her, allows her the freedom to redefine herself and escape the role of unhappy wife and victim and find love with another man when her husband is declared missing.

Land Girls also presents the WLA as providing women with purpose and identity for the duration of the war, when the roles of wives and/or mothers were temporarily suspended or reworked due to the absence of men. This is especially true for Joyce, whose family has been killed in air raids and whose husband is away on active service in the air force. The WLA offers her the chance to escape the ruins of her native Coventry and gives Joyce a purpose, a home, and an identity for the duration of the war, until she can reclaim her place as a wife and mother. Similarly for Esther (Susan Cookson), who is raising her son alone as her husband is a prisoner of war, the WLA provides a purpose as well as a surrogate family and support network until her husband returns.

However, in *Land Girls,* this transcendence of traditional gender roles is limited, fraught with danger, and must ultimately be relinquished by all of the women in order to achieve happy resolutions to their individual storylines (Mahoney, 2015). The program sets up a narrative whereby the removal of women from the safe parameters of the traditional domestic sphere exposes all of them to new and dangerous situations which, ultimately, can only be resolved by their return to, and willing acceptance of, traditional gender roles.

Bea's desire for sexual liberation exposes her to emotional danger and the sexual manipulation of an older and much more experienced American GI ("Childhood's End," 2009). Esther is reduced to selling her body when she cannot afford to pay for an operation for her son ("Final Reckoning," 2011). Annie's newfound happiness is threatened when her husband is found alive and she is called on to sacrifice her own desires and resume the role of wife to a husband with considerable physical and mental injuries ("Trekkers," 2009). Connie (Seline Hizli), who joined the WLA to escape her criminal past, is blackmailed by a former lover into helping him undertake a robbery ("Farewell My Lovely," 2011). Joyce must face the realities of war when her husband's plane is shot down and she herself is forced to kill a crashed German airman in the woods ("Final Reckoning," 2011).

In this way the series makes clear that the transcendence of traditional gender roles offered by membership in the WLA can only ever be temporary, granted in exceptional circumstances, and can offer no possibility of long term happiness or fulfillment. Furthermore, consistent with the requirements of serial prime time drama, the series provides resolution and an ultimate re-location back into more traditional feminine roles for their female leads.

Foyle's War

As the eponymous detective, narrative agency in this 2004 series is held firmly by Foyle (Michael Kitchen), who wields considerable authority as a result both of his gender and of his status as a police Superintendent. The audience follows the plot of each episode through Foyle's investigations, assisted by Foyle's driver and companion Samantha, or Sam (Honeysuckle Weeks), who was drafted to him from the Mechanized Transport Corps (MTC), and Milner (Anthony Howell), a junior male police officer.

The episode analyzed in detail here, "They Fought in the Fields," was the second in the program's third series, and was first aired by ITV on November 7, 2004. Set in 1941, this episode sees Foyle question three members of the WLA over the apparent suicide of a Hastings farmer named Hugh Jackson (Nigel Terry). As such, the WLA is here mediated through the generic conventions of television detective drama in the early 21st century. As well as highlighting the hardships of rationing and the challenges posed to the agricultural sector by limited resources, this episode also provides insights into an often overlooked branch of the WLA: the Timber Corps. Although technically a separate body, the recruitment and administration of the Timber Corps was overseen by the WLA. The solitary nature of life in the Timber Corps (women were required to scour forests and woodland, usually alone, identifying trees suitable for conversion into telegraph poles, pit props, etc.) is used to great effect in the episode, to establish one of the female characters, Barbara (Stella Gonet), as an outsider.

Physically separated from the other two Land Girls—in many shots she is seen sitting alone, or standing removed from the group—Barbara's status as outsider is also often signified by her clothing. While the other characters wear muted, utilitarian colors and uniforms, Barbara is often wearing a bright red coat; this serves not only to mark her out as different, but combined with comments made throughout the episode about her appearance and demeanor (she is visibly older than the other two Land Girls), it establishes her as the experienced and sexually threatening older woman.

As well as this visual distancing from the other women, Barbara's attitude towards men distances her from the rest of the inhabitants of the farm, who view her as cold and aloof. When asked for her first impression of Farmer Jackson during police questioning by Foyle, Barbara replies that she thought "he was not too different from most men: rude, lazy, lascivious and ignorant." Despite her attractiveness, her perceived "misandrist" attitude limits Barbara's potential as an object of male desire within the episode—which, as Charlotte Brunsdon (1987) argues, is a requirement for female characters seeking to occupy leading roles in television drama. However, throughout the episode, Barbara's sexuality and allure is repeatedly referred to; in one scene she is seen wearing a lace nightgown, and an expensive lace bra discovered in Jackson's bed is revealed to belong to her. Later on in the episode, Foyle identifies her as the "very attractive" woman with "sad eyes" as described by one of the German airmen. Her affinity with nature is also emphasized when she discusses her love of working in the forest and her familiarity with different types of plants, flowers, and trees. These traditionally feminine tropes compensate for her hostile persona, and suggest that she is in need of rescuing from self-imposed isolation and to once again occupy her "natural" role as a desirable woman. When she is discovered sobbing and alone in the woods by Foyle, she reveals to him that she was the victim of an unhappy and possibly violent marriage, and that she had lost her son at Dunkirk. Thus, the association of war and death as entirely masculine, as something carried out and perpetuated by men, is revealed as the root of her hostility. Her time in the Timber Corps has provided her with a temporary space in which she can grieve and in which she can find purpose through her participation in the national war effort. In this way, the Timber Corps, and by extension the WLA, can be seen as providers of an alternate and temporary sense of purpose for women to whom the war has denied the possibility of becoming wives and mothers— roles which are ultimately still privileged as the most natural and fulfilling for a woman to occupy.

Barbara's membership of the Timber Corps offers her the opportunity to meet Foyle, who shows her that her prejudice against men is misplaced. Her acceptance that there are good men left in the world opens up the possibility of her once more occupying the roles of wife and mother. Thus, in *Foyle's War* the Timber Corps can be read in some ways as a freeing space that offers Barbara solitude, within which she can find peace and temporary relief for her grief—however, in order to achieve true happiness and resolution, she must accept her repositioning back into a more traditional female role.

Barbara stands in almost direct contrast to Joan (Jenny Platt), one of the two Land Girls living and working at Jackson's farm. Joan is younger, working class, and although clearly an attractive girl, lacking in the refinement which defines Barbara's sexual appeal. Her working class origins are suggested, in the first place, by her Cockney accent and style of speech. When the girls' job of milking the cows is delayed by Foyle's questioning over the death of Farmer Jackson, Joan angrily confronts him, "Oi! Can't you hear them cows? Your little friend wouldn't let us get on and milk 'em. Their titties are going to explode if we don't!" Joan is uncouth, crass, and disregarding of Foyle's authority; in many ways she epitomizes the idea of the unruly woman (Rowe, 1995). As an unmarried working class woman, Joan also presents an implicit sexual threat, one which is made explicit when Farmer Jackson, after discovering her relationship with his son Tom (Joe Armstrong), promises that she "shan't get [my] boy and [...] shan't get the farm." As well as the possibility that Joan may come to possess the farm through marriage to Tom, as ultimately comes to pass, there is a suggestion within the text that Jackson's anxiety stems partly from the amount of work Joan has put into the farm, and the personal pride she visibly takes in its success. Joan's practical competency and the assumption that she is not only capable of, but also likely to replace him in running the farm, presents a challenge to Jackson's masculinity and his sense of purpose. In this way the episode taps into the initial fears and reluctance of many farmers to take on Land Girls, which stemmed, at least in part, from this very same fear of "emasculation." At a time when gender roles were in flux, the presence of women and, moreover, *competent* women in previously male-dominated industries such as agriculture, further eroded the traditional male-female binary and challenged conceptions of male competency. The episode utilizes a narrative common to most televisual depictions of women's wartime service—that is, one of women proving themselves capable of taking on male roles.

Comparisons are also drawn in the episode between Joan and Foyle's driver Sam. In contrast to Joan, Sam is obviously upper-middle class, well-spoken, and deferential to authority. Her continuous presence in *Foyle's War* ensures that she is a character with whom the audience will be familiar; however, in this episode it is initially suggested that her femininity is "delicate" and that she is perhaps incapable of the heavy, physical work undertaken by the Land Girls. At the site of the crashed German bomber, because of her gender, Sam is advised to stay back so she will not see the body of the pilot. The following shot of the pilot's bloody corpse proves that this was not a device to spare the audience unnecessary gore, but rather a deliberate undermining of Sam's character and her ability to cope with the brutal realities of war.

In contrast to the demanding, physical work undertaken by the Land Girls, Sam's role as a driver seems facile and indulgent, as evidenced when Joan spitefully asks why Foyle cannot drive himself; she asks her, "Don't you know there's a war on? Us breaking our backs, and you done up spick-and-span, your barnet done up like a Cornish pasty." Unlike Rose (Paula Jennings) and Joan, Sam's location in the male sphere is figured as superficial and frivolous in comparison with their own robust and practical contributions. Hence when Rose challenges her authority to question her, Sam meekly replies, "True."

It is only when pitching in and helping Rose and Joan in the planting of a field of potatoes that Sam gains acceptance from the two women, and that her utility to the war effort is acknowledged. In this way the episode emphasizes similar themes to those highlighted in *Land Girls*—namely that the WLA offered women a purpose during war time and an opportunity to make a tangible contribution to the war effort. When asked why she joined, Rose replies, "I wanted to do my bit. My two brothers are away in the army. I wanted to help 'em. To help bring them back alive." Furthermore, in a very similar character arc to that of Connie in *Land Girls*, the WLA allows Joan to escape a life of poverty and crime in London. Revealing that she ran away from home to escape her surroundings, Joan has found a safe and pastoral home in the countryside: "I didn't want a life of crime. I wanted something different and I found that here [...] for two years I've been my own person." As well as offering her a new and expanded physical space to occupy, the WLA offered Joan a liberating symbolic space in which she could redefine herself and escape the limitations of her previous identity.

However, as with Barbara, the transformation afforded to both Sam and Joan by the WLA is temporary. Her point proven, Sam returns to her deferential role as Foyle's driver and companion. Joan, in marrying Tom, becomes a wife and inherits a stake in the farm, thereby achieving gendered value and status in a more traditional way. Thus, as with *Land Girls,* to achieve resolution the women of *Foyle's War* must also accept the temporary nature of their freedom and allow themselves to be resituated within the parameters of normative femininity.

Backs to the Land

As Brett Mills (2009) discusses, sitcom is often dismissed as "small time," lacking in any real social value and perceived "as an alternative to work, education, seriousness" (Curtis, 1982 cited in Mills, 2009, p. 1). While this is not in itself problematic, it does suggest interesting distinctions between *Backs to the Land* and the other two programs. Unlike *Land Girls,* which has an explicitly educative and commemorative intent, or *Foyle's War,* which presents a meticulously researched and stylistically and tonally "realist" vision of the past, *Backs to the Land* is very different. Broadcast in 1977, *Backs to the Land,* like *Dad's Army,* was created at a "time sufficiently distant from the Second World War to allow laughter at it" (Nelson, 2005, p. 52). To avoid controversy, the series also shied away from any kind of explicitly political or ideological satire. This provides an interesting point of comparison to the other two series which, although having greater temporal distance from the Second World War, adopt a much more reverential approach to it as subject matter. The non-naturalistic nature of the sitcom format, evident in the style of shooting and the presence of a laughter track, also distinguishes this series from the others in that the lack of verisimilitude immediately suggests to the audience that this is not a faithful representation of the past; there is no suggestion that what they are watching is "real history."

While *Dad's Army* shares these sitcom characteristics, it also "balances laughter at its characters and situations with a reiterated respect for the readiness, if necessary, of Home Guard members to sacrifice their lives" (Nelson, 2005, p. 53). This respect is indicative of the perceived importance of male characters, even those who are the subject of light ridicule such as members of the Home Guard, to histories of the Second World War. This sense of poignancy and veneration is missing from *Backs to the Land*, because as a female-led comedy concerning women's history, the series does not carry the same cultural weight. The comedic nature of *Backs to the Land* further differentiates it from *Land Girls,* which is given more cultural weight by virtue of its status as a drama; similarly, "They Fought in the Fields" is validated by its male viewpoint supplied by Foyle, its central character. I do not wish to suggest that, as a comedy, the series is less worthy than other genres of consideration in the context of this essay. It does not make its representation of the Women's Land Army any less interesting or significant to this analysis; rather, its distinct form offers a very different space and context for the representation of the WLA.

The comic impetus (Mills, 2009, p. 6) of *Backs to the Land* is derived from the perceived incongruity of the presence of women, specifically young urban women, on a farm, and their attempts to grapple with agricultural labor. It is based on an implicit understanding between the text and the audience that such women would be fundamentally unsuited to this type of work. In the first episode of the first series, "A Miss Is as Good as a Male," farmer Tom Whitlow (John Stratton) is expecting three men to be sent as farmhands to replace his two sons who have been called up to the army. Upon discovering that he has, in fact, been sent three Land Girls, he is both furious and incredulous; he declares that he "would see 'em hung" before allowing them to work on his land. The girls listen from an upstairs window, reacting with more concern than anger, and the audience's amusement can be heard on the laugh track. The fact that the girls respond with concern that they will be unsuitable for the job and asked to leave does nothing to suggest that they will ultimately prove farmer Whitlow wrong—which is what happens in both other series considered here. Rather, there is a sense that the conceit of the episode—that a miss *is* as good as a male—has been shattered and the girls' inadequacy has been found out.

Unlike the other two series, which derived much of their narrative impetus from the desire and ultimate success of the girls in proving their capability, in *Backs to the Land* it is the incompetence of Daphne (Marilyn Galsworthy), Shirley (Philippa Howell), Jenny (Terese Stevens), and later Bunny (Pippa Page), which is foregrounded and mobilized as a source of comedy. For example, upon being told that they are not required until five the next day for milking, Daphne responds, "Won't the cows mind waiting until tea time?" In the second episode of the first series, "Nymphs and Shepherds Come Expensive," the girls encounter considerable difficulties in shearing a sheep, which causes Jenny to worry: "If we can't do what a man can do, we'll be out on our ears." Rather than providing the girls with a narrative opportunity to learn the necessary skills for shearing, the series instead introduces its central theme of the girls utilizing their sexuality to encourage and trick men into carrying out the work for them. In this case, two local farmhands discuss popular conceptions of the type of women who would join the WLA. "You know what their motto is? [...] Backs to the Land! 'Cause they're all from London and you know that sort [...] Nimblemaniacs!" This expectation that the Land Girls will be "nymphomaniacs" (the mispronunciation of which here only adds to the comedic value) plays on contemporaneous concerns about the moral danger of women living and working away from their homes and families. This, along with the series title itself, ties in with the lewd, slapstick comedy prevalent throughout much of the series.

This theme remains constant throughout the three series of *Backs to the Land,* and comedy is cultivated through its repetition; the girls encounter different challenges and problems (war games, a field which requires ploughing, an entry to a country show) and must come up with new ways of encouraging the men around them to assist them. As is common to comedies of this kind (Mills, 2009), there is little to no character development over the three series. Daphne is replaced by Bernadette, or "Bunny," in the second series with no explanation for or reference to the change, as both characters fulfill the same narrative function: in both cases their sexuality is rooted in their middle class backgrounds and associated naivety, in contrast to Shirley and Jenny, whose backgrounds are working class. It is interesting, however, to note the similarities between the stock characters used in *Backs to the Land* and the more developed characters in both *Foyle's War* and *Land Girls.* Daphne and Bunny's sheltered, middle class attitudes to and experiences of work are similar to both Sam (*Foyle's War*) and Nancy (Summer Strallen, *Land Girls*), both of whom were similarly unprepared for the physical demands of life in the WLA. Jenny's working class, criminal, East London background is almost identical to those of both Connie (*Land Girls*) and Joan (*Foyle's War*), both of whom see life in the WLA as a chance to escape their former lives and as a space in which they can start again. This is interesting in terms of the characters available to women across all genres of television and across the considerable period of time in between the broadcast dates of the three series. It would appear that those female characters that television producers and writers feel will be acceptable to audiences have remained remarkably unchanged. The key difference between *Backs to the Land* and the other two series is the progression and development of these characters. For the women in both of the more recent series, these class-based tropes are a starting point, from which they are allowed to escape and discover new, albeit more normatively traditional gender roles. In *Backs to the Land* comedy is derived from the fact that these women never escape these initial tropes, and are doomed to repeat the same mistakes as a result.

As I touched on previously, *Backs to the Land* is particularly interesting because of its startling difference to the celebratory and even reverential tone of the other two series considered here. The historical shift in tone, from a light-hearted sitcom to the more commemorative and historically "faithful" nature of the later series, reflects shifting attitudes towards the Second World War and its function in the construction of British national identity. *Land Girls* and *Foyle's War* both tap into contemporary discourses of nostalgia for an imagined Britishness that was certain, stable and confident in the wake of victory in the Second World War. It is interesting to note that the vast majority of programming depicting the Second World War which has been commissioned in recent years—including *Spies of Warsaw* (BBC 4, 2013), *Call the Midwife* (BBC 1, 2012), and *The Bletchley Circle* (ITV, 2012)—has been similarly respectful and commemorative in tone. Despite the persisting popularity of series such as, *'Allo 'Allo* (BBC1, 1982), *It Ain't Half Hot Mum* (BBC1, 1974) and *Blackadder Goes Forth* (BBC1, 1989) which deals with the First World War, the popular mood as mediated through television fiction seems to have shifted away from humor over the World Wars. This ties in with a general mood of nostalgia for ideals of traditional Britishness, in which both World Wars, and particularly the Second, are key points of reference and sites of identity construction. The analysis of the programs in this essay suggest that this nostalgia for a particular, mythologized sense of Britishness is also deeply gendered; it mobilizes potentially deviant historical femininities, but only so it can then recuperate these back into a heteronormative and traditionalized gender narrative. Ultimately, traditional gender roles are shored up by, rather than destabilized by, temporary transgression.

Conclusion

Although the three series ostensibly concern the same period and aspect of women's history, their different generic structures and conventions offer different interpretations of this period of history and a range of narrative opportunities for their female characters. The setting of the three series during the Second World War also creates an interesting space for stories of female empowerment, emancipation and non-traditional gender roles. The exceptional circumstances of the war, both as a plot device and as a contextualizing historical reference point, mean that transgressive storylines and subversive identities can be explored, based on the shared understanding that these circumstances are not permanent and a return to more traditional gender roles is inevitable. Combined with the cyclical nature of serial television and the need for closure and resolution at the end of each episode or series, this understanding engenders familiarity and reassurance "that the outcomes are known and will present no radical challenge to their conceptions of gendered identity" (Mahoney, 2015, no pagination).

While it can be seen that the WLA as a subject or setting offers potential for narratives of liberation, transcendence, and competency in women's historical television, the range of characters and narratives through which these stories can be told is limited by notions of acceptability and a concern for what the audience will find familiar and unthreatening. The mobilization of familiar narrative structures is integral to producing a sense of reassurance that plot developments will ultimately lead to a restoration of the gendered status quo, and present no lasting challenges to established concepts of gendered identity. Familiar characters, storylines, and experiences also help viewers to engage with a past that might otherwise seem quite alien.

The re-traditionalization (Ball, 2012; Adkins, 1999, 2000) of the female characters in *Land Girls* and *Foyle's War* situates the Second World War within the dominant post-feminist media discourse of women willingly returning to more traditional domestic gender roles. Similarly, in *Backs to the Land,* narrative impetus rarely lies with the three central female characters; they must cope with things happening *to* them, rather than driving the events of each episode. Given the program's broadcast date, it could be seen as a part of a backlash (Faludi, 1991) against the discourses of liberation and female empowerment of second wave feminism. While the three central characters are certainly presented as sexually aware, it is only ever to the extent of being alluring and pleasing to the men around them. Their sexuality and ability to manipulate the men around them stands in for their lack of skill and in their need to resort to this tactic; normative binary conceptions of men as active and women as passive are reaffirmed.

In this way it can be seen that the attitudes towards gendered identity depicted in the three series reveal more about contemporary concerns and norms of acceptable femininity than any particular essential "truth" of women's service in the Women's Land Army and the Second World War generally. However, as Barthes points out, the histories themselves cannot be completely eroded, or the myth image loses its linguistic framework and therefore its significance. Rather, what has and does occur is that the histories and lived experiences of British women become displaced and made to serve a secondary ideological purpose.

REFERENCES

Adkins, L. (1999) Community and Economy: A Re-traditionalization of Gender? *Theory, Culture and Society* (16) 1, pp. 119–39.
_____. (2000) Objects of Innovation: Post-occupational Reflexivity and Re-traditionalization of Gender. In: Ahmed, S., Kilby, J., McNeil, M. and Skeggs, B. (eds.) *Transformations: Thinking Through Feminism.* London: Routledge, pp. 259–72.
Backs to the Land. (1977) [TV] A Miss Is as Good as a Male. Directed by David Askey. Written by David Climie. United Kingdom: ITV, Anglia, April 15.

_____. (1977) [TV] Nymphs and Shepherds Come Expensive. Directed by David Askey. Written by David Climie. United Kingdom: ITV, Anglia, April 22.

Ball, V. (2012) The "Feminization" of British Television and the Re-traditionalization of Gender. *Feminist Media Studies* 12 (2), pp. 248–64. doi: 10.1080/14680777.2011. 597104.

_____. (2013) Forgotten Sisters: The British Female Ensemble Drama. *Screen* 54 (2): pp. 244–48. doi: 10.1093/screen/hjt014.

Barthes, P. R., Barthes, A. L. and Howard, R. (2013) *Mythologies: The Complete Edition, in a New Translation*, 1st edn. New York: Farrar, Straus and Giroux.

Brunsdon, C. (1987) Men's Genres for Women. In: Baehr, H. and Dyer, G. (eds.) *Boxed In: Women and Television*. London: Pandora Press, pp. 184–202.

_____. (1997) *Screen Tastes: Soap Opera to Satellite Dishes*. London: Routledge.

_____. (1998) Structure of Anxiety: Recent British Television Crime Fiction. *Screen* 39 (3), pp. 223–43. doi: 10.1093/screen/39.3.223.

Clarke, G. (2008) *The Women's Land Army: A Portrait*. Bristol: Sansom & Company Ltd.

Cooke, L. (2001) The Crime Series (Hill Street Blues). In: Creeber, G., Miller, T. and Tulloch, J. (eds.) *The Television Genre Book*. London: BFI, pp. 19–23.

Faludi, S. (1991) *Backlash: The Undeclared War Against American Women*. New York: Crown.

Foyle's War. (2004) [TV] They Fought in the Fields. Directed by Jeremy Silberston. Written by Anthony Horrowitz and Rob Heyland. United Kingdom: ITV, November 7. Available through: Box of Broadcasts database. (Accessed July 20, 2015).

Final Foyle's War Episode (2015) http://www.itv.com/presscentre/press-releases/final-foyles-war-episode. (Accessed October 21, 2015).

Horowitz, A. (2015) Anthony Horowitz on the Dark Truth Behind Foyle's War. *Radio Times*, January 4. http://www.radiotimes.com/news/2015-01-04/anthony-horowitz-on-the-dark-truth-behind-foyles-war. (Accessed October 21, 2015).

Kramer, A. (2011) *Land Girls and Their Impact*. Barnsley: Remember When (Kindle edition).

Land Girls. (2009) [TV] Childhood's End. Directed by Steve Hughes. Written by Roland Moore. United Kingdom: BBC, BBC1, September 7. Available through: Box of Broadcasts database. (Accessed July 25, 2015).

_____. (2009) [TV] Secrets. Directed by Steve Hughes. Written by Roland Moore. United Kingdom: BBC, BBC1, September 8. Available through: Box of Broadcasts database. (Accessed July 25, 2015).

_____. (2009) [TV] Trekkers. Directed by Paul Gibson. Written by Roland Moore and Dale Overton. United Kingdom: BBC, BBC1, September 10. Available through: Box of Broadcasts database. (Accessed July 25, 2015).

_____. (2009) [TV] Destinies. Directed by Daniel Wilson. Written by Roland Moore. United Kingdom: BBC, BBC1, September 11. Available through: Box of Broadcasts database. (Accessed July 25, 2015).

_____. (2011) [TV] Final Reckoning. Directed by Daniel Wilson. Written by Roland Moore and Dominique Moloney. United Kingdom: BBC, BBC1, January 19. Available through: Box of Broadcasts database. (Accessed July 27, 2015).

_____. (2011) [TV] Farewell My Lovely. Directed by Steve Hughes. Written by Roland Moore and Joy Wilkinson. United Kingdom: BBC, BBC1, November 10. Available through: Box of Broadcasts database. (Accessed July 31, 2015).

Land Girls Feature (2014) Interview with Becci Gemmell. http://www.bbc.co.uk/press office/proginfo/tv/2011/wk3/feature_land_girls.shtml. (Accessed October 21, 2015).

Mahoney, C. (2015) Not Bad for a Few Ordinary Girls in a Tin Hut: Re-imagining Women's Social Experience of the Second World War Through Female Ensemble Drama. *Frames, Cinema Journal 7* (no pagination).

Manvell, R. (1974) *Films and the Second World War.* South Brunswick: A. S. Barnes.

Martin, J. (2000) *The Development of Modern Agriculture: British Farming Since 1931.* Basingstoke: Palgrave Macmillan.

Mills, B. (2009) *The Sitcom.* Edinburgh: Edinburgh University Press.

Nelson, R., (2005) "They Do Like It Up 'Em": *Dad's Army* and Myths of Old England. In: Bignell, J. and Lacey, S. (eds.) *Popular Television Drama: Critical Perspectives.* Manchester: Manchester University Press, pp. 51–67.

Powell, B. and Westacott, N. (1997) *The Women's Land Army in Old Photographs.* Stroud: Sutton Publishing.

Rowe, K. (1995) *The Unruly Woman: Gender and the Genres of Laughter.* Austin: University of Texas Press.

Teletronic (n.d.) *The ITV Story Part 8: Anglia Television.* http://www.teletronic.co.uk/anglia_television.htm.

Thornton, L. P. (2002) "World War I." In: Thackeray, F. W. and Findling, J. E. (eds.) *Events That Changed Great Britain since 1689.* Westport: Greenwood Press, pp. 138–52.

Warren, A. (2010) All's Fairer Sex in Love and War in "Land Girls Series One." http://www.popmatters.com/review/134075-land-girls-series-one/. (Accessed October 21, 2015).

Why Did Women Join the Land Army? (n.d.) *Women at War.* http://www.nationalarchives.gov.uk/education/homefront/women/land/source1.htm. (Accessed October 22, 2015).

The Women's Land Army (2013) *The Land Girl Magazine.* http://www.womenslandarmy.co.uk/world-war-two/lifestyle/the-land-girl-magazine/. (Accessed October 21, 2015).

PART II

Feminism in Non-Fiction Media: Historical Narratives and Counter-Memories

"Spiced with a touch of glitz and a lot of fun"

Watch the Woman, *"Rogue" Feminism and 1980s Television for Women*

Jilly Boyce Kay

In her discussion of contemporary post-feminist media culture, Rosalind Gill argues that while in the 1960s, 1970s, and early 1980s, feminist discourses were expressed in the mainstream media as "external, independent, critical voices," by the 1990s, feminism had moved from its position of externality to become "part of the cultural field" (Gill, 2007, p. 161). For Gill, feminism's move into the mainstream, or the incorporation of feminist-inspired ideas into a new form of mediated "common sense," cannot be read as an unproblematic success for the movement. The various incorporations, appropriations, and co-optations of feminism by mainstream media and political cultures have been of deep concern to many feminist scholars, because in the processes of the "mainstreaming" of feminism, the radical impulses and collectivist politics of the movement are so often erased. Angela McRobbie (2009, p. 12) points to the ways in which certain individualist elements of feminism are "taken into account" by post-feminist popular culture, while at the same time the women's movement is positioned as a "spent force," as something that is no longer necessary, and which belongs firmly to the past. As such, a form of liberal, individualistic, depoliticized feminism has become legitimized as part of the contemporary cultural field, while the collective and radical nature of the women's movement is simultaneously cast out, pilloried, and rejected. Feminism and anti-feminism have thus become inextricably "entangled" (Gill, 2007) with one another. The "feminism" that is visible in media culture, then, is as a kind of "shadow feminism, a substitute and palliative for the otherwise forced abandonment of a new feminist political imaginary" (McRobbie, 2009,

p. 90). Elsewhere, Nancy Fraser similarly names this as feminism's "uncanny double" (Fraser, 2013, chapter 9), which has "split off" from the movement proper; it is, for Fraser, a deeply problematic form of feminism that has, she suggests, "gone rogue."

In many academic feminist accounts, it is the 1990s which marks the moment in which media culture is populated by post-feminism, and in which the radical possibilities of future feminist solidarities are closed off. While I find these arguments compelling, they give little sense of *how* feminist discourse moved from "outside" to "inside" media culture; *how* a "rogue" feminism "split off" from the movement and took on a life of its own; or, indeed, how the gender politics of pre–1990s media culture may *also* have been messy, entangled, and complex. This essay explores how one example of British media culture was tightly bound up with the shifting and contradictory gender politics of the mid–1980s, and seeks to theorize the nature of this relationship. To this end, I consider a program broadcast on Channel 4 in 1985 entitled *Watch the Woman*, which offered itself as a "glossy women's magazine" for television, and which targeted a young, "aspirational," upwardly-mobile female audience. In a book about memory, this television text may seem an odd choice for analysis, because it is now almost entirely forgotten, and it occupies no obvious or tangible place within popular memory. Even at the time, it was not heralded as culturally significant; it was summarily dismissed by critics, and it did not win a commission for a second series. However, an analysis of this rather unique program can offer critical insights into the shifting dynamics of gender politics at this moment, and contribute to a more nuanced history of gendered media culture in the late 20th century. I want to suggest that there is value in looking *back* from the contemporary neoliberal and post-feminist conjuncture to a particular moment in the mid–1980s when a "rogue" feminism was, in fact, already emerging.

While *Watch the Woman* is absent in popular memories of visual culture, the memory of the program has surfaced in some recent television scholarship, in which it has typically been cited as an example of explicitly feminist programming from an anomalously radical moment in British television history: for example, Joanne Hollows and Rachel Moseley mention it in the introduction to their edited collection *Feminism in Popular Culture*, as a rare example of "overtly feminist television programming" (Hollows and Moseley, 2006, p. 5). Jane Arthurs briefly mentions it in her book *Television and Sexuality*, suggesting that the program was "premised on an address to a politicised constituency of feminist women, [...] an address that narrowed [its] appeal" (Arthurs, 2004, p. 96). In this essay, I want to trouble some of these notions that *Watch the Woman* can be understood straightforwardly as a "feminist" text, partly by drawing on Rosalind Gill's and Angela McRobbie's theories of the entanglements, contradictions, and complexities in the relationship between popular culture and feminism. To this end, I also draw on some earlier feminist television scholarship from the 1980s which discusses the program, and which reveals its more complex and conflicted relationship to feminism. I also discuss the broader historical context of Channel 4 at this time, and its implications for the gendering of British media culture more broadly. Moreover, I seek to relate *Watch the Woman* to the complex and ambivalent gender politics of the 1980s, which I argue remain under-theorized in feminist media studies, and yet whose ambiguities and nuances are crucial for understanding the profound political problems of the contemporary moment.

Remembering the 1980s: Contested Memories of Gender Politics

In this section I sketch out some of the ways in which, somewhat in contrast to the decades preceding and following it, the 1980s is figured in highly ambivalent ways in historicizations of the recent feminist past. The second wave movement is most often characterized as having begun in 1968, before finding its fullest flourishing in the 1970s; the early years of the 1980s that are sometimes included in its periodization seem to suggest that this was a time of "tapering" off for feminism. Indeed, in many contexts, "second wave feminism" and "Seventies feminism" are terms that are used more or less interchangeably. While second wave feminism is so often demonized as "personally censorious, hairy and politically correct" (Brunsdon, 2005, p. 112), it is also the case that in much feminist historiography, the second wave is implicitly conceived as a "golden-age" for feminism (Banet-Weiser, 2008), and that the 1970s is therefore implicitly positioned as "that [to] which must be returned" (Hemmings, 2011, p. 5). While I acknowledge that there are significant contestations around the ways in which the feminism of the 1970s is remembered, what I wish to emphasize here is the clear and repeated association of this decade with the second wave movement.

In the UK context, the election of Margaret Thatcher as Prime Minister in 1979 profoundly transformed the political terrain upon which feminism operated. Neoliberalist ideology found its expression in the radical, monetarist politics of her government; Thatcher's politics were premised upon the wholesale rejection of the "post-war consensus" that had been characterized by "the belief in a common future of full employment, social justice, and a minimum level of welfare for all people" (Kingsley Kent, 1999, p. 335; see also Harvey, 2007). While the ideological underpinning of Thatcher's administration was strongly anti-feminist, and she herself explicitly disavowed feminism, the election of the first-ever female Prime Minister in Britain at this moment cannot be separated from the wider context of women's liberation. Indeed, the very fact that Thatcher was impelled to disavow feminism—"I owe nothing to women's lib," as she famously put it (cited in Smith, 2013, p. 159)—indicates the inextricable discursive entanglements of her success with the rise of the movement.

As Bonnie J. Dow argues, the 1980s is often figured in feminist histories as a depressing time (Dow, 1996, p. 86): a decade of disappointments and renewed misogyny that came after the optimism, vitality, and legislative gains of the 1970s. This particular narrative is most eloquently produced in, and reproduced through the widespread citation of, Susan Faludi's "backlash" thesis (1991). Faludi argued that throughout the 1980s, the media drove a fierce and powerful backlash against the women's movement. If this decade is often figured as a decade of feminism's demise and decline, it also represents a time when feminism became partly institutionalized within civil society and the state. Sylvia Walby (2011), for example, has argued that from the 1980s onwards, feminism became formally embedded in a number of political and civic institutions. As such, the 1980s also represents a time when feminism began to undergo a process of "mainstreaming" (ibid., p. 80). Finally, Kaitlynn Mendes suggests that the commonly held assumption that feminism "died" in the 1980s possibly has more to do with the mainstream media ignoring the movement during this period than it does with any actual demise (Mendes, 2011, p. 6). The ways in which this decade is figured in memories of feminism's recent past are, therefore, deeply ambiguous and contested.

Despite the difficulties in pinning down the specific ebbs and flows, peaks and troughs of the movement, there was clearly some kind of shift in the visibility, operation, and dominant understandings of feminism as it entered into and moved through the 1980s. These complex discursive processes and entanglements, and their productions and manifestations in media and popular culture in the 1980s, remain somewhat under-explored in feminist media studies, and it is into this under-theorized space that this essay enters.

Historical Context: Channel 4 in the 1980s

In this section, I consider how the particular historical, cultural, and institutional context of Channel 4 television in the 1980s produced a particular address to women, and how this formed the broader gendered context within which *Watch the Woman* was produced and received. Until November 1982, there were only three British terrestrial television channels: BBC1 and ITV for the "majority" audience and BBC2 for "minority" audiences. In the pre-digital era the broadcast spectrum was a scarce resource (Ellis, 2000), and the institution of each of these channels had been preceded by extended debates that were underpinned by anxieties about preserving the balanced ecology of British public service broadcasting (Hobson, 2008). These debates also attended the formation of Channel 4. Established as the fourth terrestrial channel in 1982, it was given the unique status as a "publishing house"—that is to say, not to produce its programs in-house, but rather to commission programs from the independent sector and buy in others. It was to be publicly-owned but commercially funded; this unique constitution was designed to ensure that the commercial imperatives of profit-making were institutionally separate from its remit to be innovative and distinctive from the existing channels.

From the outset, Channel 4 was tasked with catering for "minority" tastes, and the founding chief executive Jeremy Isaacs had long publicly expressed his intention to include more women in television production (Isaacs, 2006). While the channel's "programming philosophy"—which was to "cater for substantial groups presently neglected" (Lambert, 1982, p. 127)—was in many ways seen to have a clear affinity with the aims of activist women's groups, there was actually no explicit or specific remit to cater for women as a distinct audience. Women's programming thus had a peculiar, precarious, and ambiguous status within this "licence to be different" (Brown, 2007).

As Patricia Holland, Hugh Chignell and Sherryl Wilson suggest, for many women's groups and other alternative filmmaking collectives, the idea of "public service" as defined by the BBC and ITV had implied "highly restricted access to the airwaves as well a narrow and a limited range of programming styles" (Holland et al., 2013, p. 62); in this new context, Channel 4 seemed to represent opportunities for hitherto marginalized voices to gain access to the airwaves. The early years of Channel 4 are often remembered as providing a new, important, and progressive forum for marginalized identities and radical politics. However, the political impulses that drove its creation were in fact highly ambiguous and contradictory. It was, of course, under Margaret Thatcher's decidedly right-wing government that Channel 4 was given life. As Georgina Born (2003, p. 777) notes, the coalition of interests lobbying for Channel 4 were "labile" and "politically opportunistic"; this resulted in a contradictory conceptual model for the channel, one which simultaneously privileged "small businesses and leftist production collectives." Importantly, Patricia Holland et al. (2013, p. 94) note that the deregulated structure of Channel 4 was in keeping with the broader ideological project of economic liberalization, and that while the

> unapologetic radicalism of [Channel 4's] output was likely to be deeply unsympathetic to the mood and ethos of the Conservative government [...] Margaret Thatcher saw a different potential for the channel. For her, its structure demonstrated a success for market forces and the promotion of an entrepreneurial spirit.

Thatcher's distaste for radical, leftist content was thus subordinated to the overriding, more important imperative of instantiating a model of competition and free enterprise.

By the 1990s, the early promise of small independents operating in a pluralistic and open broadcasting culture had given way to "concentration and stratification" (Born, 2005, p. 141) in the independent sector; that is to say, the logic of economic liberalization eventually overwhelmed the radical, alternative potential of the channel. As such, *Watch the Woman* appeared at a highly specific moment in the history of British television, when Channel 4's intervention into the broadcasting landscape allowed—briefly—a different kind of space. At this time, it was possible to stake out spaces that were relatively radical via the legitimating discourses of diversity, plurality, and innovation. However, these spaces were simultaneously populated by the emerging logics of neoliberalism, which would ultimately subsume these radical possibilities; as such, radical politics (including those of feminism) were already becoming "entangled" with neoliberal logics at this time.

Women's Magazine Culture, Femininity and Feminism

Watch the Woman was the first production by the independent company Carol Sarler Productions. Carol Sarler had previously worked in a senior role in women's magazines, and had there encountered some controversy; in 1983 she was sacked as editor of *Honey* magazine. Janice Winship (1987, p. 20) writes that this sacking was probably "because of her efforts to introduce feminist arguments and ideas and, generally, a 'more thinking' editorial style alongside *Honey*'s usual fashion and beauty spreads" as well as Sarler's apparent "socialist sympathies." Importantly, Winship notes that while some forms of feminism are tolerated and supported in women's magazines, the combination of feminism and socialism are not (ibid., p. 21). However, as Sarler herself described it after her sacking, her approach on the magazine was to create "not so much a spare rib, more a succulent casserole with a dozen ingredients" (Sarler, 1983). It is clear that she was here distancing herself from the explicitly feminist magazine *Spare Rib* (which is discussed by Claire Sedgwick in her essay in this volume). We can begin to see here a subtle "taking into account" of feminism at the same time as a repudiation of the name and of the wider movement.

Watch the Woman represented Sarler's move from magazines into television: it explicitly sought to remediate the aesthetic qualities of "glossy" magazines for the small screen. As such, it mobilized the particular gender politics associated with "aspirational" magazines: that is to say, a notion of success as the consequence of individual effort; a notion of the identity of "working woman" as an affirmation of entrepreneurial spirit rather than a class position; and a basic, depoliticized commitment to sexual equality that co-exists with an idea that feminism's work is no longer needed. If it was defined against the austere aesthetics, explicit feminism and collectivist politics of *Spare Rib*, it also dis-identified with daytime television magazine programs. That it was intended for "working" women was consistently emphasized in the surrounding publicity, and daytime magazine programs—and their association with the stereotype of housewives economically dependent on their husbands or the state—formed a key point of disidentification. In a sympathetic *Observer* article that anticipated the new program before it was broadcast, it was described as such: "It will not, emphatically not, be in the cosy chat-on-the-sofa housewife slot in the afternoon, but up there in prime-time competing with *News at Ten*" (Lowry, 1985).

In the publicity surrounding *Watch the Woman*, then, it could be argued that the figure of the housewife was banished as an intolerable stigma. As such, the figures of both the feminist and the housewife (see Brunsdon, 2000) became key nodes of disidentification for the program's "progressive" identity; it disavowed the "regressive" identity of the housewife as well as the "militant" identity of the feminist. It can, therefore, be read as helping to forge a "new" paradigm of femininity. It should, then, be read in the context of a changing class society in which "aspiration," individual success, and economic independence were increasingly valorized at the same time as the welfare state was being radically cut back. It participated in a wider, emerging context that was shaping new individualist modes of gendered subjectivity and power.

Watch the Woman: *Conceptual Premise*

Watch the Woman's stated intention was to be a "weekly TV equivalent of a young woman's glossy, topical magazine" (Channel 4 Report, 1986, p. 10). Its publicity sought to imagine and invoke a particular demographic of "progressive and progressing" young women who, through their participation in waged labor and the consumer economy, were engaged in forging their own economic and emotional destinies. The program was first introduced in the Press Packs in the following way:

> [*Watch the Woman* is] the creation of former Honey editor Carol Sarler, and targeted precisely to women under 30, who in Sarler's words "like their broad spectrum of interests spiced with a touch of glitz and a lot of fun." The programmes will range from the serious concerns of career, health and women's rights to fashion and beauty, and onto relationships, sex and the personal issues that affect everyday contemporary living—all treated with an editorial stance emphatically on the side of this particular audience [ibid.].

Deborah Chambers notes that commercial women's magazines in the 1980s avoided addressing women as "workers" and focusing on the "unpleasurable" theme of work (Chambers, 2014, p. 292; see also Gough-Yates, 2003, p. 94). Instead, the figure of the "new woman" was mobilized through an emphasis on what Winship has called "aspirational feminism" (Winship, 1987, p. 120). Arguably, a similar mobilization occurs here through the individualist focus on "career," instead of a more collective notion of employment rights and class-based identity. In this regard, the reference to "women's rights" is very interesting here. Framed via the modalities of "glitz" and "fun," the particular use of "women's rights" mobilizes liberal discourses of freedom and individual rights, facing feminism away from questions of male power, structural inequality, and collective action.

Existing Histories of the Program

The program is briefly discussed in the 1987 edited collection *Boxed In: Women and Television* (Baehr and Dyer, 1987) in two essays by Ros Coward and Su Stoessl, respectively, indicating its significance within feminist television scholarship at the time. Coward suggests that *Watch the Woman* exemplified Channel 4's "half-hearted" approach to women's programs, which have been "allowed to fail and have been stored away in the channel's memory as 'interesting experiments'" (Coward, 1987, p. 100). While Coward viewed its relationship to feminism as "ambiguous," because of its focus on the "traditionally 'feminine' concerns of the women's magazine," she nonetheless argued that it was given far too short a time in which to "prove itself": "Any magazine programme will take time to find the right format and it will be a particularly tricky job for a women's programme which includes the highly critical feminist movement in its audience" (ibid.).

Coward also notes how Channel 4 was much more patient and generous with other types of unusual or experimental programs, which were allowed to grow, develop, and change.

Sue Stoessl (1987) discusses *Watch the Woman* from a marketing perspective in relation to women as a TV audience, and cites some important and interesting research that was done specifically on this program. Despite its explicit targeting of women under the age of 30, in reality, the audience was split 55 percent women to 45 percent men, and there was no identifiable age bias (Stoessl, 1987, p. 114). This is particularly interesting given the explicit identification of the intended primary addressees; it points perhaps to the difficulties of targeting "niche" audiences through a "mass" medium that is received within the domestic context. This is true of all "niche" or "alternative" programming, but perhaps poses the most difficult obstacles for programming marked as "feminist," because of the unequal gender power relations of the domestic sphere. I have written elsewhere about the ways in which feminist talk on television has been construed as unacceptably provocative, and even as a form of televisual "nagging" that is unwelcome on the small screens of the domestic home (Kay, 2015). Indeed, Stoessl discusses research by BARB and Channel 4, which showed that

> women found difficulties with the "feminist" tone of the programme that they had to watch in the company of others in the household [...] one of the main reasons that women did not watch was that other people in the household were in the room when the programme was being shown. They felt uncomfortable and expressed concern that the programmes appeared to be "anti-men" rather than "pro-women" [Stoessl, 1987, p. 114].

The Figuring of "Feminism" within Program Publicity and Media Reviews

The relationship of *Watch the Woman* to feminism was, as Ros Coward pointed out, highly ambivalent. In the advance press interviews, Sarler seemed to be very clear that it was *not* to be considered "feminist" television, although she correctly predicted that the Right would characterize it that way anyway. She deliberately distanced *Watch the Woman* from the women's movement by explicitly declaring that the word "feminist" had been banned from the program. In the Channel 4 Press Packs that promoted the program to the media, the term was consistently absent. However, despite the persistent moves to distance the program from the label "feminist," it was nevertheless intolerant of overt and egregious sexism—Sarler announced in a *TV Times* (1985) interview that "we'll be taking aim at the worst kind of man." The program, it seemed, promised a form of anti-sexist "common-sense," and yet was not connected to a wider political movement for gender justice.

The presenting team was made up of three women—Tina Baker (who would later go on to be a well-known TV critic on daytime television), the cabaret comic Jenny Lecoat, and Lucy Mathen (who had been the BBC's first British Asian woman presenter on the children's program *Newsround*)—and one man, Bert McIver. The class and ethnic makeup of the presenting team was accused of being studiedly and clunkily diverse; press reviews seemed to consider Mathen to be the "token" ethnic minority, Baker the "token" working class girl, and McIver the "token" man. McIver was even described as a "tame house male" and "wimpus domesticus" by the critic Julian Barnes (1985) in *The Observer*, suggesting some implicit anxieties about the "emasculating" effect that this program might have on men. Lecoat, on the other hand—white, heterosexual, educated, confident, and middle class—seemed to embody the character of the show. *The Spectator* (1985) described the program as "Channel

4's latest castration series"; the *Daily Mail* ran the headline "Radical Carol's whining wimmin" (Barrett, 1985), claiming with wearily predictable homophobia and misogyny that the program would only appeal to "a couple of embittered old dykes squatting in Islington." However, I suggest that the program's address was, in fact, quite clearly a heterosexualized one.

Complexifying the Backlash Thesis

In the midst of a full-throttled media-driven backlash against feminism in the 1980s (Faludi, 1991), these anti-feminist responses to the program are perhaps hardly surprising. However, I want to suggest that the program was *itself* implicated in a subtler, more insidious "undoing" of feminism. Angela McRobbie (2009, p. 6) has offered a "complexification of backlash" thesis, arguing that in the contemporary moment, the backlash against feminism is now not simply a force driven by the Right, but rather one that operates through multiple channels, including the seemingly more benign (feminine) elements of popular culture. In order to avert the possibility of a radical new reinvention of the women's movement, McRobbie argues, what is mobilized is a "coming-forwards" of individual women, a "movement of women" rather than a "women's movement" (ibid., p. 90). I suggest that this depoliticized invitation to women "come-forwards" can be also be read in the discourses of and around *Watch the Woman*; as such, the "memory" of *Watch the Woman* in recent scholarship as a "feminist" text somewhat obscures its contradictory and complex relationship to the movement. In the following sections I consider how the premise of the program, the address to the audience produced through its talk, and its discursive and spatial arrangements all operated in relation to the broader, emergent contexts of post-feminism and neoliberalism.

Transposing the Glossy Formula: From Print to the Tube

The following are some listings given in the *Times* newspaper's television section for *Watch the Woman*:

July 1st, 10.00pm: The first of a new magazine programme for women includes a report from the Royal College of Art's third year fashion show; the dilemma facing women who are forced to have an abortion; and an interview with Cherie Lunghi.

July 8th, 10.00pm: This week's edition of the magazine programme for women includes a profile of Irma Kurtz who is joining the series as 'agony aunt': Benda Polan reports on the politics of fashion; and an interview with Lee Rodwell.

July 15th, 10.00pm: The week's edition of the magazine programme for women includes an interview with surrogate mother, Kirsty Stevens and music from Fascinating Aida.

July 22nd, 10.00pm: This week's edition of the magazine programme for women includes a report on women returning to education in their midtwenties and Polly Toynbee talking about childbirth.

July 29th, 10.00pm: This week's edition of the magazine programme for women includes a report on women who break the law; Irma Kurtz with advice on how to break up a relationship without acrimony.

Although these listings should not be taken as an impartial rendering of information about the program, they do nonetheless help to provide a sense of the topics presented across the life of the series. The themes and interests outlined in the listings guides point to a range of topics that are not dissimilar to those that have comprised the content of other kinds of women's magazine programs on television: fashion, relationships, agony aunt advice, and celebrity interviews. As such, it might be said that the program dis-identified with "daytime" television not so much at the level of *content*, but rather in the *address* to its imagined audience. The context of the "glossy" and "aspirational" aesthetic of the studio, and the young, mixed-sex presenting team transformed the meaning of these topics and their cultural resonances: no longer for housewives, but for upwardly mobile, young, educated women. This seemed, perhaps, to lay the grounds for reclaiming those aspects of feminine culture which feminism was seen to have censoriously repudiated, and which had also historically served as markers of gender oppression and anachronism: now, fashion and beauty were no longer to be banished as culturally regressive or ideologically problematic, but could again be celebrated as part of a new, "educated" mode of femininity.

Watch the Woman *Opening Credits*

The opening titles of the program began with the bass guitar beats of a specially commissioned, upbeat song named for the series. The lyrics began: "Watch the woman, working it out/Watch the woman, hear how she shouts." The visuals accompanying the music included images of young, confident women in various "feel-good" scenarios. They began with a young, well-dressed white woman, confidently striding down a busy street. Some of the other clips included a young, smiling white woman riding a bike; a young, black female athlete performing a high-jump and then celebrating ecstatically; one of the presenters laughing as she played with a dog on the ground; a close-up of the female singer of the title song; clips showing the camerawomen working on the program; etc. Apart from one clip of Bert McIver (also laughing), and one very brief clip of a short-haired white woman looking very serious and holding up a finger to make a point emphatically, the overarching theme of the opening audio-visual montage was a promotion of the "progressive and progressing woman of the 1980s" alluded to in the Press Packs: a young, upwardly mobile, independent, happy, working woman, whose agency as an economically productive individual and pleasure in participating in public life were constantly reiterated. It is also significant that the program title invoked not the plural *women*, but rather the singular *woman*. Discursively, this semantic choice emphasized the liberatory promise of individualism, while de-emphasizing the possibility or value of, as McRobbie puts it, the political "coming-together" (2009, p. 26) of women.

The lyrics of the title song point in interesting ways to who the intended audience ought to be. Whereas the subjects of both the song and the images were young women, it seems that the subject being directed to "watch the woman" was generically male. He was *dared* to look at the archetypal 1980s career woman as a provocation and a challenge: "you cannot bear to look," the lyrics suggested, as it "shocks you." Moreover, the woman who was being watched occupied that position not as a passive object of the (male) gaze, but rather as somebody to be regarded, admired, and surprised by. She was looked at, but she looked back (she's "seeing through you"); her own gaze was knowing, her agency active, and she was loudly unafraid of coercive or traditional male power. So, the song constructed a double interpellation—both to those women hailed as confident and dynamic, embodying the entrepreneurial promise of the 1980s, and to those men who were also progressive, confident, and perhaps "man" enough to accept this new and changed terrain of gender politics. Mary Talbot (1995) has suggested that teenage girls' magazines construct a "synthetic sisterhood" through their address to a readership bound together in what she describes as a "bogus" community of consumers. I would suggest that *Watch the Woman* addressed a kind of "sisterhood" that was based not on ties of feminist solidarity, nor of pure consumerism, but rather a shared and yet highly individualized ambition to *succeed in life*. Men were not excluded as potential beneficiaries of the program's gendered "commonsense," but they were welcome on certain, qualified terms; namely, that they accepted and embraced the social, economic, and sexual mobility of young aspirational women.

Rosalind Gill (2007) has argued that in order to understand the postfeminist sensibility within contemporary media culture, attention must be paid to the key shift from objectification to subjectification; that is to say, it is no longer the case that women are straightforwardly presented as "passive, mute objects of an assumed male gaze" (p. 151). Rather, a profound shift in the operations of gender power has occurred—"a shift from an external, male judging gaze to a self policing narcissistic gaze." For Gill, this shift ultimately involves a "deeper level of exploitation," because it actively constructs girls' and women's own subjectivities. It does seem that in this regard, *Watch the Woman* cannot be understood as "post-feminist," or at least not in these particular terms; as Gill shows, in contemporary post-feminist media culture, female subjectivity is constructed and defined in relentlessly sexualized terms. In this example, the subject of the "watching" is a woman who refuses to be defined by the "watcher," unlike the subject of contemporary post-feminism, who is ostensibly endowed with agency, but actually only on the condition that she uses it to construct herself according to heterosexual male fantasies (ibid.). Nonetheless, the discourse of "being watched" here does reaffirm the "to-be-looked-at-ness" of women (Mulvey, 1975, p. 11). Attention to periodicity and context is important; I would suggest that *Watch the Woman* can indeed be read, to use Fraser's (2013) term, as "resignifying" feminism in such a way to make it more easily compatible with an increasingly individualized and privatized culture, at the same time as it was working to "disarticulate" (McRobbie, 2009) feminism as a collective social movement. However, the *extent* to which it resignified and disarticulated feminism in this way should be carefully qualified, in particular with reference to sexualization.

The opening montage ended with a camerawoman swinging the studio camera around to apparently directly face the audience, with the lens pointing straight "back" at the home viewer. This symbolically positioned the female viewer as also one of these confident, progressive, empowered women. The address to the audience, then, was towards a very historically specific figure of a young woman, who both seemed to defy the social conservatism of the incumbent Tory government and yet was, in important ways, produced by the individualism that its politics represented. The image of the camera lens facing squarely towards the home audience gave way, in a crescendo of music and the incitation to "watch the woman NOW!," to the studio setting. The four presenters—Tina, Lucy, Jenny, and Bert—were arranged across sofas and barstool seating in a space resembling something between a hotel lobby and an open-plan, informal office, with large potted plants and flowers, a bar, and a spiraling metal staircase.

As Helen Wood (2009) has shown, in morning television magazine programs, the organization of the studio set replays the arena of the domestic, where "guests sit on armchairs with cups of coffee and are thanked for 'dropping in'" (Wood, 2009, p. 44). It is significant, then, that the studio set of *Watch the Woman* evoked a hybridized space of the workplace and a bar—signaling the leisure and upwardly mobile pleasures that disposable income brings. The attractive but nondescript setting provided the presenters with sofas to chat on, and yet the context was not coded as domestic; instead, it was infused with the glamor and the promise of the non-domestic, of the "outside" world, where consumption was resignified as a gendered marker of economic independence rather than domestic confinement. The presenters had obviously been chatting just before transmission, and Tina was still smiling as she turned away from Lucy, towards the camera, and drew breath to offer the greeting "Hello, and welcome to *Watch the Woman*, it's a new series of programs 'specially for women, and we'll be with you on Monday nights, right through the summer." The greeting was offered as though the audience member had "walked in" to their conversation, and they were welcomed as participants in their talk—much as you would be welcomed to join a table of friends at a bar or in a restaurant. This is similar to the ways in which morning television talk invites its viewers to "drop in," and yet with the crucial difference that the audience was being invited to "come out" with the presenters into an exciting new world (or perhaps, to use McRobbie's term, to "come forward" as women).

Jenny Lecoat's first address to camera was as follows: "On this the glorious occasion of Princess Diana's twenty-fourth birthday, we'd like to take this opportunity ... to discuss something more interesting. We'll be meeting actress Cherie Lunghi, and asking her how politics affect her career." Lecoat's talk—in which she sarcastically affected deference for the Royal Family, before revealing her true feelings in the punchline—was addressed to an audience who would get the joke; who would understand that the spectacle of sycophantic reverence for Princess Diana was absurd. This audience was knowing, irreverent, and not beholden to retrograde feminine idolization. By defining the program against other women's media that encouraged admiration for Diana (weekly women's magazines, perhaps)—and therefore positioning itself as alert and resistant to the "stupefying" effects of feminized mass media—the program's own dealings with consumer culture were understood to be freely entered into, self-aware, and even sometimes ironic. For example, make-up was discussed in relation to ethical consumption and animal testing; health as a matter of individual choice and rights; and fashion was explored as an art form. Consumption, fashion, and beauty were treated neither as feminine frivolities, nor as oppressive gendered practices, but rather as things to be *informed about* so that they could be practiced ethically, autonomously, and knowingly.

Prickle of the Week

One of the ways in which outlandish forms of sexism were exposed and lampooned was through the weekly "Prickle of the Week" slot. Here, Tina would survey the most egregious moments of high-profile sexism from the previous seven days, and award a cactus plant "trophy" to the worst offender. This was very likely one of the segments that viewers in the market research (cited in Stoessl, 1987) found "uncomfortable" for being "anti-men." The feature highlighted particularly egregious examples of sexism, alongside Jenny Lecoat's weekly anti-sexist review of the media. While the word "feminist" had, apparently, been banned by Sarler, these weekly features did look very much like a populist form of feminism. The ridiculing of "macho" culture—for example, the masculinist cultures associated with cricket and British pubs—can be read as something of a feminist provocation in this context of primetime, national, broadcast television. This is a space in the schedule in which, historically, in talk-based television at least, masculinity has had few direct or explicit challenges, particularly in the form of ridicule. In another media context, such as a women's print magazine, or even daytime television, it would arguably not be received and understood as controversial; here, it was the context and framing of the talk in an *evening* television slot that marked it as audacious.

Conclusion

The question of whether a television program is explicitly identified as "feminist" or not is less important than how it works discursively to undermine or bolster the wider feminist movement (Kay, 2014, p. 90). Even in this case, where the word "feminist" was ostensibly repudiated, a case could still be made for the program as being partly feminist in character. However, while it clearly had a relationship with feminism—as with Thatcher, the very need to disavow the word constituted a relationship in and of itself—I would suggest that *Watch the Woman* worked in many ways to disarticulate feminism, to use McRobbie's phrase. It operated both within and against the backlash; as such, McRobbie's thesis of complexification is particularly salient here. Its particular form of address operated through an implicit dis-identification with, and even repudiation of, second wave feminism. What is significant is that the "undoing" of feminism through ostensibly "progressive" media culture was already in operation in the mid–1980s. This cues us into the ways in which post-feminism should not be understood as a straightforward or clean "break" with the feminist past; while important differences remain between the gender politics of the 1980s and today, there are also significant continuities that require close attention.

Watch the Woman attempted to address a particular demographic of women within the specific spatio-temporal context of the domestic sphere in the evening. The domestic context of television reception is particularly significant in relation to its 10:00 p.m. time of broadcast; in this case, the gender power relations structuring the "mass" domestic reception of television seemed to work against the possibility of an explicitly feminist address. However, I do not wish to insist upon an irrevocable incompatibility between feminist talk and television. Rather, following Rosalind Coward, I would suggest that the existing discursive disjuncture between the two requires that they be given much more space and time to formulate a new possibility of televisual address.

While I have generally emphasized the ways in which *Watch the Woman* worked to disarticulate feminism and repress socialist-feminist memory, it is important to note that there were also glimmers and moments of more radical politics. *Watch the Woman* presents perhaps a slightly different case to the relentlessly individualistic post-feminist media culture of the 1990s, because while its overall premise did seem to disavow a "personally censorious, hairy, and politically correct" (Brunsdon, 2005, p. 112) notion of second wave feminism, it was much more open to oppositional feminist voices than, perhaps, later programs have been. For example, it hosted interviews with feminists strongly linked with the women's liberation movement, including Beatrix Campbell, who talked at some length about her book on women in the Conservative Party, and Germaine Greer, who debated the domination of the newspaper industry by men with a senior male journalist. Notwithstanding these moments, I would still suggest that in many senses the program can be seen as complicit in the undoing of feminism, because of its discursive work in resignifying feminism as more easily compatible with the new neoliberal economy.

The producer Carol Sarler was quite open (at least according to the *Daily Mail*) that the *Watch the Woman* team was "resolutely non–Tory" (cited in Barrett, 1985), seeming to suggest that the program's sympathies lay with the Left. However, here the notions of "Left" and "Right" must be contextualized and understood within the specific context of the mid–1980s. As Stuart Hall (2011) notes, the radical zeal of Thatcher's politics, and particularly the ways in which her government seemed to win consent and shape "common sense" among the British electorate, meant that the Left was profoundly disoriented at this time. Nancy Fraser argues that the rise of neoliberalism dramatically altered the terrain on which feminism operated; this is also true for the Left more broadly, who found themselves wrong-footed by Thatcherism at every turn, and struggling to understand how this political ideology was gaining so much popular ground. For Fraser, this was a key moment when feminist critique became fragmented; a focus on political economy, socialism, and the gender politics of redistribution became subordinated to the liberal politics of recognition, which prospered more easily in this new context; it was this latter form of feminism which went "rogue," and which I suggest characterized the politics of *Watch the Woman*.

The ways in which *Watch the Woman* was "non–Tory" or otherwise "progressive" can be understood, therefore, in the terms of the politics of recognition, rather than the class politics of redistribution. Following Fraser, I am clear that this is certainly not to suggest that the liberal politics of recognition is either frivolous or intrinsically anti-feminist. The welfare state and its social protections were often strongly patriarchal, and Fraser suggests that the neoliberal resignification of feminism may well have had some positive effects, "to the extent that the protections it disintegrates are oppressive" (Fraser, 2013, chapter 10). However, the feminist gains of recent decades must be understood, in Fraser's terms, as being entwined with a tragic loss. In my view *Watch the Woman* was tightly bound up in these complex disarticulations and resignifications of feminism. Its cultural power was not such that it can be said to have been a formidable driver of these processes. However, to the extent that it mobilized an individualist, "fun" feminism, and conflated "work" with aspiration rather than class politics, it can be read as part of a much broader and pernicious culture of undoing, dismantling, and splintering of feminism as a movement of the Left.

REFERENCES

Arthurs, J. (2004) *Television and Sexuality: Regulation and the Politics of Taste.* Maidenhead: Open University Press.
Banet-Weiser, S. (2008) Girls Rule! Gender, Feminism and Nickelodeon. In: Brunsdon, C. and Spigel, L. (eds.) (2008) *Feminist Television Criticism: A Reader*, 2nd edn. Maidenhead: Open University Press, pp. 191–210.
Barnes, J. (1985) Boffing Towards Godhead: Television. *Observer*, August 18, p. 20.
Barrett, S. (1985) Radical Carol's Whining Women. *Daily Mail*, August 6, p. 12.
Born, G. (2003) Strategy, Positioning and Projection in Digital Television: Channel Four and the Commercialization of Public Service Broadcasting in the UK. *Media, Culture and Society* 25, pp. 773–99.
_____. (2005) *Uncertain Vision: Birt, Dyke and the Reinvention of the BBC.* London: Vintage.
Brown, M. (2007) *A Licence to Be Different: The Story of Channel 4.* London: BFI.
Brunsdon, C. (2000) *The Feminist, the Housewife, and the Soap Opera.* Oxford: Oxford University Press.
_____. (2005) Feminism, Postfeminism, Martha, Martha and Nigella. *Cinema Journal* 44 (2), pp. 110–16.
Chambers, D. (2014) Contexts and Developments in Women's Magazines. In: *The Routledge Companion to British Media History.* Abingdon: Routledge, pp. 285–96.
Channel 4 Report (1986). http://www.channel4.com/media/documents/corporate/annual-reports/annual_report_1986.pdf. (Accessed March 15, 2015).
Coward, R. (1987) Women's Programmes: Why Not?. In: Baehr, H. and Dyer, G. (eds.) *Boxed In: Women and Television.* London: Pandora Press, pp. 96–106.
Dow, B. J. (1996) *Prime-time Feminism: Television, Media Culture, and the Women's Movement Since 1970.* Philadelphia: University of Pennsylvania Press.
Ellis, J. (2000) *Seeing Things: Television in the Age of Uncertainty.* London: I.B. Tauris.

Faludi, S. (1991) *Backlash: The Undeclared War Against American Women.* New York: Crown.

Fraser, N. (2013) *Fortunes of Feminism: From State-managed Capitalism to Neoliberal Crisis* (e-book). London: Verso.

Gill, R. (2007) *Gender and the Media.* Cambridge: Polity Press.

Gough-Yates, A. (2003) *Understanding Women's Magazines: Publishing, Markets and Readerships.* London: Routledge.

Hall, S. (2011) The Neo-liberal Revolution. *Cultural Studies* 25 (6), pp. 705–28.

Harvey, D. (2007) *A Brief History of Neoliberalism.* Oxford: Oxford University Press.

Hemmings, C. (2011) *Why Stories Matter: The Political Grammar of Feminist Theory.* Durham: Duke University Press.

Hobson, D. (2008) *Channel 4: The Early Years and the Jeremy Isaacs Legacy.* London: I.B. Tauris.

Holland, P., Chignell, H. and Wilson, S. (2013) *Broadcasting and the NHS in the Thatcherite 1980s: The Challenge to Public Service.* Houndmills: Palgrave MacMillan.

Hollows, J. and Moseley, R. (eds.) (2006) *Feminism in Popular Culture.* Oxford: Berg.

Issacs, J. (2006) *Look Me in the Eye: A Life in Television.* London: Abacus.

Kingsley Kent, S. (1999) *Gender and Power in Britain, 1640–1990.* London: Routledge.

Kay, J. B. (2014) "The *Sunday Times* Among Them": *Good Afternoon!* and the Gendering of Afternoon Television in the 1970s. *Critical Studies in Television* 9 (2), pp. 74–93.

_____. (2015) Speaking Bitterness: Second Wave Feminism, Television Talk and the Case of *No Man's Land* (1973). *Feminist Media Histories* 1 (2), pp. 64–89.

Lambert, S. (1982) *Channel Four: Television with a Difference?* London: BFI.

Lowry, S. (1985) "Woman to watch." *Observer,* June 23, p. 42.

McRobbie, A. (2009) *The Aftermath of Feminism: Gender, Culture and Social Change.* London: Sage.

Mendes, K. (2011) *Feminism in the News: Representations of the Women's Movement Since the 1960s.* Basingstoke: Palgrave Macmillan.

Mulvey, L. (1975) Visual Pleasure and Narrative Cinema. *Screen* 16 (3), pp. 6–18.

Sarler, C. (1983) My Sour Taste of Honey. *The Times,* October 14, p. 9.

Smith, J. (2013) *Misogynies.* London: Westbourne Press.

Spectator (1985) Diary. Vol. 255, p.7.

Stoessl, S. (1987) Women as TV Audience: A Marketing Perspective. In: Baehr, H. and Dyer, G. (eds.) *Boxed In: Women and Television.* London: Pandora Press, pp. 107–16.

Talbot, M. (1995) A Synthetic Sisterhood: False Friends in a Teenage Magazine. In: Hall, K. and Bucholtz, M. (eds.) *Gender Articulated: Language and the Socially Constructed Self.* London: Routledge, pp. 143–65.

TV Times (1985) On Women for Women. June 29, p. 24.

Walby, S. (2011) *The Future of Feminism.* Cambridge: Polity Press.

Winship, J. (1987) *Inside Women's Magazines.* London: Pandora.

Wood, H. (2009) *Talking with Television: Women, Talk Shows and Modern Self Reflexivity.* Urbana: University of Illinois Press.

Feminist Magazines and Historicizing the Second Wave
Whose Histories?

CLAIRE SEDGWICK

This essay explores the ways in which two feminist magazines can be used as historical documents through which to identify key discourses disseminated within second wave feminism in the contexts of the UK and the U.S. The essay will compare these discourses to more recent feminist discourses, and as such it seeks to problematize some dominant historical narratives which posit a significant break between the second and third wave feminist movements. For the purpose of this essay, second wave feminism is identified as the period from the late 1960s until the mid–1980s; however, as this essay will attest, there has been much debate surrounding the usefulness of the term "wave" and the generational distinctions that it implies. Third wave feminism is defined as feminism that came after the late 1980s to the present.

Firstly, I outline the key arguments in the debate surrounding the usefulness of the wave metaphor within feminism, and discuss some significant problems that may arise from the use of a metaphor that is based on generational difference and change. Secondly, the essay presents evidence from *Spare Rib* and *Ms.* magazines which points to important continuities in feminist debate between the second and third wave; I argue that this complicates the idea that the third wave is a substantial departure from the second, both in terms of the issues with which it concerned itself, and the way it addressed these issues. Stacey Gillis, Gillian Howie, and Rebecca Munford (2004, p. 2) point to the fact that "the third wave has been overly eager to define itself as something different from previous feminisms," and it is my argument that the third wave's disidentification from the second means that important parallels between the two are often ignored. I argue that the main consequence of this is that the second wave movement is presented as dramatically different, which means that important opportunities for understanding across generations are curtailed.

Spare Rib and *Ms.* have been chosen because they were the most widely circulated feminist magazines during the second wave period in the UK and the U.S., respectively. Nonetheless, there were some important differences between them in terms of editorial structure, aesthetic style, and political content. *Spare Rib* was first published in 1972 by Rosie Boycott and Marsha Rowe. Boycott and Rowe had some prior experience working for the underground press (Boycott, 1984), but left in part because of the sexism within this alternative press. After originally adhering to a traditional editorial structure, the editorship of *Spare Rib* became a collective within its first year (Winship, 1987), and operated on that basis until 1992 when the final issue was published. Deborah Chambers (2014, pp. 291–92) notes that

> this monthly journal was forged by the women's movement. *Spare Rib* presented feminist debates and alternative gender roles for women. In stark contrast to glossy commercial magazines, it was a radical, anti-capitalist venture, containing no corporate advertisements and run as a collective.

In contrast, *Ms.*—also first published in 1972—was founded by Gloria Steinem and originally published as an insert in *New York* magazine. Amy Erdman Farrell (1998, p. 31) points to the magazine's aesthetic similarity to conventional women's magazines, "with lots of color, bold headlines, glossy paper, and dozens of bright advertisements." Its mobilization of a self-help ethic, and its focus on personal rather than collective transformation, mean that its political affinities were with a more liberal, individualist form of feminism. It continues to be published today and now shares space with more contemporary feminist media.

Although differing in many ways, both *Spare Rib* and *Ms.* can be described as the most well-known feminist magazines in their respective countries during this period. The historical importance of *Spare Rib* as a feminist magazine has often been emphasized, for example by Janice Winship (1987, p. 123) who in her comparison of *Spare Rib* with more general feminist lifestyle magazines, describes *Spare Rib* as a "women's liberation magazine." This meant that *Spare Rib* played an important role in articulating the debates and issues that were important to those involved in the second wave feminist movement in Britain. Similarly, *Ms.* has also been widely regarded as an important resource for the feminist movement, with Erdman Farrell (1998, p. 1) describing it as "the popular icon of the women's movement," suggesting a cultural significance that goes beyond the content of the magazine. As such, an analysis of these publications can yield unique insights into the discourses that were emphasized and circulated during the second wave.

The status of the magazines as forums for discussions of women's liberation issues makes them interesting archival material that helps enrich our understanding of feminist histories. Recently, through the work of scholars such as Clare Hemmings (2011), the importance of re-evaluating feminist history has been stressed. Hemmings (2011, p. 5) looks at those feminist stories which are often told in ways that "position their teller as a heroine of the past, present and future of Western feminism." If this is the case, it is important to compare contemporary retellings of the recent feminist past with the way in which feminist writings from the 1970s presented the movement, and the debates around it.

While Melissa Deem (2003, p. 617) asserts that "cultural memory for largely ephemeral feminist and queer practices is dauntingly limited," both *Spare Rib* and *Ms.* provide a large archive of material that, until quite recently, has been often overlooked. Given the recent launch of the full digitized archive of *Spare Rib* online via the British Library, a close analysis of its content and a re-evaluation of its wider and continuing significance is particularly timely.[1] Using archive material such as the back issues of *Ms.* and *Spare Rib* allows for a clearer understanding of the kinds of feminist discourses that were being circulated during the 1970s and 1980s.

In this essay, I analyze a range of articles published in *Spare Rib and Ms.* in 1977 which allow insights into four particular issues: these comprise key issues within the feminist movement, and are highlighted by the thematic analysis that this essay is based upon.[2] The first issue is the way that race and racism were discussed within the context of feminism. This will be considered using an article from *Ms.* by June Jordan who outlines the position of black feminism in the U.S. and the problems that mainstream white feminists have had in understanding the concerns of women of color. The second issue that will be examined is class and this will be discussed in relation to articles within *Spare Rib*. The third and fourth issues discussed here have both been characterized as controversial: these are pornography, which is analyzed in relation to a *Spare Rib* article, and transgenderism, which is discussed in the context of an article in *Ms.* This essay's analysis of these articles will be related to current debates over the particular issues that each text highlights. Finally, I will evaluate the way that *Spare Rib* engaged with the idea of post-feminism, and how this can be linked to more recent discussions of the term. Firstly, the essay discusses in more detail the importance of feminist magazines as cultural forums.

Feminist Magazines and "Multiplicity"

The second wave feminist movement provided a varied and eclectic publishing output, and Kaitlynn Mendes (2012, p. 6) has pointed to the "incredible amount of publishing taking place in alternative publications" during this time. Similarly, Thomas Flannery (2005) has pointed to both the diversity, and the cultural importance, of feminist publications. Given this, it is important to note that *Spare Rib* is one magazine among a number that were published in both the UK and the U.S., which included, for example, *Red Rag* and *Shrew* in the UK and *Off Our Backs* in the U.S. Furthermore, Joanne Hollows (2012) points to the suspicion that some feminists felt towards *Spare Rib*, meaning that it was not universally accepted within the feminist movement. As such, the magazine needs to be seen as one representative of a broader group of feminist and alternative magazines, rather than the definitive and universally representative example.

Nancy A. Walker (1979, p. 130) points to the fact that "magazines for women are not the result of monolithic editorial visions, but instead the product of complex editorial visions." When one is working within the context of a collective or an editorial team where hierarchies are not strongly imposed, and decisions are not made by a single individual, but by a group of people with collective responsibility—as with *Spare Rib*—this sense of ideological and political multiplicity in a magazine's published content is perhaps intensified further. Additionally, the fact that there are numerous philosophical positions within feminism—for example, liberal, radical or socialist (Jaggar, 1988)—further opens up the opportunity for dissenting voices and differing opinions. The existence of multiplicity, plurality, and dissent in feminist media in the 1970s suggests a continuity with some recent feminist conflicts on social media, especially regarding topics that are discussed in this essay. These include the marginalization of black feminism and transgenderism, as seen most recently in the critique of white feminism (feminism which ignores intersectionality) or the recent furor and debate surrounding Germaine Greer's comments on transgender women and the subsequent response. This suggests, therefore, that the lack of consensus between feminists today has a historical precedent. As such, the notion that the third wave represents an endless splintering of, and an unprecedented multiplicity within, feminist ideology, is somewhat overstated. As my analysis shows, feminist discourse in the 1970s was also strongly marked by debate and multiplicity. Feminist magazines, though they may represent a specific kind of feminist outlook, provide a good opportunity to gain an insight into how these contrasting views were represented in the second wave period.

Constructions of Feminist Histories

The central aim of the essay is to disrupt or challenge the ways in which feminism has been perceived, especially in retrospective accounts of the feminist movement. The stories that are told about the recent feminist past have profound implications for feminism's present and future (Hemmings, 2011); as such, they are worth reflecting on and, where necessary, they are worth contesting. Marianne Hirsch and Valerie Smith (2002, p. 11) note that "feminist art and scholarship have worked to restore to hegemonic cultural memory the stories that have been forgotten or erased from the historical record"; that is to say, feminists have long been actively engaged in contesting the dominant—most often negative—narratives about feminism that have gained currency in the culture more broadly. However, my concern here is with how feminism *itself* has constructed a problematic narrative about its *own* history through biographical, scholarly, and historical accounts. This narrative is produced by the disavowal and demonization of second wave feminism; disidentification with the women's liberation movement of the 1970s is prevalent in much contemporary feminist discourse (Brunsdon, 2005).

The "Wave" Metaphor

Feminism has been most commonly theorized through the concept of the wave. According to the logic of this metaphor, there have been three specific historical eras: the first wave representing the suffragette and suffragist movement, the second wave representing the late 1960s or early 1970s until the mid–1980s, and the third wave representing the late '80s until the present day. However, there have been conflicting opinions not only as to what these waves represent, but also as to their usefulness. Susan Arthur Mann and Douglas J Huffman (2005, p. 58) suggest that "waves are simply those historical eras when feminism had a mass base." This suggests that the wave metaphor structures the history of feminism in a fairly neutral way and has no impact on the way in which second wave feminism is regarded; I argue that this is problematic, as the invocation of the wave metaphor has much broader implications. For example, Gillian Howie and Ashley Tauchert (2007, p. 46) suggest that the "metaphor of the wave is more suggestive than its common use implies, and paradoxically runs the risk of simplifying the tradition it is called upon to describe." This suggests that by using the wave metaphor we are doing more than just applying a descriptive term, but that we are actively constructing a narrative logic that has potentially harmful implications. Victoria Bazin (2006, p. 1) argues against the use of the wave metaphor, stating that "constructing a third wave sets up a particular kind of historical narrative for feminism that implies both the end of the second wave (and the completion of its project) and the beginning of a third wave that is distinctly different to its predecessor." In this essay, the wave metaphor is challenged by a taking a detailed look at the kind of issues that were being discussed by feminists in the 1970s and '80s; the notion that these issues are so very different from the kind of issues and debates that feminists are having today is also problematized. Arguably, by ignoring the similarities between the second and third wave, both in terms of feminist struggles and feminist responses to these struggles, potentially useful lessons are lost.

The "Storying" of Feminism

The key text that informs my analysis is Clare Hemmings' 2011 book *Why Stories Matter: The Political Grammar of Feminist Theory.* Hemmings discusses the ways in which feminist theory has been historicized by and within feminist scholarship. While Hemmings is predominantly concerned with feminist theory, I suggest her ideas have a much broader application, and that they are especially useful for thinking through the mediated past of feminism. Hemmings suggests that in contemporary feminist theory, the relations between past and contemporary feminisms are narrated in three different ways. In the first instance, feminism's past is viewed through the narrative of "progress"; this suggests that feminism has become progressively more diverse and that "we used to think of 'woman' or feminism as a unified category, but [now] through the subsequent efforts of black and lesbian feminist theorists, among others, the field has diversified and feminism itself has become the object of detailed critical and political scrutiny" (Hemmings, 2011, p. 3). Such a perspective is contrasted with the second narrative of "loss" which suggests that "we used to think of 'woman' or feminism as unified, but progressive fragmentation of categories and infighting have resulted in the increased depoliticization of feminist commitments" (ibid., p. 4).

This contrasts again with the third narrative of "return," which proposes that "we have lost our way but we can get it back, if we apply a little common sense to our current situation" (ibid., p. 4). Her work is important for providing a clear framework of the differing ways in which the feminist movement has been historicized, and for encouraging feminists to reflect on the ways in which they produce and reproduce particular "stories" about feminism. For example, by implying that contemporary feminists are more enlightened, diverse, and progressive than those of the second wave, feminism's recent past is reductively positioned as regressive, simplistic, and reactionary. This functions to close off the possibility of considering the complexities, multiplicities and nuances of second wave feminism. It also functions to weaken the possibility of productive solidarities between women of different ages and generations. As such, I challenge the narrative which posits third wave feminism as significantly diverging from the issues and approaches of the second wave, and instead will point to the striking similarities between the discussions being had in the 1970s, and more recent feminist discussions.

Ms.: *Representations of Race*

In the editorial that introduced the first issue of *Ms.* (Anonymous, 1972), the editorial collective pointed to their regrets that the preview issue had not adequately represented all women, referring specifically to the marginalization of "blue-collar" and older women (ibid., p. 7). However, by 1977, there were a number of articles in *Ms.* that gave voice to those women who may have been excluded previously. The extent to which the women's movement was inclusive or exclusionary is subject to ongoing discussion, and in this context the "whiteness" of the feminist movement has been repeatedly commented on by a number of feminists. Frances E. White (2001) points to the ways in which the representation of the feminist movement as a white, middle class movement often ignores and erases the way that black feminists did actively influence feminism. She argues that, when the feminist movement is characterized as white and middle class, black feminist voices remain invisible, and that this narrative obscures the existence of a "small but vital group of black feminists" (2001, p. 28), thereby erasing the influence and importance of women of color within the movement. Nevertheless, this historical erasure must be measured against the fact that marginalization did indeed occur. Echols (1989), discussing radical feminism in the U.S., suggests that black women were accepted reluctantly within radical feminist spaces.

It is within this broader context that one must read the first article, which is here analyzed in detail: June Jordan's (1977) article "Second Thoughts of a Black Feminist." Jordan was an African-American poet, and the article identifies the difficult conflicts between black feminists and mainstream feminism. In the article, Jordan points to the profound difficulties in defining "what liberation apparently signifies to the Black Movement, the Third World Movement, and the Women's Movement. In this effort, I have encountered a woeful lack of agreement, or even goodwill" (Jordan, 1977, p. 113).

Furthermore, she questions why, when "black people are a third of the world's population" (ibid., p. 114) they not garner a proportionate amount of attention within the feminist movement. The publication of this article in *Ms.* at this time suggests that, rather than black women being "by and large silent" (hooks, 1981, p. 11), there *was* a public debate around how black women engaged with feminism, especially in relation to the civil rights movement and other black liberation movements. This also highlights the importance of recognizing that feminism cannot be viewed in isolation from other social movements that may have had an influence on it. As such, this speaks to prevalent contemporary debates around intersectionality and the role of feminism in contesting other forms of inequality. Furthermore, as Steinem (1972, p. 131) notes in an article about women's attitudes towards politics, a poll had actually found that black women were actually more "favorably disposed to the term 'women's liberation' than white women are," suggesting that black women's apparent distance from feminism may not have been to do with a lack of political engagement, but rather a marginalization within a wider feminist culture. This does suggest that the "silence" that hooks alludes to might actually be more of a silenc*ing*. While there were clearly deeply embedded power relations that structured the visibility of black feminists in problematic ways, it is nonetheless important to consider that *Ms.* at least provided some space for discussions around race. Given the magazine's wide appeal and circulation, this indicates that discourses around race and feminism were made visible in mainstream spaces. Jordan's article provides a useful argument against the totalizing notion that mainstream feminism did not include or engage with black feminism.

There has been much discussion regarding the way that second and third wave discourses on race differ. Susan Archer Mann and Douglas J. Huffman (2005, p. 57) suggest that third wave feminism can be distinguished by its "foci on difference, deconstruction and decentring." A similar sentiment is expressed by Rory Dicker and Alison Piepmeier (2003, p. 10) who argue that the "third wave [...] recognizes that the differences among women are as substantial as the differences between women and men; the category of "woman" is no longer the only identity worth examining." The implication here is that third wave feminists are different from their second wave predecessors because they acknowledge and understand difference, whereas second wave feminists did not. However, as the quote from Jordan above suggests, black feminists in the 1970s were *already* discussing the ways in which feminism needed to acknowledge the differences among feminists. Again, this complicates the view of third wave feminism as fundamentally different from the second wave in this regard.

Clare Hemmings remarks that after visiting a feminist archive she was surprised at the fact that "black and transnational critique had been a consistent component of feminist theory" (2011, p. 13) rather than one that had been historically absent and only introduced later on. This reaffirms the value of revisiting and re-evaluating feminist archive material, and points to the problematic ways in which contemporary feminist discourse often ignores the past in order to overemphasize a narrative of "progress." Catherine M. Orr (1997, p. 29) suggests that third wave feminism is "reworking what it perceives to be the successes and failures of the women's movement." However, without a clear understanding of how contemporary feminism is related to second wave feminism in terms not only of differences, but also of similarities and continuities, this job becomes harder. Bazin (2006) points to the fact that there is often a simplifying quality to third wave representations of the second wave, which is perhaps most egregious when it means that the diversity, difference, and contestation of the second wave is ignored.

One must also question the reasons *why* such a retelling of history is performed. Hemmings (2011, p. 13) argues that "which story one tells about the past is always motivated by the position one occupies or wishes to occupy in the present." Feminist attitudes are most often characterized as having been *transformed* between the second and third wave; one of the key characteristics that is seen as marking this change is the greater and more sophisticated emphasis on difference. This disidentification with second wave feminists by third wave feminists can be read as an attempt to make third wave feminism appear more progressive and inclusive. However, the recent backlash against "white feminism"[3] suggests that white third wave feminists are themselves not immune from privileging white experiences. As such, problems of marginalization, privilege, and inequality within feminism are not consigned to an obsolete past.

Furthermore, I would argue that the disidentification from second wave feminism in relation to difference allows third wave feminists to characterize themselves as "non-racist" without actually having to demonstrate or evidence that fact. By representing second wave feminism as monolithic, regressive, and anachronistic, third wave feminism can present itself as more inclusive simply by claiming its difference from the past. Sara Ahmed (2004) discusses the "non-performativity of anti-racism" in the context of British academia; I would like to use the same theoretical framework to discuss the non-performativity of anti-racism in relation to feminism. Ahmed suggests that when we talk about "admitting" our racism, we might feel bad for our racism, and that this feeling somehow "shows" we are doing something about "it." I argue that the same purpose is served when contemporary feminists "perform" anti-racism without having to substantively demonstrate this through their own actions and behavior. This idea of bad feeling being "enough" is perhaps key here—the contemporary distancing from second wave feminism and the acknowledgment of its inability to satisfactorily deal with race allows third wave feminists to assuage feelings of guilt, while at the same time ignoring the similarities with the contemporary context. The discursive "othering" of second wave feminism is thus bound up with the ways in which contemporary feminism is absolved of any imperative to reflect on race and racism. This section has discussed the ways in which an analysis of articles in *Ms.* magazine can unsettle the received wisdoms and narratives of feminist history. I will now go on to look at *Spare Rib,* and will consider the ways in which classed histories of feminism can be similarly unsettled.

Spare Rib *and Class*

The second article that this essay will now address, published in *Spare Rib,* discusses the issue of class in some detail. The title of the article—"I'm a

Working Class Woman OK"—(Bracx, 1977) provides a defiant tone, with the "OK" serving as a way in which to stop further discussion, rather than the opening up of further questions. The article involves interviews with working class women, suggesting a desire to create a space in which working class women could speak for themselves. In the article, one woman named Evelyn describes how it has "been impossible ever to talk about class" within a feminist context (Bracx, p. 14), and also points to the fact that it is only when talking to other working class women that she is able to discuss the issue properly and freely.

On the one hand, this correlates with the sense that the second wave feminism was very much middle class, which has become a widespread view of the movement; for example, Joan Wallach Scott (2002, p. 5) has argued that "while 'women' historically has served to consolidate feminist movements, it has also made race, class [...] somehow secondary." However, on the other, it is also clear that class was an issue that *was* being discussed within feminist spaces such as *Spare Rib*, and this paradoxically seems to challenge the idea of feminism as a straightforwardly middle class movement. Another respondent in the article, Hilary, suggests that she feels she has "never been able to get very far because I always felt that it was an essentially middle class movement" (Bracx, p. 14). However, as much as this is true, the fact that *Spare Rib* featured articles that allowed working class women to share their experiences means that to characterize the movement as overwhelmingly middle class silences the voices of working class women who were indeed part of the movement.

Another interviewee, Tasha, points to the fact that "with any oppressed group, you get some with more privileges than others" (ibid., p. 15). This points to an understanding within the second wave which, rather than being essentialist, acknowledges that "women" as a categorizing term is not always sufficient. Indeed, in an article on the proposed re-invigoration of *Spare Rib*,[4] contemporary feminist Reni Eddo Lodge (2013) points out that "a significant development of online feminism has been the exploration of the intersecting and complex factors that contribute to a structurally and institutionally unequal society" and "this conversation might be recent, but it's nothing new." In challenging the characterization of a move towards class and race diversity as a "new" development, it is possible to see that these are in fact *recurring* issues for the feminist movement, and not ones that contemporary feminists have newly discovered.

As Munford and Gillis (2004, p. 176) argue, such an attitude towards feminism, where the differences, rather than the common struggle between generations are highlighted, means that there is no allowance for "a collective memory of female-based thought, empowerment and activism." Furthermore, as with issues of race, the espousal of the third wave as being uniquely concerned with difference ignores the fact that contemporary feminism can also be criticized for its inability to sufficiently address class issues. For example, an article from the UK-based feminist *F Word* blog by Pavan Amara (2012) highlights that class is still an issue that needs addressing. Amara speaks to Razia, a working class mother who associates feminism with censorious behavior. For example, she suggests that feminists are "quick to shoot you down" if you don't act their way. The implication here is that particular behaviors and aesthetic codes—such as wearing a short skirt—are looked down upon from a position of class superiority. Similarly, another working class woman claims that she was spoken to by middle class feminists as though she "wouldn't understand the political issues they were talking about." The article describes a "perceived glass ceiling of class" which prevents many women from getting involved in feminism, in spite of the fact that they face many issues upon which the movement actively campaigns.

This is not to say that the anecdotal data from one blog post means that all third wave feminists are prudish and unfairly judge women based on their bodies and tastes, or that all third wave feminists are ignorant of class issues. However, it is to say that, just as second wave feminism cannot be viewed through an essentialist lens, the characterization of the third wave as more diverse, or more sensitive to difference is also reductive and misleading. It does not fully articulate the demonstrable fact that there are still women who do not identify with feminism because of a continuing perception of the movement as white and middle class. Furthermore, it may be more useful to acknowledge that the women in the second wave also dealt with this issue, rather than to present the second wave as the antithesis to the third.

Sexuality and Gender in Spare Rib *and* Ms.

The next section in this essay aims to address the ways in which issues of gender and sexuality were addressed during the second wave, and how these can be linked to the on-going debates surrounding these issues today. Specifically, it will look at an article in *Spare Rib* in 1977 which discussed pornography and the conflict between protecting freedom of speech with the potential harm of pornography. Secondly, the section will discuss an editorial by Gloria Steinem (1977) that accompanied an article about a transgender tennis player. The section will compare the attitude towards transgenderism expressed in the article, which was openly hostile towards transgender women, with the on-going contemporary debate between trans-inclusive and trans-exclusive feminists.

Spare Rib and Pornography

The first article that this section will analyze was published in *Spare Rib* in December 1977, and is entitled "Pornography: Between the Devil and the True Blue Whitehouse" (Wallsgrove, 1977). It articulates a debate around the conflict between viewing pornography as harmful to women, countered with the discomfort caused by the fact that taking an anti-pornography stance often ran the risk of sharing opinions with the conservative Right. The author Ruth Wallsgrove suggests that she finds "pornography disturbing, chilling— even sometimes physically disgusting" (ibid., p. 44). However, Wallsgrove distances herself from campaigners such as Mary Whitehouse[5] by asserting that "Mary Whitehouse and the Festival of Light seem as opposed to what I want for the world as do pornographers" (ibid.). The fact that Wallsgrove needs to assert the difference between herself and campaigners such as Whitehouse suggests that feminism's collusion with the Right is an assumption that may well be made. Academic Gayle S. Rubin (1984, p. 164) argues that "the right wing opposes pornography and has already adopted elements of feminist anti-porn rhetoric." This suggests that there was a very real sense of danger that the Right would infiltrate or co-opt feminism in a way that would fundamentally discredit a movement that has traditionally been on the Left.

The article stages an ambiguity surrounding pornography and its relationship to feminism that still exists today. The fact that the debate still continues can be seen in an article on the *F-Word* blog from 2014. The article "Feminist Porn: Revolution or Reinvention" (Vibes, 2014) articulates similar debates that were discussed in Wallsgrove's article from 1977. For example, a question that the author Isadora Vibes asks is whether "fundamentally feminism and porn [are] diametrically opposed?" This is a question that has been challenging feminism since at least the second wave, and it is clear from the article that consensus has still not been reached. The difference, however, is Vibes' acknowledgment that "pornography has been defined and produced by men for far too long," and its foregrounding of feminist porn in the discussion. This does contrast with the perspective presented in the *Spare Rib* article, which does not present the possibility of a feminist-produced pornography. This suggests that the terms of the feminist debate around pornography have shifted, and that they have done so in relationship with broader cultural changes, such as the proliferation and greater visibility of pornographic images in an online context. Nonetheless, there are again important continuities between contemporary and earlier feminist debates which should be acknowledged.

It is important to note that neither article can be read as advancing the definitive or even prevailing opinion among the feminist movement; instead, they must be read as one opinion among many from their particular moments in time. In a later article in *Ms.*, Barbara Ehrenreich, Elizabeth Hess, and Gloria Jacobs (1982) point to the fact that "nowhere is it written that women's liberation and sexual liberation go hand in hand" (ibid., p. 61); indeed, the fact that this is still a tension that is continually discussed in feminist discourse suggests that it is an on-going concern. This, again, disrupts the idea of a substantial generational break between second and third wave feminisms.

Ms. and Transgenderism

Transgenderism—or "transsexuality" as it is referred to in the texts I discuss here—is an issue that has traditionally caused numerous shockwaves within the feminist movement. Patricia Elliot (2010, p. 3) traces through the various framings of transgenderism within the feminist movement: "with respect to feminism, transsexuality has been variously described as a betrayal of feminist goals [...] 'the next logical phase of feminism' [...] or like feminism, one example of gender dysphoria." This suggests a multiplicity of views on the politics of transgenderism within feminism, and the range of these divergent views correlates with the frequency and visibility of the issue as a topic of discussion and debate.

Gloria Steinem's 1977 article views transgenderism as "a titillating idea and a phenomenon far removed from most people's lives" (p. 85). In the article on the tennis player Renee Richards, who was a transgender woman, "transsexuality" is positioned in opposition to feminism. Steinem suggests that it is problematic that "the right of a transsexual to enter a women's tournament was being immediately and generously defended" by the authorities, while women who were assigned female at birth as a general class are not supported within sport. This is mobilized in the article as evidence that transsexual women have advantages over other women.

Increasingly, the visibility of high profile trans people (for example, Caitlyn Jenner, Laverne Cox, and Janet Mock in the U.S. and Paris Lees in the UK) has proven that transgenderism is neither titillating, nor removed from most people's lives. While it is clear that the awareness of transgender issues has dramatically increased in recent years, for example with *Time* magazine declaring 2014 as the year of the "Transgender Tipping Point," it is also clear that feminism is still internally conflicted with regard to its attitudes to transgender people (Steinmetz, 2014). Julia Serano (2013, p. 62) discusses the fact that the Michigan Womyn's Festival still chooses to exclude trans women, and also points to a 2012 *Ms.* blog piece where transgenderism was framed as a "debate," flagging that "when transfeminism is reduced to a debate about whether trans women 'count' as women or as feminists, it's a disservice not only to us, but to feminism as a whole." This suggests that feminism still has a way to go with regards to inclusivity.

Again, emphasizing the similarities between second and third wave feminists in questions around pornography and transgenderism is not to deny that developments and changes have taken place, for with the passage of time and through the energies of social movements there will always be an evolution in the way that we think about things. However, pointing to the ways in which similar themes and issues can be drawn out across time makes clear that presenting feminism as a movement of linear progress—where a clear break has occurred between past and present—obscures the complexities and multiplicities of feminism's recent past. Furthermore, in regards to transgenderism, Serano (2013, p. 145) argues that the framing of second wave feminists as essentialistic and therefore opposed to transgenderism, and of more recent feminisms as progressively embracing transgenderism, constitutes a narrative that "both misrepresents the concerns of radical and lesbian feminists and overlooks the high degree of ambivalence that social constructionists have expressed towards transsexuality over the years." A simplistic narrative that posits third wave feminism as straightforwardly more progressive in relation to attitudes towards trans women ignores the fact that prevailing attitudes also bear the marks of essentialism.

Conclusion

Feminist magazines from the 1970s provide an interesting insight into the discussions that feminists were having with each other at that particular moment in time. Furthermore, as the analyses of *Spare Rib* and *Ms.* in this essay show, the magazines also served as loci for discussions of conflict, which complicates the idea that the second wave feminist movement can be simply characterized according to a set of shared beliefs that were forged straightforwardly according to white, middle class perspectives. Through an analysis of articles from *Spare Rib* and *Ms.* from the 1970s, as well as contemporary feminist media texts, it has been shown that the issues mediated during the second wave period were not so dissimilar to those which concern contemporary feminists. Furthermore, my analysis has shown that *Spare Rib* and *Ms.,* while still exclusive and excluding in many ways, did in fact attempt to address these questions, and that the notion of the second wave as white and middle class is an oversimplification that obscures the nuances of feminism's recent past, and renders invisible the participation of black and working class feminists in the movement. The positioning of the second wave as monolithic and regressive is used as a rhetorical device to show contemporary feminism to be more diverse and inclusive, therefore eliding the *continued* lack of representation of black and working class women.

Secondly, the essay discussed the ways in which two key issues, pornography and transgenderism, were framed in *Spare Rib* and *Ms.*. These were again contrasted with more recent discussions, and I emphasized that while the framings of these issues have been subject to certain changes, there are still powerful continuities and connections. This should warn against any figuring of second wave feminism as anachronistic, and of the contemporary moment as incontestable in its enlightenment. Overall, the essay has demonstrated that a range of key questions have been the purview of feminists since at least the second wave. A more rigorous analysis of contemporary issues should start with an appreciation—rather than a demonization—of second wave debates. This will help develop a feminist cultural memory that would situate current debates in the context of a much larger and longer discussion.

NOTES

1. Full public access to the *Spare Rib* Archives is available through the British Library website via JISC: https://journalarchives.jisc.ac.uk/britishlibrary/sparerib. (Accessed February 24, 2016).
2. In the broader doctoral study from which this essay is drawn, thematic analysis analyzed five years of magazine content for both *Spare Rib* and *Ms.* and calculated how often each topic was mentioned.
3. Although White Feminism was discussed earlier by Aziz (1997), this has gained wider prominence recently on social media and blogs. It can be most usefully understood as a feminism which ignores intersectionality and perpetuates white privilege. The Huffington Post recently published a post called "Taylor Swift's Tweets to Nicki Minaj are Peak White Feminism," http://www.huffingtonpost.com/entry/taylor-swift-minaj-white-feminism_55afa165e4b08f57d5d30d1e, which highlights how the term has been used to critique mainstream feminism.
4. It was proposed that *Spare Rib* would be relaunched, but eventually this did not happen due to arguments between the original editors and Charlotte Raven, who was to be the editor of the new magazine.
5. Mary Whitehouse was a conservative campaigner whose activism often focused on depictions of sex and violence on television.

REFERENCES

Ahmed, S. (2004) Declarations of Whiteness: The Non-performativity of Anti-racism. *Borderlands* (3) 2. http://www.borderlands.net.au/vol3no2_2004/ahmed_declarations.htm. (Accessed May 10, 2015).
Amara, P. (2012) Feminism: Still Excluding Working Class Women? *F Word*, http://www.thefword.org.uk/features/2012/03/feminism_still_. (Accessed May 10, 2015).
Anonymous. (1972) A Personal Report from *Ms. Ms.*, July, pp. 4–7.
Aziz, R. (1997) Feminism and the Challenge of Racism: Deviance or Difference?. In: Mizra, H. S. (ed.) *Black British Feminism: A Reader*. London: Routledge, pp. 70–78.
Bazin, R. (2006) "[Not] Talking 'Bout My Generation": Historicizing Feminisms in Caryl Churchill's Top Girls. *Studies in the Literary Imagination* 39 (2), pp. 1–11.
Boycott R. (1984) *A Nice Girl Like Me*. London: Simon & Schuster.
Bracx, A. (1977) I'm a Working Class Woman OK. *Spare Rib*, October, pp. 14–17.

Brunsdon, C. (2005) Feminism, Postfeminism, Martha, Martha and Nigella. *Cinema Journal* 44 (2), pp. 110–16.

Chambers, D. (2014) Contexts and Developments in Women's Magazines. In: Conboy, M. and Steel, J. (eds.) *The Routledge Companion to British Media History.* Abingdon: Routledge, pp. 285–96.

Deem, M. (2003) Disrupting the Nuptials at the Town Hall Debate: Feminism and the Politics of Cultural Memory in the USA. *Cultural Studies* 17, pp. 615–47.

Dicker, R. and Piepmeier, A. (eds.) (2003) *Catching a Wave: Reclaiming Feminism for the 21st Century.* Boston: Northeastern University Press.

Echols, A. (1989) *Daring to be Bad: Radical Feminism in America 1967–1975.* Minneapolis: University of Minnesota Press.

Eddo Lodge, R. (2013) Let Spare Rib Reflect all the Richness of Online Feminism. *Guardian,* April 30. http://www.theguardian.com/commentisfree/2013/apr/30/spare-rib-online-feminism. (Accessed May 10, 2015).

Ehrenreich, B., Hess, E. and Jacobs, G. (1982) A Report on the Sex Crisis. *Ms.,* March, pp. 61–64, 87.

Elliot, P. (2010) *Debates in Transgender, Queer, and Feminist Theory: Contested Sites.* Farnham: Ashgate.

Erdman Farrell, A. (1998) *Yours in Sisterhood: Ms. Magazine and the Promise of Popular Feminism.* Chapel Hill: University of North Carolina Press.

Flannery, K. T. (2005) *Feminist Literacies: 1968–1975.* Urbana: University of Illinois Press.

Gillis, S., Howie, G. and Munford, R. (2004) Introduction. In: Gillis, S., Howie, G. and Munford, R. (eds.) *Third Wave Feminism: A Critical Exploration.* Basingstoke: Palgrave Macmillan, pp. 9–12.

Gillis, S. and Munford, R. (2004) Genealogies and Generations: The Politics and Praxis of Third Wave Feminism. *Women's History Review* 13, pp. 165–81.

Hemmings, C. (2011) *Why Stories Matter: The Political Grammar of Feminist Theory.* Durham: Duke University Press.

Hirsch, M. and Smith, V. (2002) Feminism and Cultural Memory: An Introduction. *Signs,* 28, pp. 1–19.

Hollows, J. (2012) *Spare Rib,* Second Wave Feminism and the Politics of Consumption. *Feminist Media Studies* 13 (2), pp. 268–87.

hooks, b. (1981) *Ain't I a Woman? Black Women and Feminism.* Boston: South End Press.

Howie, G., and Tauchert, A. (2007) Feminist Dissonance: The Logic of Late Feminism. In: Gillis, S., Howie, G. and Munford, R. (eds.) *Third Wave Feminism: A Critical Exploration (Expanded Second Edition).* Basingstoke: Palgrave Macmillan, pp. 46–58.

Jaggar, A. M. (1988) *Feminist Politics and Human Nature.* Towata: Rowman and Allanheld.

Jordan, J. (1977) Second Thoughts of a Black Feminist. *Ms.,* February, pp. 113–15.

Mann, S. A. and Huffman, D. J. (2005) The Decentring of Second Wave Feminism and the Rise of the Third Wave. *Science and Society* 69, pp. 56–91.

Mendes, K. (2012) "Feminism Rules! Now Where's My Swimsuit?" Re-evaluating Feminist Discourse in Print Media 1968–2008. *Media, Culture and Society* 34, pp. 554–70.

Orr, C. M. (1997) Charting the Currents of the Third Wave. *Hypatia* 12, pp. 29–45.

Rubin, G. S. (2007 [1984]) Thinking Sex: Notes for a Radical Theory of the Politics of Sexuality. In: Parker, R. and Aggleton, P. (eds.) *Culture, Society and Sexuality: A Reader.* Cambridge: Cambridge University Press, pp. 150–87.

Serano, J. (2013) *Excluded: Making Feminist and Queer Movements More Exclusive.* Berkeley: Seal Press.

Steinem, G. (1972) Women Voters Can't Be Trusted. *Ms.*, July, pp. 47–51, 151.

_____. (1977) If the Shoe Doesn't Fit, Change the Foot. *Ms.*, February, pp. 75, 85–86.

Steinmetz, K. (2014) The Transgender Tipping Point. *Time.* http://time.com/135480/transgender-tipping-point/. (Accessed May 10, 2015).

Vibes, I. (2014) Feminist Porn: Revolution or Reinvention? *F Word*, http://www.thefword.org.uk/blog/2014/07/feminist_porn_r. (Accessed May 10, 2015).

Walker, N. A. (1979) *Ladies Home Journal:* "How America Lives." *Media History* 6 (2), 129–38.

Wallach Scott, J. (2002) Feminist Reverberations. *Differences: A Journal of Feminist Cultural Studies* 13 (3), pp. 1–23.

Wallsgrove, R. (1977) Between the Devil and the True Blue Whitehouse. *Spare Rib*, December, pp. 44–46.

White, E. F. (2001) *Dark Continent of Our Bodies: Black Feminism and the Politics of Respectability.* Philadelphia: Temple University Press.

Winship, J. 1987. *Inside Women's Magazines.* London: Pandora.

Discursive Activism and Counter-Memories of SlutWalk

KAITLYNN MENDES

In January 2011, when delivering a routine talk to a group of York University students about campus safety, Toronto Police Constable Michael Sanguinetti stated: "I'm told I'm not supposed to say this, but women should avoid dressing like sluts in order to avoid victimization" (Kwan, 2011). Little did PC Sanguinetti realize when he delivered this "common sense" advice about sexual assault prevention, which in fact reproduces long-standing myths that women are somehow responsible for the violence perpetuated against them, that it would ignite a global anti-rape and victim-blaming movement which would soon spread to over 200 cities in 40 nations, attracting unprecedented mainstream and alternative media coverage along the way. Drawn from a larger project which explores representations of SlutWalk in mainstream news and the feminist blogosphere (see Mendes, 2015), this essay focuses specifically on the ways feminist bloggers, many of whom attended SlutWalk, used personal blogs and photo-sharing sites such as *Flickr* to disrupt the mainstream "storying" of the movement, creating their own "counter-memories" of SlutWalk. In doing so, they reframed mainstream visual representations of the movement, from one in which young, mainly white women in various states of undress pursued their right to dress like a "slut," to one which unpicked and exposed patriarchy and rape culture in action. As a result, this study provides one of the first contemporary examples which document the ways feminists are increasingly employing new media technologies to "talk back" to a patriarchal culture in which women's bodies are sexualized (see Gill, 2007) and their voices are marginalized or ignored (for example see Keller, 2011; Peipmeier, 2009; Shaw, 2012a).

101

The Emergence of SlutWalk

Not long after York University's student newspaper published an article detailing PC Sanguinetti's "advice" on sexual assault prevention (see Kwan, 2011), Toronto resident Heather Jarvis read the article via *Facebook* and became angered by the ways that those with authority, such as the police, continued to perpetuate a number of rape myths—or generalized false ideas or beliefs about rape, including why rape happens, who commits it, and who is likely to be a target. In particular, Jarvis was frustrated by the particular myth stating that women who dress "provocatively," drink alcohol, or who enjoy sex, are themselves liable for blame if sexually assaulted (Bonnes, 2013; Meyer, 2010). In response, she shared the story on *Facebook*, creating an online dialogue between friends. After several exchanges with fellow Toronto resident Sonya Barnett, the two agreed to stage a protest at the Toronto Police Headquarters with three demands (Jarvis, 2012). These included a restructuring of police education and training with regards to sexual assault; the implementation of a third party review of police training and education; and an increase in police outreach and educational programs for the public surrounding sexual assault, informed consent, and rape myths (SlutWalk Toronto, 2011).

In order to publicize their protest, the two created a website, *Facebook* page, and *Twitter* account. While they initially hoped to attract around a hundred people, on the day of the march, thousands turned up, and sparked the organization of hundreds of other SlutWalks all around the globe (Jarvis, 2012). Although the Canadian mainstream media began its coverage in the run up to the first march, SlutWalk's momentum really began to grow when it went "viral" among the vibrant feminist blogosphere (McNicol, 2015; Mendes, 2015). This was made possible because of the strength of community ties among feminists, who regularly speak with and connect to one another online (Keller, 2011; Shaw, 2012b). While 2011 was the pinnacle of activism, marches have continued to take place over the years in major cities such as Chicago, Washington, D.C., Miami, New Orleans, Melbourne, Vancouver, and Los Angeles. That being said, while the movement initially attracted what I have argued is unprecedented mainstream media coverage for feminist activism, this has dwindled dramatically since 2012, particularly as the movement is now "old" news, and has lost its news appeal (Mendes, 2015).

There is ample evidence that feminist activism is experiencing a resurgence in popularity, attention, and support (see Valenti, 2014), and I have argued elsewhere that SlutWalk is part of a series of initiatives which helped rejuvenate feminism and give it public visibility (Mendes, 2015).[1] While Slut-Walk was overwhelmingly supported in the mainstream news media, there were still undoubtedly ways that coverage was problematic and gave particular emphasis to a small, but visible, minority of young, white, "scantily" clad women at the marches, at the expense of the diversity of people who were actually there. As a result, it is important to go back and think critically about how feminists have historically engaged with the mainstream media. In doing so, we also need to reconsider how we define "activism," keeping in mind that the work women often do in this regard is not as highly valued as men's because of its personal sphere of reference, its highly personalized nature, and its aims of engaging in ideological and cultural, rather than political, economic, or legal change. These issues become increasingly important as we acknowledge the ways the internet offers "feminist pockets or zones in cyberspace" (Piano, 2002 cited in Keller, 2013, p. 31) in which various types of activism, including that at the discursive level, can take place.

What Counts as Activism?

There is no doubt that the world of activism has undergone a dramatic shift since the rise of new technologies and the internet. This has resulted in a fundamental shift in the ways social movements function (Wolfson, 2012, p. 150), particularly regarding the growing importance of new media technologies, the internet, and social networking sites in building, organizing, networking, and choreographing physical assembly and collective identities (see Downing, 2000; Diani and McAdam, 2003; Castells, 2007, 2009, 2012; Juris, 2008; Staggenborg, 2008; Atkinson, 2009; Gerbaudo, 2012). As a result of the rise of new media technologies, we have witnessed the emergence and development of activism which increasingly takes place online, or which relies on new technologies to facilitate it. In tandem with this, we have also witnessed the rise in debates over the legitimacy of online activism, which has been derogatorily named "slacktivism" (Morozov, 2011), "clicktivism" or "armchair activism" (see Lim, 2013), and which is seen as less meaningful and capable of bringing about change than activism which takes place in the "real" world (see Friedman, 2007).

Although by no means alone, feminist scholars have long questioned the politics and implications of privileging certain types of activism over others (Mendes, 2015; Shaw, 2011; Taft, 2011; Young, 1997). Privileged forms of activism have historically included marches, protests, demonstrations, and sit-ins, which seek political or policy change and which require people to physically occupy public spaces. In contrast, feminists have long taken part in linguistic and discursive interventions in the form of newsletters, zines, poetry, speak-outs, meetings, film, and theatre, which often take place in "private" settings or are cultural in orientation. Feminists argue that these constitute legitimate forms of political activism, along with lobbying, protests, and marches (Berrington and Jones, 2002; Maddison, 2013; Peipmeier, 2009; Shaw, 2011, 2012a, 2012b; Young, 1997). In part, women have had to turn to these alternative types of activism because they have long been excluded from the public sphere (Fraser, 1990), and their presence and participation in "political" activism has not always been encouraged, or deemed "appropriate" (see Mendes, 2011).[2]

Limited notions of "legitimate" activism are particularly problematic for feminists, whose tactics have not historically been recognized as "political," and which seldom lead to policy or regime change (Young, 1997, p. 167). As Stacey Young (1997) argued, in the fight to transform power relations and social structures, discursive politics is just as important as other types of politics (such as electoral politics), because it aims to fundamentally change the way people think. Consequently, many feminists advocate the importance of sharing personal experiences about common problems and developing new discourses to articulate them (e.g., rape is about power, not sex), as a necessary first step in enacting social change (Maddison, 2013; Young, 1997). Known as consciousness raising (CR), this activist practice has been used by feminists since the 1970s and has been fundamental to the development of counter-hegemonic discourses about women and their place in the world (Maddison, 2013; Shaw, 2011; Young, 1997), and is central to the activism of SlutWalk. Because SlutWalk aims to challenge hegemonic discourses about the nature of rape, what causes it, and who is to blame, it requires "discursive activism"— or "political speech […] that intervenes in hegemonic discourses, and that works at the level of language to change political cultures" (Shaw, 2011); it requires this form as activism as much, if not more so, than protests in the street. So, although the physical aggregation of bodies in public spaces can be a powerful means of enacting change, CR and discursive activism are necessary to get people to the streets in the first place. It is in this domain of discursive activism where feminist blogs played a crucial role.

Discursive Activism in Practice

Drawing on the importance of discursive politics in her research on the Australian feminist blogging community, Frances Shaw (2011) demonstrated the ways that many bloggers take part in discursive activism. Yet such discursive interventions have historically been undervalued (Maddison, 2013; Shaw, 2012a; Young, 1997), and perceived as "less noteworthy than men's by the nature of their often domestic and personal spheres of reference" (Gregg, 2006, p. 85). This is despite the fact that such activities can and do challenge dominant ideologies, and that "rhetorical struggle" is seen as crucial to politics—however defined (Williams, 1995).

For example, Young (1997) wrote about how "language acts" including published writings played a crucial role in both individual and collective social change in the second wave women's movement. More recently, Meenakshi Gigi Durham (2013) documented the ways in which (feminist) bloggers, columnists, and op-ed writers forced *The New York Times* to apologize for its coverage of the gang rape of an 11-year-old girl in Texas. Bloggers in particular were quick to condemn the story's use of patriarchal and victim-blaming tropes which made it seem that "the girl had it coming" (Knox, 2011 cited in Durham, 2013, p. 1). Shaw (2012b) also detailed the ways feminist bloggers in Australia intervened in a radio contest to highlight how the history of rock music excluded and erased women. Similarly, Jessica Mowles (2008) showed how the U.S. feminist blog *Feministing* has reshaped conventional political discourse, particularly around gender roles and the hyper-sexualization of women. Mowles quoted the "About" section of *Feministing*'s blog, which describes the site as "a platform for us [young women] to comment, analyse, and influence" (2008, p. 33).

While the aggregation of bodies on the streets via SlutWalk protests are certainly important (and newsworthy) signals that rape culture is increasingly being subjected to challenge and protest, hegemonic ideologies can only be challenged through discursive interventions. This requires talking, listening, and debate, for which the internet, at least theoretically, provides significant opportunities. Because the development of feminist discourse has been regarded as having a "profound effect on women's expectations for their own lives" (Maddison, 2013, p. 31), this essay will analyze the ways that feminist bloggers used a range of online tools and platforms to engage with discursive activism in order to challenge the mainstream and hegemonic representations of sexual assault and rape culture. The widespread challenge to these ideologies has been made possible because of the formation of networked publics and counterpublics.

Networked Publics and Counterpublics

In order to understand the concept of networked publics or counterpublics, one first must be familiar with Jürgen Habermas' (1989) famous essay on the structural transformation of the public sphere, which outlined the importance of public spaces in which individuals come together to talk, debate, and form opinions. Habermas discussed the public sphere as a crucial part of a healthy democracy, in which everyone was welcome to come together as equals and discuss issues of public concern. Although Habermas' theory was criticized by many, Nancy Fraser's (1990) critique is one of the most well-known. Where Habermas talked about the bourgeois public sphere as an idealized space open to all individuals who were free to discuss a range of social, economic, and political issues and reach consensus, Fraser (1990) pointed out the ways in which this "idealized" public sphere actually functioned to exclude significant groups of people such as women and the working class. In response to their exclusion, these groups formed, and continue to form, their own subaltern counterpublics. These counterpublics are not only places where marginalized groups withdraw and regroup, but spaces where they plan agitation and protest activities directed at wider publics (ibid., p. 68). Consequently, a key function of counterpublics is wider social transformation (see also Warner, 2002). Both these concepts—the public sphere and counterpublics—are important for this essay, as are the ways scholars have adapted them in light of technological developments.

For example, new media scholar danah boyd combined the concepts of networks and publics to theorize the concept of "networked publics" (boyd, 2008, 2010), which she defined as publics that have been restructured by network technologies. Like other types of publics, boyd (2010) argued that networked publics provide a space for people to gather for social, cultural, and civic purposes, and to connect individuals with a world beyond their close friends and family. Accordingly, social media sites are networked publics because of the ways in which they connect many people and provide space for interactions and information (ibid., p. 45). While this concept is undoubtedly useful for understanding how mainstream groups come together to interact with one another and discuss issues, like Habermas' theory of the public sphere, it does not fully address the ways that marginalized groups create their own subaltern networked counterpublics in virtual spaces. For example, feminist media scholar Jessalynn M. Keller (2013) has discussed the ways that feminists have used social media platforms and blogs to form their own networked counterpublics which emerge "around particular discursive feminist identities and issues, coming together, dissolving, and reconvening in a fluid manner" (ibid., p. 160). In this essay, I argue that feminist blogs act as a series of networked counterpublics, which among other things were used to engage in discursive interventions into mainstream media narratives.

Methods

As someone who has been closely following the SlutWalk movement since its inception, has participated in a march, and is deeply interested in the media's potential for dismantling rape culture, it is perhaps unsurprising that this research was undertaken using a feminist cultural studies perspective. Inherent in this approach is the analysis of power structures and the ideologies which uphold them. Cultural studies scholars are also interested in resistance to these structures (see D'Acci, 2005), as exemplified by those who participated in SlutWalk marches, as well as discussions about the movement in mainstream news, feminist media, and social media. A key question asked is: to what extent have feminists used blogging and social media to engage in discursive activism, and to form networked counterpublics around rape culture and sexual assault? Informed by my feminist cultural studies perspective, the larger project from which this essay was drawn employs a variety of methods including frame analysis, qualitative content analysis, and critical discourse analysis (CDA) of mainstream news, feminist media, and social media posts. It also employs ethnographic methods including in-depth interviews with 22 SlutWalk organizers and close observations of social media sites (netnography), from eight nations around the world (Australia, Canada, India, South Africa, Singapore, UK, and U.S.). For the purposes of this essay, the main focus will be on critical discourse analysis of the ways feminists engaged in discursive activism and created their own counter-memories of SlutWalk.

Gathering Data

Although I could have analyzed representations of SlutWalk in popular culture more generally, I specifically focused on the news media because of its crucial role in maintaining and (re)producing hegemonic ideologies (Dow, 1996; Meyers, 2006). As with many other contemporary social movements, such as Occupy Wall Street, there is a public perception that SlutWalk is "over" (Midgley, 2013), despite the fact that walks continue to be organized in major cities all around the world. Because of this perception, I deliberately expanded the time frame beyond SlutWalk's first anniversary to explore the extent to which the movement still generated copy in news and feminist media. Material was collected between February 17, 2011, when the SlutWalk Toronto Facebook page was created, and December 31, 2013, providing me with nearly three years' worth of data. Online news items were gathered both via databases such as Nexis, and through searching well-known online news sites in each of my eight nations. Using the search terms "SlutWalk" and "Slut Walk," I collected 304 mainstream news articles about the movement from 35 news sites.[3] I was also careful to try to include a range of publications, from those concerned with the more "serious" issues such as formal politics and the economy, as well as those covering more "entertainment-based" issues such as celebrity, gossip, human interest, and scandal; this was to ensure that my sample would include variations in the possible ways SlutWalk might be addressed.

Before I embarked on this project, I became increasingly interested in the rising popularity of a number of feminist blogs, such as *Feministing* in the U.S., *The F-Word* in the UK, *Hoyden Around Town* in Australia, and *Feminist Current* in Canada. Concurrently, I became aware of research highlighting the increased importance of blogs both as sources of information and inspiration in mainstream news (see Fenton, 2010; Perlmutter, 2008; Thorsen, 2009). I began to read academic studies demonstrating the ways that feminist blogs were helping to cultivate feminist identities and discourses which challenged mainstream hegemonic ideologies (see Keller, 2013; Rentschler, 2014; Shaw, 2011). Using the same search terms, I collected 390 posts from 96 feminist blogs.[4] Given that feminist bloggers invest time and energy into cultivating online feminist communities (see Keller, 2013; Shaw, 2011), snowball sampling was selected as an appropriate way of collecting material for my feminist media sample. Snowball sampling involves the researcher using existing participants to help recruit additional participants via their own contacts and networks, most often because the research population is small or difficult to find. Following in the footsteps of other research on feminist media (Shaw, 2011), I based my initial selection on my pre-existing knowledge of feminist blogs which I regularly read, and searched these for articles on Slut-Walk. Next, I went through their blogrolls—or list of links to other blogs which the blogger likes—and searched these for articles on SlutWalk. Finally, I made a rule that I would follow all embedded links in each post about Slut-Walk and include these texts in my sample. My only real criteria for selection were that the individual author or site identified as feminist (this was often evident in the blog or post title), that the blog/article was related to SlutWalk, and that it was published between February 17, 2011, and December 31, 2013.

Representations of SlutWalk in the News Media

Over the past several decades, a range of scholars have become interested in representations of feminism and feminist activism in the media (see Morris, 1973; Pingree and Hawkins, 1978; Tuchman, 1978; van Zoonen, 1992; Douglas, 1994; Costain, Braunstein and Berggren, 1997; Ashley and Olson, 1998; Goddu, 1999; Barker-Plummer, 2000; Freeman, 2001; Bradley, 2003; Sheridan, Magarey and Lilburn, 2007; Mendes, 2011, 2015). While all social movement actors run the risk of receiving unfavorable coverage, feminists in particular have long been cast as "deviant." As they have demanded equal access to the public sphere and challenged a range of patriarchal ideologies (predominantly middle class, white), they have been constructed as passive, asexual, heterosexual, maternal, unskilled, irrational, and so forth (see Douglas, 1994; Goddu, 1999; Hinds and Stacey, 2001; Lind and Salo, 2002; Mendes,

2011). As a result, it has been particularly surprising to note that SlutWalk was supported in nearly 70 percent of all mainstream news and feminist media coverage (Mendes, 2015). Overwhelmingly, when reading through the texts, SlutWalk was framed as a movement which legitimately challenges rape culture, creates awareness over sexual assault related issues (e.g., conviction rates, the impact on victims, prevention strategies, etc.), and validates the experiences of sexual assault survivors (Mendes, 2015). Given that previous research demonstrates that feminist activism has not always attracted mainstream media support (see Molotch, 1978; Pingree and Hawkins, 1978; Douglas, 1994; Mills, 1997; Goddu, 1999; Barker-Plummer, 2000; Hinds and Stacey, 2001; Lind and Salo, 2002; Bradley, 2003; Hollows and Moseley, 2006; Mendes, 2011), these supportive frames are undoubtedly a positive development in the "storying" of feminism.

Yet despite the fact that the news media frequently supported the movement, and sometimes even engaged more deeply with issues surrounding rape culture and patriarchal power, there was a distinct difference in the ways the movement was visually and discursively represented in mainstream news texts. For example, while it was often discursively constructed as a movement which challenged rape culture in the written text, the use of visuals created a contrasting meaning, at least in the mainstream news. As someone who had been closely following the SlutWalk movement since it started in April 2011, I had become familiar with the typical range of images accompanying news coverage: mainly young, white women in various stages of undress. Some had words such as "slut" or "don't touch" written on their exposed flesh, while others carried signs with statements such as "It's My Hot Body, I Do What I Want," "Don't Tell Us How to Dress," "My Vagina, My Rules," and "Still Not Asking for It." While some marchers look serious, defiant or even angry, many others are smiling, cheering, or jumping.

Yet in contrast to the wide range of photos found on feminist blogs, few mainstream news photos focused on women in jeans, T-shirts, or other "unprovocative" attire; men; the elderly; the disabled; or people of color (see also McNicol, 2015). Furthermore, when I attended my first SlutWalk in London, 2012, I was surprised at not only the diversity of marchers, but how few were "provocatively" dressed. Those who attended in various states of undress were easy to spot, as they were often surrounded by (mainly male) photographers. Therefore, while it would be incorrect to argue that the mainstream news media "misrepresented" SlutWalk, it nonetheless provided an interpretive framework (Hall, Critcher, Jefferson, Clarke, and Roberts, 1978) in which the movement, at least visually, was seen to be by, for, and about young, thin, white, women who, rather than simply challenging rape culture, were marching to "celebrate" their sexuality, individual bodily autonomy, and right to dress as they please (see also McNicol, 2015).

My personal observations were also confirmed by other SlutWalk organizers, who expressed a range of emotions at the ways the news media (visually) represented the movement. These ranged from irritation (Brodie, 2014), to disappointment (Castieau, 2012; Gray, 2014a; Pillay-Siokos, 2013; Wraith, 2013), to disillusionment (Govender, 2014), to infuriation (Ho, 2012). For example, SlutWalk Aotearoa 2011 and 2012 organizer M.J. Brodie said she was "irritated" by media coverage which emphasized all the "slutty sluts with these slutty clothes," when in fact most participants were wearing jeans and hardly showed any skin (Brodie, 2014). SlutWalk Newcastle 2011–13 organizer Lizi Gray stated that although some coverage was nuanced and thorough, she was disappointed by other coverage which focused on "short skirts and sensation stories" and failed to discuss the purpose of the march (Gray, 2014b). When asked her views on how SlutWalk Singapore was reported, organizer Vanessa Ho stated she was "infuriated" with "gut-wrenchingly disgusting" coverage which represented the movement as a "two dimensional issue by simply flocking to the scantily clad women" (Ho, 2012). When thinking about the implications of the media's treatment of the movement, Slut-Walk Chicago 2011 organizer Stephanie Sutton concluded that the focus on scantily clad women is "one of the flaws of SlutWalk in general" (Sutton, 2014). While she went on to defend the movement's celebration of sexuality, sex positivity and openness, she acknowledged that the media's disproportionate focus on these aspects "limited the movement in a way." So, while the promise of sexy photo opportunities was likely a draw for mainstream media attention, organizers were concerned that it also limited the ways the movement was interpreted and understood and was a distraction away from the true purpose of the march—to challenge rape culture.

Feminist Interventions into Mainstream Media

In studying the feminist blogosphere in Australia, Shaw (2011, 2012b) noted that the mainstream media was a key and frequent topic of discussion and debate. In particular, Shaw commented upon the ways that feminist bloggers experience a dislocation in which mainstream discourses jarred against their own (feminist) views and beliefs. As a result, they use blogging as a way to demonstrate the "absurdity" of mainstream discourses and to expose their contradictions (Shaw, 2011). When examining the results from my study of SlutWalk, it also became clear that feminist bloggers were both attuned to the mainstream media, and that they frequently felt this sense of dislocation with mainstream news coverage. Out of 390 feminist posts from 96 feminist blogs/websites, nearly 40 percent (146 posts) discussed the mainstream news at some point. What is worth noting is that the reasons for discussing mainstream coverage varied. That being said, few, if any, spoke out to praise the mainstream news. Instead, feminists frequently used their blogs to "call out" the media on what they saw as misrepresentative coverage, and disgraceful tactics. In "This is What a SlutWalk (Really) Looks Like" (Corinna, 2011) the blogger protested that the visual representations of the march in the mainstream media ranged from the "incorrect to [the] exceptionally dishonest." The blogger went on to note that "as [far as] I can tell, the images that keep getting picked aren't those which are most representative of the protests as a whole, but which are most representative of what a given person either found most provocative or most interesting" (Corinna, 2011). Writing on the Canadian website *Rabble.ca* another blogger shared in disgust how a CBC cameraman "asked two 'slutty' young women to dance for his camera" (Kraus, 2011). The blogger recounted that after she told the young women they didn't have to dance for the media, "the CBC cameraman went off hunting elsewhere."

What became clear after reading these 146 posts is that for the most part, these bloggers were not just complaining about coverage, but attempting to make an active intervention into how the movement was understood, represented, and remembered. At times, the bloggers spoke directly to the mainstream media, imploring them to provide more nuanced coverage. In a speech at SlutWalk Aotearoa in 2011, organizer M.J. Brodie challenged the media to "not be so distracted by the 'slutty' outfits that you forget that this march is about rape and sexual assault. We would beg you to cover this march properly, and fairly—show the range of people, men and women, who are here today, not just close ups of tits and ass" (Brodie, 2011).

Writing on the morning of SlutWalk Wellington and Auckland in 2011, another New Zealand blogger wrote that she hoped the media would "pull up their socks and actually engage in the issues and practice some legitimate journalism!" (Lady News, 2011). Although there is no way of measuring the extent to which the mainstream media were aware of these critiques, nor how they might have altered their coverage as a result, it is clear that feminists are using online spaces to "talk back" to a patriarchal culture in which women's bodies are sexualized (see Gill, 2007) and in which their voices are marginalized or ignored (hooks, 1989, p. 5; Keller, 2011; Peipmeier, 2009).

Through thinking about, and "talking back" to the mainstream news media, these feminist bloggers are participating in discursive politics and activism, and in doing so, are developing alternative discourses and understandings of themselves, the SlutWalk movement, and the world around them (see Maddison, 2013; Shaw, 2012b). On their own, these contributions might seem irrelevant, but as scholars have noted, blogs are highly social, and it is the interlinkage of blogs, with frequent updates and "dense" connections which make them politically significant (Shaw, 2011, p. 375). According to

Alison Peipmeier (2009, p. 20), these "micropolitical" interventions "are so personalized that they are often invisible as activism to scholars who are searching for the kinds of social change efforts that were prevalent in the social justice movements of the earlier twentieth century." Yet, in "talking back," feminist bloggers are not only challenging mainstream media accounts of the movement, they are also creating their own "counter-memories." Drawing on the work of Michel Foucault, Red Chidgey (2012, p. 87) argued that "feminist media can become discursive 'weapons' [...] to contest hostile framings [of feminism] and to put forward counter-understandings of what feminism is, what feminism can do, and who a feminist can be." In the section below, I therefore argue that many feminists in my sample used blogs to challenge post-feminist constructions of SlutWalk as a movement about women's freedom to dress as they please. Blogs were also frequently used to challenge the visual whitewashing of the movement—or the ways the movement ignored women of color (see also McNicol, 2015).

Discursive Activism and Counter-Memories

A critical discourse analysis of my feminist media sample provides ample evidence of the various ways feminist bloggers sought to disrupt mainstream constructions of SlutWalk and provide alternative accounts, or counter-memories, of the movement, primarily through the use of photos, video, and hyperlinks. While this served various purposes, one of the key aims was to challenge both the mainstream whitewashing of the movement and its focus on "slutty" women, and instead to represent the diversity of participants. For example, one blog embedded a short film of SlutWalk NYC 2011 in their post, as well as a quote from the filmmaker who explained why she felt the need to provide an alternative account of the movement:

> For me, one of the truly frustrating things about coverage of SlutWalks all over the world has been the media's focus on the most elaborately undressed and risqué marchers, leading people to believe the events are solely about demanding the right to dress like a slut. I hope this video gives people a sense of the range of participants (gender, orientation, background, race, age) that were there marching, chanting and generally raising some hell [Seltzer and Kelley, 2011].

The embedded trailer to the documentary, just over 30 seconds long, features panned out shots of diverse crowds, close-ups of signs ("I will be post-feminist in the post-patriarchy"), and a clip from a protester who, making reference to PC Michael Sanguinetti's comments that women could avoid being "victimized" if they didn't dress like "sluts," explained what was needed to combat sexual assault and rape culture: "What we need from police is enforcement, what we need from the larger culture is anti-violence education, not fashion tips" (Trixie Films, 2011).

Although some bloggers embedded videos and photos into their posts, the vast majority used hyperlinks instead, perhaps as a deliberate strategy to avoid the problematic focus on women's bodies. In her post titled "An Open Challenge to Mainstream Media re SlutWalk Sydney" Australian blogger tigtog (2011) used hyperlinks to the photo-sharing site *Flickr* to demonstrate the ways the news media flocked to the provocatively dressed, while ignoring those in "normal" clothes. One image shows a woman in a black corset and feather boa literally surrounded by between 30 to 50 (mostly male) photographers. A second photo shows two women in "normal" dress standing right beside the media swarm, being ignored. Angered by the media's omission of the broad range of people attending the walks, she asked:

> Do any of you publishers and editors have the integrity to instruct your field reporters to gather images and stories of more than just the sexy young things marching in their skimpies tomorrow? Does a single one of you have the guts to forego predictable titillation and let the public know the truth about SlutWalk and the hundreds and hundreds of other women and male and queer allies who will be marching in non-skimpy wear, and why they are there? [tigtog, 2011].

Similarly, in her effort to showcase the diversity of participants at SlutWalk London 2011, blogger Lipsticklori (2011) directed viewers to the photojournalism site Demotix in an effort to "give you an idea of the dedication and strength of the views of many of those in attendance." In going through the photos, it becomes clear that yes, SlutWalks certainly did attract white, middle class women who turned up in skimpy attire. However, it also attracted hordes of women, men, and children, of diverse backgrounds, wearing mostly "everyday" items of clothing.

Although some feminist bloggers embedded professional photos of marches taken by news agencies such as Reuters and Associated Press into their posts, the majority appeared to use photos they took themselves, or borrowed from others who attended the march. In total, 130 posts, or 33 percent of my feminist media sample, included at least one photo of a SlutWalk event, poster or advertisement.[5] Of the images present, only a minority focused on explicitly or provocatively dressed women (11 percent of all photos coded). The majority captured crowds, placards, posters or "ordinary" women and men (89 percent of all photos coded).

Even a cursory examination of the visuals used in my mainstream news and feminist media samples indicates a significant difference in their representations of various marches, with the former focusing on provocatively dressed women as previously discussed, and the latter on large crowds, signs and posters, and "ordinary" women and men. As a result, while I will not try to claim that the feminist media more "accurately" represented SlutWalk marches, its coverage certainly is more diverse—something which I think needs celebrating. Just as there is no one definition of feminism, there should not be one image of what feminism is, or what a feminist looks like. As evidenced by the range of photos on various photo-sharing websites, those attending SlutWalk are not in fact only young, white, thin women, but are also old, curvy, (dis)abled, gay, straight, and bisexual. They are black, white, and brown. They are men, women, and transgendered people. The diversity evident in photos shared by feminist bloggers is a challenge in itself to the visual representation put forward by the mainstream news media. And while convincing the mainstream news to reframe the narrative might indeed be a "fruitless endeavor" (Echo Zen, 2012), the feminist blogosphere has at least provided counter-memories of what the movement is about and who did, or did not, attend. Thinking about this in terms of the "storying of feminism," and how the feminist movement comes to be remembered and told, feminist blogs have revealed their potential in expanding the number and types of voices heard, people seen, and experiences recounted.

Conclusion

This essay focused on the ways feminist bloggers not only felt a sense of dislocation with the mainstream "storying" of SlutWalk, but how they used blogs to engage in discursive activism. This important form of activism allowed feminists to create counter-memories of SlutWalk, and as such enabled them to re-frame the movement from one where women pursued their right to dress like a "slut," to one with more radical potential to shatter patriarchy. Although there is no way to prove all such bloggers acted with specifically political intent, there is no doubt that in identifying and responding to the "discursive crisis" (Shaw, 2011) that constitutes rape culture, they were certainly engaged in activism in challenging mainstream discourses. As such, it is clear that these feminist bloggers have not reinvented the wheel— instead they are merely using new tools to continue a long legacy of protesting cultural injustices and oppression (see Bryson, 2003; Frank and Fuentes, 1987), and to "talk back" to mainstream patriarchal culture.

NOTES

1. Other examples include the British campaign group Object, the U.S. based Hollaback! against street harassment, India's Blank Noise Project, and various other types of social media activism, including *Twitter* campaigns, and photo-sharing/blog projects.

2. For example, during the 2011 Egyptian uprising, women protesting in Tahrir square were routinely harassed, groped, and assaulted in efforts to dissuade them from protesting, and to reinforce the idea that their place is at home (see "Rape and

Sexual Assault: The Hidden Side of Egypt's Protests," 2013; Trew, 2013). In fact, the sexual assault of female protesters has become such an issue that several groups have formed which aim to "rescue" women who are attacked. These include Operation Anti-Sexual Harassment (OpAntiSH) and Tahrir Bodyguard.

3. My mainstream news sample consisted of the following: *Calgary Herald* (Canada); *Canberra Times* (Australia); *Cape Times* (South Africa); *Daily Dispatch* (South Africa); *Daily Mail, Mail on Sunday,* and *Mail Online* (UK); *Daily News* (U.S.); *Globe and Mail* (Canada); *Hobart Mercury* and *Sunday Tasmanian* (Australia); *Indian Express* (India); *New Indian Express* (India); *New York Times* (U.S.); *New Zealand Herald* (New Zealand); *Ottawa Citizen* (Canada); *Sowetan* (South Africa); *Sunday Star-Times* (New Zealand); *The Australian/Weekend Australian* (Australia); *The Straits Times* (Singapore); *The Guardian* (UK); *The Observer* (UK); *The Sun* (UK); *The Telegraph* (India); *The Times* (UK); *Times of India* (India); *Toronto Star* (Canada); *Washington Post* (U.S.); *Washington Times* (U.S.); *Sydney Morning Herald* (Australia); *Herald Sun and Sunday Herald Sun* (Australia); *Australian Broadcasting Company* (Australia); *BBC* (UK); *CBC* (Canada); *Huffington Post* (Canada, UK and U.S.); *South African Broadcasting Company* (South Africa); *TV New Zealand* (New Zealand); *The New Paper* (Singapore).

4. My feminist media sample consisted of the following sites: *The F-Word* (UK); *Bitch Media* (U.S.); *Bad Reputation* (UK); *Rarely Wears Lipstick* (UK); *Red Pepper* (UK); *Lesbilicious* (UK); *Here. In My Head* (UK); *Slutwalk London* (UK) *Bust Magazine* (U.S.); *Feministing* (U.S.); *Thought Catalogue* (U.S.); *To the Curb* (U.S.); *AlterNet* (U.S.); *Jezebel* (U.S.); *Women's Views on News* (U.S.); *The Pursuit of Harpyness* (U.S.); *Life in a Pickle* (U.S.); *Crunk Feminist Collective* (U.S.); *AfroLez femcentric perspective* (U.S.); *Queer Black Feminist* (U.S.); *Feministe* (U.S.); *Ms. Magazine* (U.S.); *Where is Your Line?* (U.S.); *Dissent* (U.S.); *David Wraith* (U.S.); *Racialicious* (U.S.); *The F Bomb* (U.S.); *Yasmin Nair Blog* (U.S.); *Intersectional Activism* (U.S.); *Feminist Frequency* (U.S.); *Black Women's Blueprint* (U.S.); *Feminist Current* (Canada); *People of Color Organize* (U.S.); *I Blame the Patriarchy* (U.S.); *Rookie* (U.S.); *Hugo Schwyzer* (U.S.); *Big Think* (U.S.); *Feminists for Choice* (U.S.); *The Good Men Project* (U.S.); *Gender Focus* (Canada); *Rabble.ca* (Canada); *Emma W. Wooley* (Canada); *come again?* (New Zealand); *The Hand Mirror* (New Zealand); *Feminist Catalyst* (Canada); *Rmott62* (Canada); *Ideologically Impure* (New Zealand); *Lady News* (New Zealand); *Pickled Think* (New Zealand); *Craft is the new black* (New Zealand); *Luddite Journo* (New Zealand); *Stop Street Harassment* (U.S.); *SlutWalk Toronto* (Canada); *Too Fat for our Pants* (New Zealand); *Kiwiana* (New Zealand); *Brooklynne Michelle* (New Zealand); *The Lady Garden* (New Zealand); *Scarleteen* (U.S.); *News With Nipples* (New Zealand); *Hoyden About Town* (Australia); *Definataliewww* (Australia); *Versatile Identities* (UK); *Iced Chai* (New Zealand); *Scuba Nurse* (New Zealand); *Clarisse Thorn* (U.S.); *Feminists SA* (South Africa); *SlutWalk Johannesburg* (South Africa); *The Feminist Wire* (U.S.); *Open Democracy* (International); *Just a South African Woman* (South Africa); *Thought Leader* (South Africa); *Women's Web* (India); *Crazy Dumbsaint of the Mind* (India); *Pratiksha Baxi* (India); *Ramblings of a Feminist Abroad* (India); *Asian Window* (India); *Just Femme* (India); *The Dancing Sufi* (India); *Rendezvous* (India); *This Is My Truth* (India); *Textual Orientation* (India); *From A SlutWalker, With Love* (India); *SlutWalk Singapore* (Singapore); *Aware* (Singapore); *Juice* (Singapore); *Diva* (Singapore); *Rachel Zeng* (Singapore); *Feminaust* (Australia); *Zero at the Bone* (Australia); *Two Feminists* (Australia); *DragOnista* (Australia); *Dangers Untold and Hardships Unnumbered* (Australia); *Green Left Weekly* (Australia); *Insanity Works* (Australia); *The Conversation* (Australia); *Godard's Letterbox* (Australia).

5. While my coding scheme allowed me to count the number of photos in each post, I only coded the content for the first image presented.

REFERENCES

Ashley, L. and Olson, B. (1998) Constructing Reality: Print Media's Framing of the Women's Movement, 1966–1986. *Journal of Mass Communication Quarterly* 75 (2), pp. 263–77.

Atkinson, J. (2009) Networked Activists in Search of Resistance: Exploring an Alternative Media Pilgrimage Across the Boundaries and Borderlands of Globalization. *Communication, Culture & Critique* 2, pp. 137–59.

Barker-Plummer, B. (2000) News as a Feminist Resource? A Case study of the Media Strategies and Media Representation of the National Organization for Women, 1966–1980. In: Sreberny, A. and van Zoonen, L. (eds.) *Gender, Politics and Communication.* Cresskill, N.J.: Hampton Press Inc., pp. 121–59.

Berrington, E. and Jones, H. (2002) Reality vs. Myth: Constructions of Women's Insecurity. *Feminist Media Studies* 2 (3), pp. 307–23.

Bonnes, S. (2013) Gender and Racial Stereotyping in Rape Coverage. *Feminist Media Studies* 13 (2), pp. 208–27.

boyd, d. m. (2008) Why Youth [Heart] Social Network Sites: The Role of Networked Publics in Teenage Social Life. In: Buckingham, D. (ed.), *Youth, Identity, and Digital Media.* Cambridge: MIT Press, pp. 119–42.

_____. (2010) Social Network Sites as Networked Publics: Affordances, Dynamics, and Implication. In: Papacharissi, Z. (ed.) *Networked Self: Identity, Community, and Culture on Social Network Sites.* New York: Routledge, pp. 39–58.

Bradley, P. (2003) *Mass Media and the Shaping of American Feminism, 1963–1975.* Tuscaloosa: University Press of Mississippi.

Brodie, M. (2011) M.J.'s SlutWalk Aotearoa Speech. *Kiwiana*, August 15. https://kiwianainked.wordpress.com/2011/08/15/mjs-slutwalk-aotearoa-speech-civic-square-wellington-june-25th-2011/. (Accessed February 24, 2016).

_____. (2014) SlutWalk Aotearoa 2011 and 2012 Organizer. Personal Interview, May 25.

Bryson, V. (2003) *Feminist Political Theory: An Introduction*, 2nd edn. New York: Palgrave Macmillan.

Castells, M. (2007) Communication, Power and Counter-power in the Network Society. *International Journal of Communication* 1, pp. 238–66.

_____. (2009) *Communication Power.* Oxford: Oxford University Press.

_____. (2012) *Networks of Outrage and Hope: Social Movements in the Internet Age.* Cambridge: Polity Press.

Castieau, B. (2012) SlutWalk Perth 2011 Organizer. Personal Interview, September 5.

Chidgey, R. (2012) Hand-made Memories: Remediating Cultural Memory in DIY Feminist Networks. In: Zobl, E. and Drueke, R. (eds.), *Feminist Media: Participatory Spaces, Networks and Cultural Citizenship.* Bielefeld: Transcript, pp. 87–97.

Corinna, H. (2011) This is What a SlutWalk (Really) Looks Like. *Scarleteen*, July 26. http://www.scarleteen.com/blog/heather_corinna/2011/07/26/this_is_what_a_slutwalk_really_looks_like. (Accessed February 24, 2016).

Costain, A. N., Braunstein, R., and Berggren, H. (1997) Framing the Women's Movement. In: Norris, P. (ed.) *Women, Media and Politics.* New York: Oxford University Press, pp. 205–20.

D'Acci, J. (2005) Cultural Studies, Television Studies, and the Crisis in the Humanities. In: Spigel, L. and Olsson, J. (eds.) *Television After TV: Essays on a Medium in Transition*. Durham: Duke University Press, pp. 418–46.

Diani, M. and McAdam, D. (2003) *Social Movements and Networks*. Oxford: Oxford University Press.

Douglas, S. (1994) *Where the Girls Are: Growing up Female with the Mass Media*. New York: Three Rivers Press.

Dow, B. J. (1996) *Prime-time Feminism: Television, Media Culture, and the Women's Movement Since 1970*. Philadelphia: University of Pennsylvania Press.

Downing, J. (2000) *Radical Media: Rebellious Communications and Social Movements*. Thousand Oaks: Sage.

Durham, M. G. (2013) Vicious Assault Shakes Texas Town. *Journalism Studies* 14 (1), pp. 1–12.

Echo Zen (2012) Feminist Advocacy and Social Media (or How We Achieved Critical Mass). *AlterNet*, April 28. http://www.alternet.org/newsandviews/article/909806/feminist_advocacy_and_social_media_%28or_how_we_achieved_critical_mass%29. (Accessed February 24, 2016).

Fenton, N. (2010) News in the Digital Age. In: Allan, S. (ed.) *The Routledge Companion to News and Journalism*. Abingdon: Routledge, pp. 557–67.

Frank, A. G. and Fuentes, M. (1987) Nine Theses on Social Movements. *Economic & Political Weekly* 22 (35), pp. 1503–9.

Fraser, N. (1990) Rethinking the Public Sphere: A Contribution to the Critique of Actually Existing Democracy. *Social Text* 25/26, pp. 56–80.

Freeman, B. (2001) *The Satellite Sex: The Media and Women's Issues in English Canada, 1966–1971*. Waterloo: Wilfred Laurier Press.

Friedman, T. (2007) Generation Q. *The New York Times*, October 10. http://www.nytimes.com/2007/10/10/opinion/10friedman.html?_r=0. (Accessed June 3, 2014).

Gerbaudo, P. (2012) *Tweets and the Streets: Social Media and Contemporary Activism*. London: Pluto Press.

Gill, R. (2007) *Gender and the Media*. Cambridge: Polity.

Goddu, J. (1999) "Powerless, Public-spirited Women," "Angry Feminists," and "The Muffin Lobby": Newspaper and Magazine Coverage of Three National Women's Groups from 1980–1995. *Canadian Journal of Communication* 24 (2), pp. 105–26.

Govender, U. (2014) SlutWalk Cape Town 2011 Organizer. Personal Interview, April 24.

Gray, A. (2014a) SlutWalk Melbourne 2012 and 2013 Organizer. Personal Interview, September 8.

Gray, L. (2014b) SlutWalk Newcastle 2011–13 Organizer. Personal Interview, May 19.

Gregg, M. (2006) Posting with Passion: Blogs and the Politics of Gender. In: Bruns, A. and Jacobs, J. (eds.) *Uses of Blogs*. New York: Peter Lang, pp. 151–60.

Habermas, J. (1989) *The Structural Transformation of the Public Sphere: An Inquiry into a Category of Bourgeois Society*. Malden: Polity Press.

Hall, S., Critcher, C., Jefferson, T., Clarke, J. N., and Roberts, B. (1978) *Policing the Crisis: Mugging, the State and Law and Order*. Basingstoke: Palgrave Macmillan.

Hinds, H. and Stacey, J. (2001) Imaging Feminism, Imaging Femininity: The Bra-burner, Diana, and the Woman Who Kills. *Feminist Media Studies* 1 (2), pp. 153–77.

Ho, V. (2012) SlutWalk Singapore 2011 and 2012 Organizer. Personal Interview, December 6.

Hollows, J. and Moseley, R. (2007) *Feminism in Popular Culture*. New York: Berg.

hooks, b. (1981) *Ain't I a Woman? Black Women and Feminism*. Boston: South End Press.

_____. (1989) *Talking Back: Thinking Feminist, Thinking Black*. Boston: South End Press.

Jarvis, H. (2012) SlutWalk Toronto Co-founder and 2011–14 Organizer. Personal Interview, December 7.

Juris, J. S. (2008) *Networking Futures: The Movements Against Corporate Globalization*. Durham: Duke University Press.

Keller, J. M. (2011) Virtual Feminisms. *Information, Communication & Society* 15 (3), pp. 429–47.

Keller, J. M. (2013) *"Still Alive and Kicking": Girl Bloggers and Feminist Politics in a "Postfeminist" Age*. PhD Dissertation. Austin: University of Texas at Austin.

Kraus, K. (2011) SlutWalk: Changing a "Don't Get Raped" Culture to a "Don't Rape" Culture. Rabble.ca, April 5. http://rabble.ca/news/2011/04/slutwalk-changing-don%E2%80%99t-get-raped-culture-don%E2%80%99t-rape-culture. (Accessed March 3, 2016).

Kwan, R. (2011) Don't Dress Like a Slut: Toronto Cop. *Excalibur*, February 8. http://www.excal.on.ca/dont-dress-like-a-slut-toronto-cop/. (Accessed June 5, 2014).

Lady News (2011) SlutWalk. *Lady News*, June 24, http://www.ladynews.co.nz/?p=241. (Accessed February 24, 2016)

Lim, M. (2013) Many Clicks But Little Sticks: Social Media Activism in Indonesia. *Journal of Contemporary Asia* 43 (4), pp. 636–57.

Lind, R. A. and Salo, C. (2002) The Framing of Feminists and Feminism in News and Public Affairs Programs in U.S. Electronic Media. *Journal of Communication*, 52 (1): pp. 211–27.

Lipsticklori (2011) Let's Talk About Slutwalk London. *Rarely Wears Lipstick*, June 14. http://www.rarelywearslipstick.com/2011/06/lets-talk-about-slutwalk-london/. (Accessed February 24, 2016).

Maddison, S. (2013) Discursive Politics: Changing the Talk and Raising Expectations. In: Maddison, S. and Sawer, M. (eds.) *The Women's Movement in Protest, Institutions and the Internet: Australia in Transnational Perspective*. Abingdon: Routledge, pp. 37–53.

McNicol, L. (2015) A Critical Reading of SlutWalk in the News: Reproducing Postfeminism and Whiteness. In: Silva, K. and Mendes, K. (eds.) *Feminist Erasures: Challenging Backlash Culture*. Basingstoke: Palgrave, pp. 235–57.

Mendes, K. (2011) *Feminism in the News: Representations of the Women's Movement Since the 1960s*. Basingstoke: Palgrave Macmillan.

_____. (2015) *SlutWalk: Feminism, Activism and Media*. Basingstoke: Palgrave Macmillan.

Meyer, A. (2010) "Too Drunk to Say No": Binge Drinking, Rape and the Daily Mail. *Feminist Media Studies* 10 (1), pp. 19–34.

Meyers, M. (2006) News of Battering. *Journal of Communication* 44 (2), pp. 47–63.

Midgley, C. (2013) I Don't Give a Monkey's…. *The Times*, February 23, p. M14.

Mills, K. (1997) What Difference Do Women Journalists Make? In: Norris, P. (ed.) *Women, Media and Politics*. New York: Oxford University Press, pp. 41–56.

Molotch, H. L. (1978) The News of Women and the Works of Men. In: Tuchman, G., Daniels, A. K. and Bennett, J. (eds.) *Hearth and Home: Images of Women in the Mass Media*. New York: Oxford University Press, pp. 176–85.

Morozov, E. (2011) *The Net Delusion: How Not to Liberate the World*. London: Penguin.

Morris, M. B. (1973) The Public Definition of a Social Movement: Women's Liberation. *Sociology and Social Research* 57 (4), pp. 526–43.

Mowles, J. M. (2008) Framing Issues, Fomenting Change, "Feministing": A Contemporary Feminist Blog in the Landscape of Online Political Activism. *International Reports On Socio- informatics* 52, pp. 29–49.

Peipmeier, A. (2009) *Girl Zines: Making Media, Doing Feminism.* New York: New York University Press.

Perlmutter, D. D. (2008) *Blog Wars.* Oxford: Oxford University Press.

Piano, D. (2002) Congregating Women: Reading 3rd Wave Feminist Practices in Subcultural Production. *Rhizomes* 4. http://www.rhizomes.net/issue4/piano.html. (Accessed 3 March 2016).

Pillay-Siokos, K. (2013) SlutWalk Johanessburg 2013 Organizer. Personal Interview, May 25.

Pingree, S. and Hawkins, R. P. (1978) News Definitions and Their Effects on Women. In: Epstein, L. K. (ed.) *Woman and the News.* New York: Hasting House, pp. 116–35.

Rentschler, C. A. (2014) Rape Culture and the Feminist Politics of Social Media. *Girlhood Studies* 7 (1), pp. 65–82.

Seltzer, S. and Kelley, L. (2011) "Hey Rapists, Go Fuck Yourselves": SlutWalk arrives in NYC. *AlterNet*, October 3. http://www.alternet.org/story/152603/'hey_rapists,_go_fuck_yourselves'%3A_slutwalk_arrives_in_nyc. (Accessed February 24, 2016).

Shaw, F. (2011) (Dis)locating Feminisms: Blog Activism as Crisis Response. *Outskirsts*, May 24. http://www.outskirts.arts.uwa.edu.au/volumes/volume-24/shaw. (Accessed May, 5 2013).

_____. (2012a) *Discursive Politics Online: Political Creativity and Affective Networking in Australian Feminist Blogs.* Ph.D. Thesis. Sydney: University of New South Wales.

_____. (2012b) "Hottest 100 Women": Cross-platform Discursive Activism in Feminist Blogging Networks. *Australia Feminist Studies* 27 (74), pp. 373–87.

Sheridan, S., Magarey, S., and Lilburn, S. (2007) Feminism in the News. In: Hollows, J. and Moseley, R. (eds.) *Feminism in Popular Culture.* New York: Berg, pp. 25–40.

SlutWalk Toronto (2011) SlutWalk Toronto. *Facebook*, April 2. https://www.facebook.com/notes/214633831886772/. (Accessed February 14, 2013).

Staggenborg, S. (2008) *Social Movements.* Oxford: Oxford University Press.

Sutton, S. (2014) SlutWalk Chicago 2011 Organizer. Personal Interview, May 27.

Taft, J. K. (2011) *Rebel Girls: Youth Activism & Social Change Across the Americas.* New York: New York University Press.

Thorsen, E. (2009) Blogging the Climate Change Crisis from Antartica. In: Allan, S. and Thorsen, E. (eds.) *Citizen Journalism: Global Perspectives.* Oxford: Peter Lang, pp. 107–17.

tigtog (2011) An Open Challenge to Mainstream Media re SlutWalk Sydney. *Hoyden About Town*, June 12. http://hoydenabouttown.com/2011/06/12/an-open-challenge-to-mainstream-media-re-slutwalk-sydney/. (Accessed February 24, 2016).

Trew, B. (2013) Egypt's Sexual Assault Epidemic. *Al-Jazeera*, August 13. http://www.aljazeera.com/indepth/features/2013/08/201381494941573782.html. (Accessed June 10, 2014.

Trixie Films (2011) #slutwalk nyc 2011. Vimeo. https://vimeo.com/73893505. (Accessed October 31, 2014).

Tuchman, G. (1978) *Making News: A Study of the Construction of Reality.* New York: The Free Press.

Valenti, J. (2014) Beyoncé's "Flawless" Feminist Act at the VMAs Leads the Way for Other Women. *The Guardian*, August 25. http://www.theguardian.com/commentisfree/2014/aug/25/beyonce-flawless-feminist-vmas. (Accessed February 24, 2016).

van Zoonen, L. (1992) The Women's Movement and the Media: Constructing a Public Identity. *European Journal of Communication* 7 (4), pp. 453–76.

Warner, M. (2002) *Publics and counterpublics*. New York: Zone.

Williams, R. H. (1995) Constructing the Public Good: Social Movements and Cultural Resources. *Social Problems* 42 (1), pp. 124–44.

Wolfson, T. (2012) From the Zapatistas to Indymedia: Dialectics and Orthodoxy in Contemporary Social Movements. *Communication, Culture & Critique* 5, pp. 149–70.

Wraith, D. (2013) SlutWalk St. Louis 2012 Organizer. Personal Interview, April 28.

Young, S. (1997) *Discourse, Politics and the Feminist Movement*. London: Routledge.

PART III

Media Histories and Discarded Technologies: Recycling Memory in the Information Age

The Same Handful
of Images
Submarine, *Indie Retro*
and 2000s Youth Cinema

CAITLIN SHAW

Independent production company Warp Films' *Submarine* (Richard Ayoade, 2010), a coming-of-age adolescent comedy, was released in the wake of Warp's successful 1980s-set youth drama *This Is England* (Shane Meadows, 2006). More broadly, it surfaced amidst widespread Eighties revivalism in British media and pop culture that had inspired such recent popular film and TV outputs as *Son of Rambow* (Garth Jennings, 2007) and *Ashes to Ashes* (BBC, 2008–10). Given these contexts, alongside subtle textual details in *Submarine* that imply a pre-digital setting—characters, for instance, listen to music on cassette tapes and records but not CDs—critics and audiences might be forgiven for having assumed that it, too, was set in the 1980s. Several UK critics, including *The Observer*'s Philip French (2011) and *The Telegraph*'s Sukhdev Sandhu (2011), labeled it as 1980s-set, as did American critics like *The Christian Science Monitor*'s Peter Rainer (2011) when it eventually reached North American screens. Yet, *Submarine* lacks many of the typical signifiers commonly associated with period cinema. A year is not denoted, characters do not sport stereotypically Eighties fashions, instead wearing school uniforms or nondescript clothing, and the soundtrack's featured songs are not from the 1980s but are rather original works by indie rock band Arctic Monkeys' lead singer Alex Turner. In fact, despite being dubbed a 1980s period film in multiple media sources, Ayoade has insisted in interviews that his film is not set in a particular decade. Asked about it in a BBC interview, he responds, "I definitely didn't want to make it all 1980s, with hilarious clothes and music" (Jones, 2011). In another interview, he likens *Submarine* to other

122

coming-of-age films like Satyajit Ray's *The World of Apu* (1959) and François Truffaut's *The 400 Blows* (1959), which have unclear time settings and are merely set "in a slightly remembered past" ("Production Notes," 2010).

Ayoade reveals here his disinterest in either reconstructing or deconstructing a specific era; instead, his decision to evoke pastness stems from what he sees as an established coming-of-age cinematic mode with which he expects his audiences to be familiar. It is this use of pastness—as a tool for expression, a language—that differentiates *Submarine* from most traditional period dramas while simultaneously likening it to a growing number of so-called "indie" outputs like, for instance, certain Wes Anderson films. These productions tend less to recall a particular past, instead invoking aesthetic codes of pastness as modes of expression for their globalized, media-savvy audiences. Using *Submarine* as a case study, this essay will consider this process and its relationship to contemporary indie youth and young adult film culture. I will explore *Submarine*'s positive critical and popular reception not just in Britain but in North America as well, and I will suggest that its popularity was due to a quirky, retro style that likened it to other indie coming-of-age teen dramas like the American *Juno* (Jason Reitman, 2007). However, the film's effectiveness simultaneously lay in its self-aware, ironic stance toward invoking past referents, and toward indie-ness more generally, preventing it from appearing commodified or fabricated. At once operating within and just far enough outside indie youth culture, *Submarine*'s style speaks to the irreverent and ironic appropriations of the past that are characteristic of 2000s adolescents and young adults living in highly globalized, digitized, and participatory cultures.

Global Indie Cinema and Submarine*'s Transatlantic Success*

Set almost as vaguely in Wales as it is in the 1980s, *Submarine* is adapted from Joe Dunthorne's 2008 present-day-set novel of the same name. It follows a reasonably ordinary teen romantic comedy narrative: 15-year-old protagonist Oliver Tate (Craig Roberts) seeks to simultaneously save his parents' marriage and court his classmate Jordana Bevan (Yasmin Paige). Despite this straightforward set-up, *Submarine*'s cast of characters is decidedly eccentric; Oliver is an intelligent but alienated and self-absorbed teen who spends his time reading the dictionary, while his love interest Jordana is a stone-faced pyromaniac. Oliver's dissatisfied accountant mother Jill (Sally Hawkins) is on the verge of leaving his meek, depressive marine biologist father Lloyd (Noah Taylor) for her ex-lover Graham Purvis (Paddy Considine), a New Age mystic. Stylistically, *Submarine* is also unusual and is highly allusive. As already noted, it is set in an undefined past, and the presence of outdated technologies like VHS tapes and home footage shot on Super 8 lend it a cool, retro feel that is enhanced by stylistic references to 1960s and '70s art film movements. These and other features, on which I will elaborate below, differentiate *Submarine* from typical adolescent fare, marking it as an "arty" feature for independent cinemagoers.

Given this, as well as Warp Films' emerging reputation as a producer of high-quality screen fiction and comedian Ayoade's previous successes in the television series *Garth Marenghi's Darkplace* (Channel 4, 2004) and *The IT Crowd* (Channel 4, 2006–08, 2013), *Submarine* could have been expected to receive some attention from British critics and audiences of non-mainstream films. Even still, its degree of UK box office success appears to have surprised its domestic distributor, Optimum Releasing; the magazine *NME* reported that in *Submarine*'s first week of release, it brought in $400,068 USD from only 60 screens, achieving the highest per-screen ticket sales of any film that week. This result, to which *NME* attributed "rave reviews and word-of-mouth" ("Richard Ayoade's 'Submarine,'" 2011), prompted Optimum to nearly double the film's screens in the following week. *Submarine* also performed well in North America, where it achieved unusually wide viewership for a British teen comedy with a relatively modest budget of $1.9 million USD ("Submarine (2011)," n.d.). This was in part due to a well-received premiere at the 2010 Toronto International Film Festival; *Variety* later reported that several distributors expressed avid interest in buying North American distribution rights, which were ultimately acquired by The Weinstein Company (McClintock, 2010; Dawtrey, 2011). Also contributing to its North American appeal was American comedian Ben Stiller's involvement as executive producer: Stiller explains that in the film's early stages, Warp sent him the screenplay, requesting promotional assistance. Pleased with the script and impressed by Ayoade's previous work as a music video director, Stiller agreed to act as supportive executive producer, participating in press conferences and agreeing to have his name attached to American publicity materials (Hay, 2011; White, 2011).

Requesting Stiller's involvement indicates Warp's anticipated difficulty in selling, to American audiences, a Wales-set youth film starring actors either entirely unknown or only marginally recognizable to non–British viewers. Yet, it also reveals Warp's recognition that *Submarine* had transatlantic potential as an "indie" hit. Useful here is Michael Z. Newman's (2011) identification and analysis of "indie"; he notes that the term came into prominent usage in the 1990s as a catch-all term for non-mainstream American culture and has been assigned to such films as *The Big Lebowski* (Joel and Ethan Coen, 1998), *Ghost World* (Terry Zwigoff, 2001) and *Little Miss Sunshine* (Jonathan Dayton and Valerie Faris, 2006). He suggests that while the term partly functions as a mere shorthand for "independent," it also mystifies the latter's meaning, diminishing the term's importance as an economic distinguisher and embedding in it additional connotations concerning style and social identity (ibid., p. 4). These connotations center on indie cinema's general aim to define itself against mainstream stylistic, tonal, and character conventions by developing a quirky, eccentric aesthetic. Although this aligns indie with previous art film movements, Newman notes that its motivation for deviating from the mainstream is different: it is "located in play rather than in meanings, in a field of signifiers rather than an authorial signified, in fun that can be had by mixing and matching conventional narrative and cinematic elements" (2011, p. 35). In other words, indie cinema's predominant aim is not to shock or alienate audiences or to provoke intellectual discussion, but rather to play with cinematic codes that are familiar to its media-savvy, "mature, urban, college-educated" (2011, p. 38) audiences while exploring challenging characters and subject matter, thus engaging its viewers' sense of non-mainstream social identity without compromising wide appeal. The term "indie" is broad and is used to label a variety of films and other pop cultural outputs and, as such, Newman writes that it can be understood primarily as "a cluster of interpretative strategies and expectations" (2011, p. 11) that are shared by those who produce, distribute, critique, and view films.

Although Newman's analysis is restricted to American cinema and it has chiefly been the American film industry that has developed and exploited the label, several non–American films have achieved moderate to widespread global visibility in part due to their indie appeal, such as *Amélie* (Jean-Pierre Jeunet, 2001, France/Germany), *Good Bye Lenin!* (Wolfgang Becker, 2003, Germany) and *Eagle vs Shark* (Taika Waititi, 2007, New Zealand). It is clear that Warp was aware that *Submarine*'s unique, referential style, unusual characters, and sharp-tongued dialogue could qualify it, too, for the "indie" label. Tellingly, the film's New York City press conference featured only Ayoade, Stiller, and songwriter Alex Turner (Hay, 2011). Participation from Stiller and Turner could stimulate American interest, as Stiller's occasional cross-overs from mainstream to indie comedy in films like *The Royal Tenenbaums* (Wes Anderson, 2001) and *Greenberg* (Noah Baumbach, 2010) lend him some anti-mainstream credibility and Turner is familiar to American listeners of indie music as the frontman of the Arctic Monkeys. Furthermore, *Submarine*'s release not just at the Toronto International Film Festival but also subsequently at the London and Sundance Film Festivals before its official UK release reflects the tendency, as noted by Newman, of aspiring indie films to "capitalize on buzz" by being "screened at multiple festivals to make them available to critics well before their release date" (2011, p. 234). These tactics almost certainly assisted *Submarine* in achieving visibility both in and outside the UK, establishing it both as a quality film and, by extension, an off-beat, hip movie that would appeal to fans of the Arctic Monkeys and *The Royal Tenenbaums*.

Submarine's indie status was not merely established in retrospect as a means of boosting ticket sales; it is obvious that Ayoade and others on set were aware of the film's indie-ness, drawing comparisons between it and American counterparts. In an interview for the BBC, Craig Roberts confirms that what he calls the film's "American feel" was acknowledged during production, commenting that it "was a standing joke on set that this is the kind of story that Michael Cera would be playing if it had been made in the US. [...] Whenever my acting was bad, Richard would threaten me with: 'I'm going to call Michael Cera'" (Jones, 2011). Roberts' reference to Cera emphasizes the film's superficial resemblance to indie American teen comedies for which Cera has become known, such as *Juno* and *Scott Pilgrim vs. the World* (Edgar Wright, 2010). In particular, *Juno*, whose eponymous protagonist is a teenage girl (Ellen Page) who becomes pregnant after first-time sex with her boyfriend (Michael Cera) and who initially plans to abort the child but eventually decides to give it up for adoption, had by *Submarine*'s 2010 release become a hallmark of the indie adolescent romantic comedy. Its racy but nonetheless accessible subject matter, as well as its witty screenplay and quirky protagonist who, as Newman describes, is "at once offbeat—a 'real character'—and adorable, from the cherries on the underwear she removes before having sex to her use of well-turned phrases like 'I need to procure a hasty abortion'" (2011, pp. 236–37), resonated with a broad audience, and the film recouped well in excess of its $7.5 million USD budget, grossing $231 million USD worldwide ("Juno," n.d.). Implied comparisons to *Juno* reveal that *Submarine*'s cast and crew were conscious of American indie youth cinema's popularity and aware that, on some level, *Submarine* was itself also indie, and this active engagement with global, contemporary constructions of anti-mainstream undoubtedly contributed to *Submarine*'s transatlantic success.

Retro, Digital Mediation and the Past as Anti-Mainstream Language

To some extent, then, *Submarine*'s positive reception in art house circuits was pre-engineered: the film was produced and distributed in accordance with trends in American and global indie cinema. Still, I will suggest that there is something more particular about *Submarine* than a generalized stylistic and tonal resemblance to other indie films that resonates with its adolescent and young adult viewers, and this rests in its approach to pastness. Indeed, although Newman is not explicitly concerned with pastness in his discussion of American indie, implied is the significance of retro to contemporary notions of "quirkiness": especially since the 2000s, indie films have often either been set directly in the past or have recalled it through retro cinematic conventions and references to outdated popular cultures. Joel and Ethan Coen, Quentin Tarantino, and Wes Anderson, who rank among Hollywood's most visible and prolific indie directors, are similarly recognized for styles that rely heavily on generic and formal cinematic allusion, and in recent years they have increasingly turned to past settings (for instance, the Coen brothers' *True Grit* [2010] and *Inside Llewyn Davis* [2013]; Tarantino's *Inglourious Basterds* [2009] and *Django Unchained* [2012]; and Anderson's *Moonrise Kingdom* [2012] and *The Grand Budapest Hotel* [2014]). Among indie cinema directed at youth audiences, retro aesthetics are also often notable; *Juno*, for instance, is set in the present but stylistically invokes the past, from Juno's taste in 1970s punk bands like Iggy and the Stooges and The Runaways to the film's iconic opening song, Barry Louis Polisar's "All I Want Is You," borrowed from his 1977 children's album, *My Brother Thinks He's a Banana and Other Provocative Songs for Children*.

As described briefly above, *Submarine* is also very retro, and much of its quirkiness is rooted in its fluid, cut-and-paste incorporation of disparate media pasts. A vague late 1980s setting is implied in the film's pre-digital *mise-en-scène*: videos are viewed on VHS, music is listened to on records and cassette tapes and Jordana carries a Polaroid camera. Pre-digital datedness is also established stylistically; Super 8 home footage is used to depict Oliver's and Jordana's exploits as their young love develops, and segments of artificially dated pseudo-media are occasionally incorporated, including a self-help film featuring Graham Purvis, *Through the Prism*, and a documentary on aquatic life presented by Oliver's father called *Mysteries of the Deep*. The former's archaic computerized effects and low-fi electronic music and the latter's retro fonts, washed out colors and 4:3 aspect ratio framing with curved corners signal 1980s documentary production. In *Through the Prism*, Purvis dons a mullet and sits in front of a glass block wall, drawing associations with yuppie consumerism; indeed, Purvis' involvement in what Oliver calls "mystic bullshit" can be seen to stand in for the burgeoning "me" culture of which New Age spiritualism was a part and, as a threatening figure, Purvis evokes anxieties felt in Britain in the wake of encroaching Thatcherism.

However, the details that mark *Submarine*'s 1980s setting are confounded by stylistic citations from 1960s and '70s cinematic movements such as French New Wave and New Hollywood. For instance, the justified, colored capital lettering used for its titles explicitly references Jean-Luc Godard films like *Tout va bien* (1972), while expressive shots that evoke Oliver's alienation recall the cinematography of New Hollywood films about alienated young men like *The Graduate* (Mike Nichols, 1967). Meanwhile, Alex Turner's original soundtrack has a double function. On one hand, it avoids conjuring associations with a particular era; Craig Roberts notes that Ayoade "didn't want audiences to hear a track they already associated with a memory or a movie" (Jones,

2011). Simultaneously, however, Turner has commented that the film's songs were inspired by those of The Velvet Underground's John Cale (Hay, 2011), and they produce a tone of vague recollection rather than explicit recycling that contributes to the film's ambiguous pastness.

Of course, the retro styles in *Submarine* and other 2000s and 2010s indie films do not constitute an entirely new phenomenon. The growing tendency toward allusion in both mainstream and anti-mainstream popular cultures was identified as far back as the 1980s, perhaps most famously by Fredric Jameson (1991) and Jean Baudrillard (1994), and has since been discussed extensively in and outside of academic literature. It was succinctly described by Jim Collins in 1993 as a by-product of what he calls the "reality of the array" in contemporary "techno-sophisticated cultures" (1993, p. 255) that depend, for communication, on a shared knowledge of "the array," or "the perpetual circulation and recirculation of signs that forms the fabric of post-modern cultural life" (1993, p. 246). He suggests that this array of mediated signs—which can include shared memories of specific televised events, or of old films or TV shows, but also the shared recognition of broader signs like genre codes and conventions—is so engrained in people's day-to-day experiences that it is considered as real as the material world (1993, p. 255). The significance of recycled culture to pre–2000s British youth cinema has also been identified and theorized. Karen Lury, for instance, suggests that the British hit *Trainspotting* (Danny Boyle, 1996) was a domestic and international success because "it was not about its apparent subject matter—British youth—but was made to appeal to the youth of a global, hybrid culture" (2000, p. 107). She argues that much of its popularity was owed to its careful mixture of past and present music and pop cultural references, which enabled it to resonate with a youth audience that increasingly encompassed a wider age range than the term "youth" had traditionally denoted and which now derived pleasure, due to the proliferation of VCRs and rental outlets, from watching both new and old films (2000, pp. 103–04).

It can be said that *Submarine*'s integration of 1980s details, '60s and '70s cinematic citations and a contemporary retro-folk soundtrack represents an extension, 14 years on, of the formula that worked so well for *Trainspotting*. To an extent, this is true; both are British youth films set in regions that are relatively foreign to non–British viewers—*Submarine* in Wales and *Trainspotting* in Scotland—and achieve wider interest by appealing to global and "techno-sophisticated" cultures that consume and recycle a vast range of media from multiple nations and eras. However, they differ in their stylistic approach to pastness: unlike *Submarine*, *Trainspotting* does not foreground it. The latter still feels quite contemporary, integrating its past and present elements subtly and seamlessly to affect late '90s youth who were at once influenced by old movies, music, and other media and by the recent wave of

"New Britain" optimism. Popularized by the British media and exploited by the Blair government, the "New Britain" brand sought to shed the UK's international reputation as stuffy and conservative by globally redefining it as cool, modern, and decidedly un-nostalgic, and due to a combination of media hype and government incentives, it is seen in academic literature to have impacted on several pop cultural forms, including various film genres.[1]

Submarine, by contrast, is explicitly retro. In this way it, and other 2000s and 2010s indie films, British or otherwise, respond to evolving globalized notions of "cool" that increasingly tend toward what post-punk historian Simon Reynolds (2011) labels "retromania." Focusing on 2000s music trends, Reynolds notes their tendency to reference past styles rather than inventing their own, attributing the retro-steeped contemporary music scene to the easy accessibility of popular music pasts via internet platforms like *YouTube* and *iTunes*. Reynolds' assessment is largely pessimistic—he suggests that these platforms have "insidiously" hampered the present's ability to develop its own unique identity (2011, p. 57)—but he is correct to identify the correlation between the predominance of retro in post–2000 popular culture and the internet. If, in the 1990s, VCRs and video rental stores enabled youth to watch films from a variety of eras, the mass digitization of media technologies and proliferation of online media-playing platforms, as well as the convergence of these two phenomena in video-streaming services like Netflix, have extensively widened the scope of available media and rendered their access simple and immediate. As a result, the "array," to use Collins' term, of media knowledge that 2000s and 2010s youth have amassed is incomparable to previous decades. In turn, the accruement of obscure (and often, as a result, non-contemporary) media knowledge has become a fixture of the anti-mainstream, and citation its stylistic outlet: in contemporary notions of "indie," sophistication is marked by the ability to identify little-known media references. In addition, Henry Jenkins (2006) has noted the growing importance, in the era of media convergence, of participation to 2000s and 2010s popular cultures. Advances in technology have enabled youth not just to consume but also to recycle and manipulate media content, and Jenkins likens this process to folk cultural practices wherein stories are actively shared, appropriated, and adapted (2006, p. 140). As such, indie identity is constructed not just around knowledge of obscure media references, but also around the clever and quirky appropriation, re-contextualization and modification of the media's disparate pasts.

Submarine's incoherent approach to invoking the past is therefore pertinent to its 2010 indie youth and young adult audience. The irreverent incorporation of pre-digital 1980s *mise-en-scène*, codes associated with '60s and '70s art cinema movements and contemporary but Velvet Underground-inspired folk music, appeals to viewers who take pleasure in both recognizing the references and seeing them called up and adapted in new, creative ways. Furthermore, its incorporation of artificial "old" media which, apart from the documentaries produced for the film described above, also include a false news segment in which Oliver imagines how others would react to his death and the ensuing media coverage, speaks to contemporary DIY, cut-and-paste storytelling practices observable, for instance, in home-edited *YouTube* video montages wherein archival media are appropriated to express the interests, concerns and anxieties of the present. Graham Purvis' self-help film *Through the Prism* is also available to view in its entirety on the UK DVD release, broadening the film's diegetic world and consequently appealing to convergence-era media consumers who, as Jenkins argues, are now "encouraged to seek out new information and make connections among dispersed media content" (2006, p. 3). These pseudo-media productions, as well as the Super 8 home footage and Polaroid photographs, also work tonally: while recycled "old" media act as components of a language among youth living in highly digitized contemporary societies, their associated codes of technological outdatedness simultaneously conjure a general sense of reminiscence for viewers whose personal memories have been refracted through photographs and home videos and are intertwined with memories of pop cultural media. As such, *Submarine's* artificial media evokes a "slightly remembered past" which, as noted in the introduction, Ayoade considers characteristic of coming-of-age cinema.

Irony, Nostalgia and Indie Authenticity

Submarine's success can therefore be credited both to successful exploitation of its potential for "indie" status and to its incorporation of pastness in a manner accessible to contemporary indie youth and young adults. The same can be said of other indie youth films like *Juno*; as I have posited above, it too uses retro as a basis for quirky style. In his analysis of *Juno*, Newman notes that it was, like *Submarine*, given a "rollout" release: it was pre-viewed at the Tellu-ride Film Festival before an official premiere at the Toronto International Film Festival, enabling it to take advantage of critical buzz (2011, p. 234). Newman additionally points out that, much like *Submarine* was compared to *Juno* and implicitly linked through Ben Stiller to other indie films like *The Royal Tenenbaums*, *Juno* was compared in its paratexts to previous American off-beat comedies like *Napoleon Dynamite* (Jared Hess, 2004) and *Little Miss Sunshine*, thus "reproducing [its] indieness" (2011, p. 234). However, *Submarine* was not subjected to the eventual critical backlash that *Juno* experienced. Newman traces this phenomenon, writing that after initially positive reviews, *Juno* was "de-authenticated by the indie community when its popularity pushed it beyond the art house theater and audience and into the mainstream" (2011, p. 235). As the film gained momentum, it was increasingly criticized for seemingly manipulating audiences into believing it was "indie" when, in fact, it was financed by Fox Searchlight and ultimately favored accessibility over genuinely challenging subject matter (Newman, 2011, pp. 240–44).

The most obvious reason why *Submarine* did not suffer the same backlash is that, unlike *Juno*, it was not financed by the niche division of a major Hollywood studio and it did not achieve the same degree of popularity. Despite comparatively wide American distribution for an off-beat British youth comedy, *Submarine* did not, ultimately, cross over into the mainstream, and it is impossible to say if it would have sustained its critical credibility had it done so. However, there is also something fundamentally different in *Submarine*'s approach to indie retro. Newman describes *Juno*'s approach as an instance of a film "performing its own indieness, its own alternative sensibility" (2011, p. 235), and its carefully plotted appeal to contemporary indie culture, partly founded on the integration of retro style, had much to do both with *Juno*'s massive popularity and its eventual critical backlash. It is safe to guess that some of *Submarine*'s cast and crew were likely aware of this backlash and, as such, their on-set comparisons of *Submarine* to Michael Cera films are tinged with retrospective irony toward the process of manufacturing an indie product. That such a standpoint informed *Submarine*'s production is further suggested by a comment made by Ayoade; when asked by an interviewer what inspired his film's "cool" and "quirky" style, he responds that "the idea, really, was that the character was directing the film, and so the character would want to be seen in a light that was flattering to him and he wishes to be an existential hero. [...] Hopefully the choices that you make [...] [are] motivated by this particular character rather than putting stuff in that you think is cool" (Weintraub, 2011). Here, Ayoade implies that, aesthetically, his film seeks not to replicate pre-conceived notions of "cool" but instead to draw comedy from protagonist Oliver's desire to blazon his eccentric, original identity through references to other media and texts.

Ayoade's self-conscious approach to indie style manifests in the film text's employment of pastness. While retro elements seemingly appear in *Juno* "just because"—as trivial details that enhance its quirkiness—*Submarine*'s version of retro aligns with certain academic conceptions of ironic postmodern nostalgia. Among these is Linda Hutcheon's (2000) assertion that although little commercial nostalgia is ironic, some—what she calls postmodern nostalgia—is ironic, and in so being "undermines modernist assertions of originality, authenticity, and the burden of the past" (2000, p. 206). Theorized this way, nostalgia does not have to function as Reynolds suggests it does in "retromanic" contemporary music cultures, as the antithesis to originality; instead, it can call into question the modernist belief in true originality. A similar assertion is made by Elizabeth E. Guffey (2006), who writes that when used ironically, nostalgia can put modernist "visions in perspective, to see the unshakeable faith in Modernity as limited in scope" (2006, p. 25). Guffey calls this ironic nostalgia "retro," qualifying it as contemporary retro and disassociating it from previous usages of the term. She argues that it "regards the past from a bemused distance" (2006, p. 12), tempering "ideas of exile and longing" with "a heavy dose of cynicism or detachment" (2006, p. 20). It is true that the citations in *Submarine* are in part influenced by Ayoade's own cinematic nostalgia; in *Sight and Sound*, he comments that he admires films like *The Graduate* and *Badlands* (Terence Malick, 1973), as well as French New Wave films, claiming that his "favourite film for a long time was *Zazie dans le metro* (Louis Malle, 1960). I guess when you really love a film you end up subconsciously ripping it off" (Charity, 2010, p. 18). However, Guffey defines retro as a process of both longing and detachment, wherein an ironic stance tempers nostalgic sentiment, and this particular process is at play in the film's references to 1960s and '70s political/art film movements. While *Submarine* "rips off" the visual styles of these films, it simultaneously ironizes the modernist notions of directorial vision, originality, and formal destabilization that drove them, knowingly poking fun at the individualistic desire to express oneself through original forms and at the ultimate impossibility of doing so in a postmodern context.

This process is evident from the film's opening. After the Godardian titles, Oliver narrates, "Most people think of themselves as individuals. That there's no one else on the planet like them. This thought motivates them to get out of bed, eat food and walk around like nothing's wrong. My name is Oliver Tate." Jump cuts then close in on Oliver and he looks at the camera. Assuming a vague familiarity among its audience with French New Wave conventions and their auteurist connotations, and suggesting that Oliver is invoking this style to express his ultimately imaginary individuality, the sequence establishes a tongue-in-cheek stance toward its own stylization. In a later scene, Oliver composes a pamphlet to help a classmate who is being bullied, suggesting that she must discover who she is, and writes, "I don't quite know what I am yet; I've tried smoking a pipe, flipping coins, listening exclusively to French crooners. Other times I go to the beach and stare at the sea. Someone made a documentary about a prominent thinker who struggled with unspeakable loss." As he narrates this in voiceover, excessively expressive shots picture Oliver performing these tasks; while staring at the sea, for instance, he is pictured from the side with the sun setting behind him, his hands in his pockets and a pensive expression on his face. Comedy is derived here from the shared recognition that the pictured actions—smoking, listening in solitude to music, staring at the sea—are common signifiers of thoughtfulness, depth, and alienation in films and other media. In other words, they constitute what Jim Collins describes as the "icons, scenarios, [and] visual conventions" characteristic of heavily mediated societies which, due to constant recycling, "carry with them some sort of cultural 'charge' or resonance" (1993, p. 256). The scene is funny because it draws attention to the audience's shared recognition of the "charge" the images carry and, in turn, to the fact that they are artificial markers of originality whose meaning has been constructed and sustained through media repetition.

While *Submarine* maintains an aura of ironic detachment in its references to the past, it does not descend into cynicism. Ayoade self-consciously calls up indie culture's tendency to depend for expression on media citation, but instead of criticizing or mocking it, his film explores both positive and negative ways that the media can shape identity. This is notable in the differing ways that *Submarine*'s artificial media are integrated into the film text. On one hand, Graham Purvis' *Through the Prism* is presented as a threatening exploitation of media technology; its combination of colorful computerized effects, orientalist Native American–style music, and false information that includes Purvis' claim that he can see colors in people, evokes the media's abilities to distort truth and destructively impact perspectives. However, on the other hand, when Oliver reveals to his parents that he is dating Jordana, his father Lloyd offers him a cassette tape—as he describes it, "a compilation of songs I used to listen to during some of my early formative relationships"—to help Oliver process his newfound emotions. As Oliver presses the "play" button, Alex Turner's original song "Hiding Tonight" begins to play, ensuring that the audience will not be moved by nostalgic impulses and will instead experience the song as Oliver might: as a cultural media product that is positively shaping his identity in the present by helping him to understand his youthful love for Jordana.

By self-reflexively engaging with its retro quirkiness, *Submarine* manages to simultaneously appeal to the contemporary indie market and avoid making a commodity of indie culture. Arguably, it was the film's ironic tone that helped to sustain its authenticity among critics and indie audiences, as it assists in bridging gaps between viewers in what Lury, as noted previously, identifies as an ever-expanding and ever more global youth cinema market. While *Submarine*'s eccentric adolescent protagonists and stylistic retro quirkiness appeal to the teenage viewers targeted by off-beat American youth films like *Garden State* (Zach Braff, 2004), *Juno, Nick and Norah's Infinite Playlist* (Peter Sollett, 2008) and *The Perks of Being a Wallflower* (Stephen Chbosky, 2012), the ironic playfulness that counterbalances its indie-ness prevents it from alienating the increasingly university-educated, widely-read, middle class 20- and 30-somethings who now also form part of indie youth cinema's audience. Its self-consciousness is also appropriate for young film viewers who, in an era of proliferating media technologies and platforms, have progressively honed the ability to recognize and be suspicious of media manipulation. In such a context, a backlash against *Juno*'s premeditated exploitation of the contemporary alternative, anti-mainstream sensibility might be seen as having been inevitable among certain discerning viewers. *Submarine* evades this by neither exploiting nor censuring indie culture. Instead, it highlights, while simultaneously praising and gently mocking, the ways in which film, television, and other media references are engrained in postmodern realities and shape identities.

Conclusion: The Past as Language

If, as Lury suggests, *Trainspotting* spoke to the interests of late 1990s global youth by hybridizing the past and present, *Submarine* can be said to speak to those of youth in 2010. It invokes incongruent elements from the array of "old" media knowledge at their fingertips, not to signal a past setting but as building blocks for its protagonist's self-expression. As such, it establishes an eccentric, nostalgic aesthetic for young viewers who project their anti-mainstream identity by sharing in the recognition of, cleverly reappropriating, and fusing obscure remnants from art and popular culture's mediated pasts. It is evident that much of *Submarine*'s appeal in indie circuits was founded on this aesthetic, as well as on Warp Films' recognition that the film could consequently qualify for "indie" status. The film's off-beat, cool aura—extratextually assisted in the UK by Richard Ayoade's and Warp's good reputations among indie audiences and internationally by Ben Stiller's involvement and Alex Turner's retro-folk soundtrack—enabled it to garner significant critical and indie attention. In this way, its star Craig Roberts was correct to compare it to American youth films starring Michael Cera, like *Juno*, which also project anti-mainstream status through the textual incorporation of quirky, retro details and which promotionally take advantage of the indie label.

Yet, *Submarine* simultaneously ventures beyond the average indie product. It mildly mocks the affectedness of contemporary films that blankly replicate indie conventions to appeal to youths who identify themselves outside the mainstream. Ultimately, *Juno* strives for sincerity; its formal eccentricities are suggested to be in natural harmony with its quirky identity. *Submarine*'s irony abates this, while paradoxically lending it a degree of honesty that is lacking *Juno*. In a pivotal moment in *Submarine*'s epilogue, tragic non-diegetic music swells as Oliver stares at the sea and narrates, "I feel shrunken, as if there's a tiny ancient Oliver Tate inside me operating the levers of a life-size Oliver-shaped shell. A shell on which a decrepit picture show replays the same handful of images. Every night I come to the same place and wait till the sky catches up with my mood." As he narrates, shots depict him staring longingly out to sea; then, when he mentions the "handful of images," a montage of artificial home footage depicts him and Jordana playing happily on the beach. A shot of the waves at sunset accompanies his final comment. Like those discussed above, this scene comically highlights the affectation inherent in expressing one's identity through referential idiosyncrasy, setting it apart from *Juno*'s sincere quirkiness. Yet, at the same time, it embraces the impact of media on young contemporary identities: far from being depthless, the "same handful of images" Oliver describes is held up here as a vital tool with which to work through his emotions. *Submarine*'s earnestness rests in this oscillation: at once, it acknowledges both the absurdity and, in spite of this, the value of using the media's pasts as a language for the present.

NOTE

1. New Britain's relationship to the film industry is discussed in depth by Monk (2000, 2001) and Wayne (2006). Steve Chibnall (2011) has noted its impact on "lad" films, while Robert Murphy (2009) has highlighted its impact on the romantic comedy.

REFERENCES

Anonymous. (n.d.) Juno. *Box Office Mojo*, n.d. http://www.boxofficemojo.com/movies/?id=juno.htm. (Accessed June 8, 2015).

Anonymous. (n.d.) Submarine (2011). *The Numbers*, n.d. http://www.the-numbers.com/movie/Submarine#tab=summary. (Accessed May 28, 2015).

Anonymous. (2010) Submarine Production Notes. *Optimum Releasing*, n.d. http://press.optimumreleasing.net/dyn/SUBMARINE_PRODUCTION_NOTES_2011.pdf. (Accessed June 2, 2015).

Anonymous. (2011) Richard Ayoade's "Submarine" Achieves Highest UK Per-screen Figures. *NME*, n.d. http://www.nme.com/filmandtv/news/richard-ayoades-submarine-achieves-highest-uk-per-screen-figures/209358. (Accessed May 28, 2015).

Baudrillard, J. (1994) *Simulacra and Simulation*. Ann Arbor: University of Michigan Press.

Charity, T. (2010) Above Us the Waves: Richard Ayoade Talks "Submarine." *Sight and Sound*, November, pp. 18–20.

Chibnall, S. (2001) Britain's Funk Soul Brothers: Gender, Family and Nation in the New Brit-pics. *Cineaste* 26 (4), pp. 38–42.

Collins, J. (1993) Genericity in the Nineties: Eclectic Irony and the New Sincerity. In: Collins, J. (ed.) *Film Theory Goes to the Movies*. London: Routledge, pp. 242–63.

Dawtrey, A. (2011) Richard Ayoade: Comic's Sensibility Anchors "Submarine." *Variety*, January 7. http://variety.com/2011/film/news/richard-ayoade-comic-s-sensibility-anchors-submarine-1118029637/. (Accessed May 28, 2015).

French, P. (2011) Submarine—Review. *The Guardian*, March 20. http://www.theguardian.com/film/2011/mar/20/submarine-richard-ayoade-philip-french. (Accessed May 26, 2015).

Guffey, E. (2000) *Retro: The Culture of Revival*. London: Reaktion.

Hay, C. (2011) Ben Stiller, Richard Ayoade, Alex Turner Dive into Making the Movie "Submarine." *Examiner*, June 3. http://www.examiner.com/article/ben-stiller-richard-ayoade-alex-turner-dive-into-making-the-movie-submarine. (Accessed June 2, 2015).

Hutcheon, L. (2000) Irony, Nostalgia, and the Postmodern. In: Estor, A. and Vervliet, R. (eds.) *Methods for the Study of Literature as Cultural Memory*. Atlanta: Rodopi, pp. 189–207.

Jameson, F. (1991) *Postmodernism, or, the Cultural Logic of Late Capitalism*. Durham: Duke University Press.

Jenkins, H. (2006) *Convergence Culture: Where Old and New Media Collide*. New York: New York University Press.

Jones, E. (2011) Richard Ayoade Takes the Helm for Submarine. *BBC News*, March 15. http://www.bbc.co.uk/news/entertainment-arts-12730794. (Accessed December 4, 2013).

Juno. (2007) [Film] Directed by Jason Reitman. USA: Fox Searchlight Pictures.

Lury, K. (2000) Here and Then: Space, Place and Nostalgia in British Youth Cinema of the 1990s. In: Murphy, R. (ed.) *British Cinema of the 90s*. London: BFI, pp. 100–08.

McClintock, P. (2011) Buyers Dive for "Submarine." *Variety*, September 13. http://variety.com/2010/biz/markets-festivals/buyers-dive-for-submarine-at-tiff-1118024077/. (Accessed May 30, 2015).

Monk, C. (2000) Underbelly UK: The 1990s Underclass Film, Masculinity and the Ideologies of "New" Britain. In: Ashby, J. and Higson, A. (eds.) *British Cinema, Past and Present*. London: Routledge, pp. 274–87.

_____. (2001) Projecting a "New Britain." *Cineaste* 26 (4), pp. 34–7, 42.

Murphy, R. (2009) Citylife: Urban Fairy-tales in Late 90s British Cinema. In: Murphy, R. (ed.) *The British Cinema Book*. London: BFI, pp. 357–65.

Newman, M. Z. (2011) *Indie: An American Film Culture*. New York: Columbia University Press.

Rainer, P. (2011) Submarine: movie review. *The Christian Science Monitor*, June 3. http://www.csmonitor.com/The-Culture/Movies/2011/0603/Submarine-movie-review. (Accessed May 26, 2015).

Reynolds, S. (2011) *Retromania: Pop Culture's Addiction to its Own Past*. London: Faber & Faber.

Sandhu, S. (2011) Submarine, Review. *The Telegraph*, March 18. http://www.telegraph.co.uk/culture/film/filmreviews/8390132/Submarine-review.html. (Accessed May 26, 2015).

Submarine. (2010) [Film] Directed by Richard Ayoade. UK: Warp Films.

Wayne, M. (2006) The Performing Northern Working Class in British Cinema: Cultural Representation and its Political Economy. *Quarterly Review of Film and Video* (23) 4, pp. 287–97.

Weintraub, S. (2011) Writer/Director Richard Ayoade Video Interview Submarine. *Collider*, June 2. http://collider.com/richard-ayoade-interview-submarine/. (Accessed June 8, 2015).

White, J. (2011) Ben Stiller talks Submarine. *Empire*, January 14. http://www.empireonline.com/movies/news/ben-stiller-talks-submarine/. (Accessed June 2, 2015).

To Hold On or to Let Go?

Small-Gauge Amateur Filmmaking and Nostalgia in Super 8 *and* Frankenweenie

MARTA WĄSIK

"It is among the lasting and the novel that we find an orientation between the past and the present, rather like a compass."—Charles Acland, *Residual Media*, p. xix

In contemporary popular culture we are observing a surge of interest in the texts and textures of the recent past (Reynolds, 2011; Niemeyer, 2014; Olivier, 2014). The films *Super 8* (J.J. Abrams, 2011) and *Frankenweenie* (Tim Burton, 2012) are two examples of this trend, combining an investigation of cinematic heritage with a fascination with obsolete image-making technologies. Both works are cinephilic homages—*Super 8* to the blockbuster cinema of the 1970s and 1980s, and *Frankenweenie* to B-grade horror film—and their pronounced interest in the past has often been perceived in terms of nostalgia, a bittersweet longing; in this case, for bygone cinematic cultures (Gustini, 2011; Orr, 2011; Papamichael, 2012). This yearning is perceptible both in how Abrams and Burton strive to imitate the styles of the films of the past (in the frequent use of the lens flares in *Super 8* or in *Frankenweenie*'s monochrome tonality and use of low key lighting) and also in the films' depiction of filmmaking. The protagonists of both films are adolescent movie-makers whose 8 mm productions (a zombie horror entitled *The Case* which closes *Super 8* and a dinosaur disaster movie *Monsters from Beyond* which opens *Frankenweenie*) are, like the films in which they are embedded, intertextual homages. In interviews, both directors have spoken about their own roots in Super 8 filmmaking (Puckrick, 2011; Burton and Salisbury, 2006) and their choice to depict their heroes as young amateurs can be read as a semi-autobiographical gesture, suggesting nostalgia not only for a cinema of the past but also for a tradition of non-professional filmmaking and its obsolete tools. Studying the amateur films as focusing the directors' interest in bygone cinematic cultures, this essay will interrogate what the representation of small-gauge productions reveal about these directors' attitudes towards the past. I will argue that the amateur films-within-the-films function as a self-reflexive device and as such occupy a privileged space, as at once the vehicle for and objects of nostalgia, as well as a lens through which that longing can be interrogated.

As Katharina Niemeyer (2014) argues, nostalgia not only describes an attachment to the past but also often functions as a reflection on change. Studying nostalgia thus allows us to interrogate the attitudes towards both the obsolete and the novel, and to gauge and assess the fantasies and anxieties which accompany the transitions between them. Negotiating the relevance of the past for the present is a central concern to the projects of *Super 8* and *Frankenweenie* and is apparent through both directors' choice to frame their nostalgic exploration via narratives of grief: the death of the mother in *Super 8* and the beloved dog in *Frankenweenie*. In depicting their protagonists' struggles to come to terms with loss, the films pose broader questions about their own attachment to the past. Yet, while they propose different resolutions—*Super 8* foregrounding the need to overcome mourning, and *Frankenweenie* refusing to accept separation—their representation of past and present media do not always support those resolves. Drawing on Stanley Cavell's (1981) concepts of the contained and containing film (that is to say, both the amateur films that appear in the films, and the films themselves), this essay will interrogate the different mobilizations of nostalgia in *Frankenweenie* and *Super 8*. Furthermore, it will ask what the directors' attachment to the texts and technologies of the past can tell us about their perception of the contemporary cultural landscape in which the films are developed and consumed.

Small-Gauge Cinema, Large Format Mourning

Set in the town of Lilian, Ohio, in 1979, *Super 8* tells the story of a group of teenagers shooting an amateur zombie film *The Case*. The film's protagonist Joe (Joel Courtney) is struggling to come to terms with his mother's death and his bourgeoning romantic feelings for his friend Alice (Elle Fanning). The narrative of the young filmmakers is interwoven with an extra-terrestrial plot of an alien who escapes military confinement following a train derailment in Lilian. Taking revenge for his mistreatment by the army, the enraged creature wreaks havoc on the small town, kidnapping many of its inhabitants, including Alice. Joe and his friends set out to save her; the rescue concludes as the hero faces the monster and persuades it to let go of its grudge against humans. While the encounter leads to the alien's departure, it also facilitates the resolution of the protagonist's grief, which is symbolically enacted in the film's finale when Joe relinquishes his mother's locket—a cherished souvenir—to the departing spaceship.

Super 8 is a film fascinated with small-gauge filmmaking. It contains a diverse range of non-professional films which include: the amateur zombie film *The Case*; Joe's childhood home movies depicting his mother; accidental footage of the alien captured by the camera which the teenagers abandoned while fleeing the train crash; and 16 mm films shot by the military. Already the film's title indicates its interest in small-gauge movie making. "Super 8" is a reference to an Eastman Kodak motion picture format which was released in 1965 as an improvement on their previous "Regular" 8 mm stock.[1] Technology historian Alan Kattelle has praised the system, writing that: "with the arrival of Super 8, motion picture equipment for the amateur had reached a high plateau of versatility and sophistication" (Kattelle, 1986, p. 57). Super 8 was also one of the final developments in the history of small-gauge film, which declined in popularity in the 1980s following the introduction of video for the commercial market (Zimmermann, 1995; Moran, 2002). *Super 8* thus takes place at the end point of the format's commercial popularity and the sense of an end of an era subtly shades Abrams' film, infusing its representation of domestic media with a melancholic sense of impending loss.

While *Super 8* takes place just as small-gauge filmmaking was facing impending obsolescence, *Frankenweenie* is set in the loosely defined 1950s sometime during the post-war consumer boom. As Patricia Zimmermann (1995) points out, this era marked the widespread popularity of domestic filmmaking.[2] Inspired by James Whale's *Frankenstein* (1931) and a remake of Burton's own 1984 short film of the same title, *Frankenweenie* focuses on young Victor Frankenstein (voiced by Charlie Tahan), a reclusive amateur movie maker with a love for science. When his beloved dog (and the star of his films) Sparky is hit by a car, Victor decides to re-animate his deceased pet. As the word of Sparky's resurrection spreads, the other children conspire to steal Victor's secret for life beyond the grave in order to win the first prize at the science fair. The experiments get out of hand and a horde of undead pets is unleashed upon the fictional town of New Holland. The most dangerous of these is Weird Girl's (Catherine O'Hara) mutant bat-cat Mr. Whiskers. Facing the feline in a final showdown at a mini golf course, Sparky manages to save the day at the cost of his own life. No longer terrified by the dog's monstrosity, the townspeople gather together to (re-)resurrect Victor's beloved pet, and he is revived once more in the film's finale.

Unlike *Super 8*, *Frankenweenie* is arguably not a film about amateur filmmaking. The films-within-the-film are nonetheless of crucial importance to the project of the work, offering a condensation of its central themes and preoccupations. Like *Super 8*, *Frankenweenie* communicates its interest in small-gauge image making from the outset. The film opens with a family screening of Victor's film—*Monsters from Beyond*—which stars Sparky as the dinosaur Sparkysaurus. The contained film is, like *Frankenweenie* itself, a mix of stop-motion animation (using toys and appliances as characters and props) and live action in the scenes featuring the dog (live action, that is, within the diegetic world). The pet is the only living presence within Victor's film, establishing the boy as a lonely auteur, and mirroring Burton's own creative persona (in contrast, *The Case* is presented as a collective endeavor). Focusing on the story of dinosaurs rampaging a modern day city, the amateur film foreshadows *Frankenweenie*'s broader concern with the persistence of the past which comes to the fore in Victor's resurrection of Sparky. As Svetlana Boym argues in *The Future of Nostalgia* (2001), in Northern American culture the dinosaur features as a privileged figure of nostalgia, symbolizing "an attempt to make the past come alive" (Boym, 2001, p. 33) and frequently also charting the consequences of seeing that desire fulfilled.[3]

Similarly to *Monsters from Beyond*, *The Case* also demonstrates a preoccupation with persistence and return. It follows a detective (played by Joe's friend Martin portrayed by Gabriel Basso) investigating the spread of a mysterious virus which turns humans into zombies. The living-dead arguably symbolize *Super 8*'s broader preoccupation with the past and its hold on the present.[4] In their article "Zombie Media: Circuit Bending Media Archaeology into an Art Method" Garnet Hertz and Jussi Parikka (2012) recognize the critical potential of the zombie as a metaphor for the endurance of the obsolete which, by hanging around long past its due date, grates against the dominant thrust towards incessant innovation and disposability. Like the dinosaur, the living dead thus indicate a concern with the persistence of the old in the new; at the same time, both also possess a potentially monstrous dimension. Yet, in contrast to the representation of home movies in the analog horror film *Sinister* (Scott Diedrickson, 2012)—which depicts home movies as haunted media inhabited by a murderous demon—the small-gauge films in *Super 8* and *Frankenweenie* are not particularly horrifying.[5] The living-dead depicted in *The Case* and the dinosaur in *Frankenweenie* are both perceptibly non-threatening and their potentially abject qualities (such as leaking blood or other fluids), voracious appetites and destructive capacities are diffused by the humor which arises from their clumsy special effects. If, as Marc Olivier argues, Diedrickson's mediaphobia indicates a weariness with the contemporary predilection for nostalgia, and attempts to turn this cultural fasciation into revulsion (Olivier, 2014), Abrams and Burton offer a contrary message about persistence, indicating that while the proliferation of the past in the present may initially appear unsettling, it is fundamentally harmless and charming.

Abrams' and Burton's deployment of the dinosaur and the zombie as metaphors for return is further communicated by their status as intertextual references to cinematic heritage. Both Victor's film and *The Case* are cinephilic homages which mirror, albeit on a smaller scale, the referencing of *Super 8* and *Frankenweenie*. *The Case* alludes to George A. Romero—a prominent horror filmmaker of the 1970s known for his zombie films such as *Night of the Living Dead* (1968) and *Dawn of the Living Dead* (1978)—by naming the chemical plant which manufactures the zombie virus "Romero Chemicals" and in the Romero film posters in the bedroom of the film's director, Charles (Riley Griffiths). The latter obliquely reflects *Super 8*'s preoccupation with Steven Spielberg—the executive producer of the film and Abrams' nostalgic hero—whose influence is palpable in the tone and style of the production.[6] A key inspiration for *Monsters from Beyond* is *The Lost World* (Harry O. Hoyt, 1925), an adaptation of Arthur Conan Doyle's novel. This reference is identifiable not only through their shared narrative preoccupation with dinosaurs running amok in a modern day city (Hoyt's film ends with a Brontosaurus set loose in London), but also in the use of stop-motion animation (*Lost World*'s dinosaurs were animated by stop-motion pioneer Willis O'Brian). Thus, while *Frankenweenie* has often been read as a semi-autobiographical film—particularly in its representation of Victor and his relationship with Sparky (see Adams, 2012; Fischer, 2012)—it is also a cinematic autobiography, an homage to Burton's formative influences and inspirations.[7]

Notably, the amateur films-in-the-films are not only vehicles for but also objects of nostalgia. As Charles Acland (2007), Simone Natale and Gabriele Balbi (2014), and Katharina Niemeyer (2014), among others, have shown, bygone media frequently becomes the object of sentimental attachment, so much so that Natale and Balbi argue that nostalgia is one of the key fantasies attached to obsolete media (together with an anxiety over their potential disappearance). The prevalence of this association can be witnessed in the ways that contemporary uses of 8 mm film characterize the format's identity as a medium of the past.[8] This association is illustrated by online promotional material of Pro8mm, the company which supplied 8 mm cameras for *Super 8*, who on their website write that "nostalgia, grit and grain are some of the most popular aesthetics of the format that attract filmmakers to Super 8" (Pro8mm, n.d.). The film's title thus not only informs the viewers of the director's interest in old media, but also shores up associations with nostalgia which have become attached to small-gauge filmmaking following its obsolescence.

In their depiction of amateur films, *Super 8* and *Frankenweenie* are unique in their prevalent usage of small-gauge imagery which, as my doctoral research into the history of cinematic home movies has shown, since the 1980s has tended to privilege the "degraded" aesthetic of the format (as part of the cinematic vocabulary for the depiction of past) over a representation of its technology.[9] In contrast, both Abrams and Burton foreground the *material* culture of the past practices of domestic image making. The focus on materiality is apparent in *Frankenweenie*; as the screening of *Monsters from Beyond* concludes, the camera lingers on the dismantling of the machinery—as Victor takes the projector up to his studio in the attic, while Mrs. Frankenstein folds the screen away in the living room and hides it behind the chimney—prominently foregrounding the physical dimension of the equipment which sets images in motion.[10]

Representing the now obsolete technologies at a time of their dominance, *Super 8* and *Frankenweenie* fondly recall a time of their commercial ubiquity. In both cases the protagonists occupy a world saturated with home movies and home movie makers. When Charles' camera is broken during the train crash, the young filmmakers simply borrow a substitute from Joe's father; similarly, Victor's friend Toshiaki (James Hiroyuki Liao) is also shown to have a small-gauge camera which he uses to record his own undead pet, an oversized turtle called Shelly. The nostalgic yearning for the media of the past which the films engender is thus predicated upon a disjunction: between the widespread availability of the technology at the time of the films' setting and its contemporary scarcity.[11] *Super 8* offers a poignant illustration of this in a scene in which Joe and Charles take the broken camera to the camera store where numerous accessories and boxes of film are prominently on display. A cardboard Kodak logo hovers over a pyramid of KodaChrome films and its appearance is wistful, a product placement with nothing to sell; it fuels the film's nostalgic longing by igniting a desire for the things of the past which are largely unavailable for contemporary consumption, and which the digital remediation of analog aesthetic cannot alleviate.

As Niemeyer and others have observed, nostalgia is a bittersweet sentiment, and as such entails not only a celebration of the past, but also a melancholic recognition of its inevitable passing. Both Abrams and Burton recognize this ambiguity, and foreground it by framing their nostalgic explorations through narratives of grief. *Super 8* opens with the death of Joe's mother and her absence is central to the project of *Super 8* not only narratively—providing Joe with an arc for his maturation—but also tonally, overshadowing the film with a sense of longing.[12] Victor similarly seeks to keep a hold of the past after he loses his beloved dog. In an attempt to prolong his encounters with Sparky, after the dog's death the boy revisits *Monsters from Beyond*; the somber tone of the scene, however, contrasts starkly with the exuberance of the opening.[13] The screening emphasizes the ephemerality of the images—the film is projected on a bed sheet, with folds and crevices of the fabric perceptible beneath—intensifying the illusory sense of presence which the home movies convey. In a parallel scene, Abrams too presents cinema as a ghostly medium, as, watching the home movies of his mother, Joe remarks: "It's weird seeing her like this, like she's still here." The sequence offers a mediation on the protagonist's loss, but can also be read self-reflexively as a comment on the film's own nostalgic projects and the directors' attempts to return to the past in the form of moving images.

Framing their nostalgic explorations through narratives of grief allows Abrams and Burton not only to add poignancy to their yearning, but also poses questions concerning coming to terms with loss. However, *Super 8* and *Frankenweenie* diverge in their proposed resolutions. On the one hand, *Super 8* advocates letting go, and the final scene of the film symbolically enacts laying the past to rest as Joe relinquishes the mother's locket which he had clung to throughout the narrative. *Frankenweenie*, on the other hand, refuses to accept separation; rejecting the finality of the pet's death, Victor converts his film studio in the attic into a science laboratory to bring Sparky back to life.[14] Considering these dissimilar conclusions, it is instructive to study how the directors' narrative resolutions relate to the nostalgia for the things of the past professed by the films. Studying how both Abrams and Burton locate their fascination with the obsolete in the new media landscape, the following sections will investigate the films' attitudes towards nostalgia which at times contradict the resolutions proposed by their narratives.

CGI Meets DIY

While it is fascinated with the past, *Super 8* embraces contemporary forms of visual storytelling. Its dual interest in the filmmaking of the past and the media of the present is apparent in the film's promotional material. The posters for *Super 8* pay tribute to those of the 1970s and 1980s, signaling the film's affinity with the Blockbuster Renaissance by replicating the characteristic composition and hand-drawn style of the posters of the time.[15] However, the marketing also includes a smartphone application entitled "Super8" which promises to "turn your iPhone into a vintage camera," and a tie in with the video game *Portal 2* which features a hidden level that transports the players to the inside of the train which carries the alien. The marketing appears to present two different readings of the project of *Super 8*; while the posters signal the film's commitment to a nostalgic exploration of cinematic heritage (fostering a fantasy that *Super 8* belongs to the time of its setting) the transmedia tie-ins suggest a negotiation around the position and status of the obsolete in the new media landscape. The marketing's ambiguous stance echoes *Super 8*'s own hesitancy in gauging its attitude towards the past. Captivated by the possibilities of digital special effects, Abrams' work dramatizes the attempt to reconcile the new with his longing for the obsolete.

An interest in the potential of digital media is evidenced in *Super 8* itself and comes to the fore in the frequent deployment of computer generated imagery. The delight which the film takes in CGI is seen in the train crash sequence which occurs early in the film. The crash's cascade of fiery computer-generated debris is the film's most spectacular moment; the force and duration of the explosion are extensive, and practically gratuitous. The derailment of the train is one of the film's many moments of magnificent destruction, all of which are occasioned by or produced in response to the film's key CGI figure, the alien. Although the appearance of the creature is withheld until the film's finale, because of the consistent depiction of digital effects as metonyms for the monster, the extra-terrestrial is arguably *Super 8*'s symbolic figure of new media (in the manner in which the zombie can be perceived as its metaphor for the obsolete). This is suggested not only visually (the creature's body is entirely computer generated), but also at the level of characterization which emphasizes the unknowability of the alien and its technological sophistication.[16] Inserted into a faithfully recreated 1979 diegesis, the CGI alien anticipates the media transitions yet to come, anchoring the film's concern with the place and role of new media in narratives about the obsolete.

The train crash offers not only a thrilling sequence of digital spectacle, but also a key moment of intersection between the DIY and CGI narratives.[17] The derailing of the military transport is witnessed by the film's protagonists, who had been in the process of shooting a scene at the station. As the children frantically seek safety from the explosion, they leave the equipment behind, including a camera which is left running and acts as witness to the crash and its aftermath. The recording references a horror genre trope of "found footage" films, in which horror is enhanced by stylizing the footage to resemble amateur recordings. Alexandra Heller-Nicholas argues that found footage horror relies on film's aesthetic appeal to realism, "to create a space […] where spectators can enjoy having their boundaries pushed, where our confidence that we know where the line between fact and fiction lies is directly challenged" (2014, p. 13). The "accidental" footage in *Super 8* functions in a similar way, except the boundary it blurs is not between fact and fiction, but rather between analog home movie and digital special effects.

At first, the accidental footage suggests the incompatibility of the technologies of the past and present. The train crash—the spectacular center of Abrams' work—is depicted as un-representable on small-gauge film. The camera's view is clouded by thick smoke and the film makes a point of emphasizing this as Charles draws attention to the inferiority of the footage, saying: "look at all that smoke. We can't use this." However, as the sequence progresses, its representation of the relation between *Super 8*'s different media forms shifts. When the smoke settles, the film reveals an image of a creature climbing out of the train wreckage. In contrast to the train crash which show-cases its own spectacularity, the alien is integrated into the home movie, its computer-generated body subject to the small-gauge's technological limita-tion: it is barely visible in the poorly lit conditions and partially obscured by the crack in the lens which cuts across the screen. Introducing the alien through the analog found footage "authenticates" the creature (anchoring it as part of the world of Abrams' film as it is depicted through the media of the period) but exposes an extra-diegetic tension between the director's stated ambition to shoot the amateur sequences on Super 8 film and the difficulties involved in representing the CG creature on the particular format. As Larry Fong (the film's cinematographer) elucidates, unlike *The Case* and the home movie, the accidental footage was not recorded on Super 8 but on Super 16, as the special effects team was unable to work on 8 mm to generate the image of the alien (Stasukevich, 2011). Fong argues that Abrams was at first reluctant to give in to the special effects team's request to shoot on 35 mm, but finally he settled for a compromise to use 16 mm. He states: "it bummed J.J. and me out but we couldn't ignore ILM's [Industrial Light&Magic, the special effects studio] predicament." (Stasukevich, 2011, p. 27) The found footage scene is built upon a compromise, one which suggests a successful integration between the CGI and DIY narratives, but which comes at the price of sacri-ficing a nostalgic fidelity to technological purism.

Should we read this compromise as symbolic of the film's message about nostalgia? Abrams' conclusion appears to indicate a positive resolution, sug-gesting that an encounter with the new propels Joe to let go of the past. The ending of *Super 8* is, however, more problematic than it first appears. After Joe relinquishes the medallion, the alien also takes his leave and the characters remain standing among the burning debris of Lilian. The final images offer a summary of the impact of the CGI extra-terrestrial on the nostalgic setting, which appears to have been exclusively negative: throughout the film the creature has done little else but devour the supporting cast and demolish the *mise-en-scène*. The film's positive resolution thus entails not only Joe's over-coming of grief (the message to let go of the past), but also the alien's depar-ture and an end to the destruction. This, however, brings into question the success of the integration between the novel and the obsolete, and suggests that while Abrams is prepared to envisage their coexistence, he is ultimately unable to embrace it. Rather than an anticipation of the arrival of new media, *Super 8*'s depiction of the alien communicates an anxiety about the impact the new will have on the obsolete. Its consistent characterization as voracious, vengeful, and incomprehensible betrays a profound fear of change. The film's ending on the image of ruins rather than on regeneration can thus be read as visualizing the film's wider inability to move on, and Abrams' difficulty in envisaging a time after Super 8 and the Blockbuster Renaissance.

Good and Bad Monsters

In contrast to Joe, who relinquishes the material remnant of his attachment to the mother, Victor refuses to let go of the past. An intertextual nod to James Whale's *Frankenstein* (1931) Sparky's resurrection also reverberates with references to Burton's own work, specifically to the 1984 live action short film *Frankenweenie* which provided the template for the 2012 animation. The short was shot early in the director's career, at a time when Burton was working as an animator for Disney. It was intended to be shown as an accompaniment to the 1984 re-release of *Pinocchio*; it was, however, shelved after receiving a PG rating (which meant it could not be screened alongside a G-rated film) and soon afterwards Burton and Disney parted ways.[18] Between the two *Frankenweenies* Burton had collaborated with Disney on occasion, yet as Tim Adams points out in an interview with the director, the remake is of particular symbolic importance and the parallels between Victor's resurrection of Sparky and Burton's (re-)animation of *Frankenweenie* are hard to overlook.[19] Is the film's transformation, like Sparky's, merely superficial (the pet's character remains essentially unchanged by the transformation) or does it signal a fundamental change of attitude towards the material? In order to evaluate this, it is instructive to look at the amateur movies that open the two films—*Monsters from Long Ago* in the 1984 version and *Monsters from Beyond* in 2012—which offer a condensation and intensification of the concerns of the containing works.

The two differences between the *Frankenweenie* films (and the amateur films contained within them) which become immediately apparent are technical: a shift from live-action to stop-motion and from 2D to 3D. As Burton's biographer Mark Salisbury illuminates, Burton had always intended for *Frankenweenie* to be an animation but the costs proved prohibitive at the time (Burton and Salisbury, 2006).[20] Remaking the film as it was originally envisaged, the director's use of stop-motion can therefore be read as a restorative gesture. This choice, however, resonates differently in the contemporary media landscape than it would have done 28 years before, and this becomes apparent in the critics' consistent reading of the film's stop-motion as an opposition to digital cinema. Adams (2012) positions *Frankenweenie* as a respite after the director's turbulent experience of digital animation in *Alice in Wonderland* (2010), while David Cox (2012) perceives it as an example of "digital-disdain": a snobbishly high-brow rebuttal of the popular contemporary media. While I would disagree that Burton's film displays high-brow pretensions (its intertextual references are drawn from the popular end of the spectrum) I am inclined, in this case, to read stop-motion as oriented towards the cinema of the past, particularly in light of the intertextual acknowledgment of Willis O'Brian in Victor's amateur film.

Burton's use of 3D has similarly been perceived as a nostalgic reference. As Mark Kermode (2012) argues, stereoscopic filmmaking in *Frankenweenie* has "an appropriately nostalgic feel," stylistically referring to the films of the 1950s 3D boom such as *The Creature from the Black Lagoon* (Jack Arnold, 1954) and *The House of Wax* (André De Toth, 1953). The director's commitment to a nostalgic (re-)appreciation of the history of stereoscopic filmmaking is already apparent in the opening small-gauge film, which forges an association between 3D and obsolete technology. While the connection which Burton draws is an *imaginative* one (his home movie is an animated approximation) it is not purely *imaginary*. Intentionally or not—the director himself remains evasive on the subject (Ross, 2012)—*Frankenweenie*'s portrayal of amateur 3D filmmaking indicates a factual but little discussed facet of small-gauge film (Zone, 2011). Locating 3D within the context of domestic small-gauge filmmaking, Burton's film functions as a media archaeological text, bringing a forgotten history of the practice to light. In contrast to Abrams' attempts to combine DIY and CGI, *Frankenweenie* appears to bypass the novel altogether, using past texts, technologies, and techniques to tell a story concerned with the endurance of the obsolete.

It is, however, not only the media landscape that has shifted between 1984 and 2012: the cultural attitudes towards nostalgia have also undergone significant changes. *Frankenweenie* reflects on these cultural transitions through its depiction and defense of monstrosity. While both works open with Victor's dinosaur spectaculars, there are important differences in their depiction of the creatures and their environment (already suggested by the adjustments to their titles). While *Monsters from Long Ago* takes place in a pre-modern setting, *Monsters from Beyond* is set in a modern day city in which the dinosaurs appear distinctly out of their time. The changes to the *mise-en-scène* are accompanied by further modifications to the narratives. In *Monsters from Long Ago*, Sparkysaurus emerges as neither the hero nor the villain of the piece. The plot is somewhat loose, as the dog comes on screen, walks off, tries to catch a pterodactyl, but then distractedly trips over the cardboard volcano. *Monsters from Beyond*, however, has a clear-cut narrative, where the pterodactyl angrily menaces the town and is stopped in his tracks by the heroic Sparkysaurus. While these changes humorously reflect on the realities of working with real vs. animated dogs, they also suggest a more profound shift in *Frankenweenie*'s perception of nostalgia. The change in the character and role of Sparkysaurus anticipates a narrative shift which occurs between the two films; while in the 1984 film the conflict is centered on the town's growing acceptance of Sparky's monstrosity, the 2012 film maintains this narrative but adds a further tension between good and bad monsters: Sparky and the pets reanimated by the other children.

It is possible to read the added distinction between good and bad monsters as Burton's defense of the film's nostalgia against a broader cultural landscape flooded with texts and textures of the recent past. This comes to the fore as Sparky's characterization is contrasted with that of the other un-dead pets, and particularly with the film's chief antagonist Weird Girl's bat-cat Mr. Whiskers (whose winged apparition echoes the menacing pterodactyl of *Monsters from Beyond*). Unlike the other resurrected animals, whose return is, at least in part, motivated by a longing for reunion, the cat's transformation is accidental and arises from curiosity rather than grief. Striving to imitate Victor's experiment, Weird Girl chooses as her subject a dead bat brought in by her feline companion. Mr. Whiskers, however, is unwilling to part with his prey and when the lightning strikes it hits both the cat and the bat, fusing them together into a single monstrous entity. The difference between the two types of return envisaged by Burton is reminiscent of the distinction proposed by Paul Grainge (2003) between "nostalgia mode" and "nostalgia mood." Mr. Whiskers represents the former, standing for a hollow fascination with the past which takes the form of repetition of surface styles. The feline symbolizes a "nostalgia without loss" and this is made clear as, unlike the other resurrected pets, the cat is alive when he is hit by lightning. In contrast, Sparky is the film's figure of "good" nostalgia, an attachment to the past that arises from grief and whose return is fueled by love and not merely a morbid or superficial curiosity. *Frankenweenie* culminates in a showdown between them and, like in the opening home movie, "good" nostalgia triumphs over its shallow counterpart, allowing *Frankenweenie* to justify his attachment to the past in, to quote Simon Reynolds, "an age gone loco for retro and crazy for commemoration" (2011, p. ix).

Burton's definition of "good" nostalgia is, however, fundamentally underlain by an inability to fully come to terms with the inevitability of loss. This is foregrounded in the film's finale which stages a re-resurrection of Sparky, who dies saving Victor from Mr. Whiskers.[21] Convinced of the dog's heroism, the New Holland community embraces his otherness and comes together to save the pet by lining up their automobiles to create a supply of power which will jolt Sparky back to life.[22] Initially the revival appears to fail, and Sparky continues to lie lifelessly in a circle of car lights. Faced with his dog's inanimate body Victor indicates that he is ready to let go of the past as he hugs the dog and says: "It's ok boy, you don't have to come back. You'll always be in my heart." Burton's resolution, however, contradicts this message, and after a dramatic pause Sparky is revived once more. This repetition is not without repercussions and the cyclicality of the ending suggests that *Frankenweenie*, like *Super 8*, betrays a deep unease about finality. If the first resurrection expressed a fantasy for a prolonged engagement with the object of one's affection, the second one fails to recognize the limits of that fantasy. This perception is amplified by the similarities between the finale of the 2012 remake and that of the 1984 film, both of which conclude with Sparky's second resurrection. If the first instance conveyed Burton's refusal to lay the past to rest, the second *Frankenweenie* is the intensified and enduring product of this attitude, forcefully signaling the director's commitment to nostalgic return.

Conclusion (Or Is It?)

The words "the end" seal the kiss between Sparky and his canine sweetheart, the bride of Frankenstein-styled poodle, Persephone. The final image of *Frankenweenie* declares a closure not only of the film itself, but also implicitly of its project and genesis which after 28 years can finally be put to rest. Yet to what extent should the viewers trust the finality which it imposes? We may recall that the 1984 film ended with the very same words. Fresher in mind is perhaps the ending of *Monsters from Beyond* which suggests the illusory nature of closure, following a similar proclamation of finality with a questioning title card: "or is it?"

The finale offered by *Super 8* is equally ambiguous. The film ends with a lens flare, a line of light emanating from the departing spaceship slashing across the darkness of the screen. The slow fade to black indicates closure, which aligns with the film's wider message of laying the past to rest. These "final" images, however, are not actually the film's last. As the credits roll, the viewers are treated to a screening of Charles' amateur film. *The Case* itself also contains two endings: the first of which resolves the zombie threat (as the detective reverses the transformation of his infected wife by injecting her with a vaccine), while the second shows the living dead return (the zombified wife attacks Charles as he addresses the audience, urging them to vote for the film in the Cleveland Amateur Film Festival). A movie about zombies, *The Case* is itself zombie-like in its persistence, contradicting the apparently firm and final conclusion proposed by Abrams. Returning to the amateur film in its credit sequence, *Super 8* thus once more reinstates its commitment to the obsolete, communicating that, contrary to the film's message, the director is reluctant to lay the past to rest.

The return of the living-dead in the conclusion of *Super 8* mirrors the double resurrection of Sparky in *Frankenweenie*. Both Abrams and Burton champion the prolongation of engagement with the past, and use the figure of the zombie as a mascot for nostalgia. Diffusing their monstrosity with humor, both films use the living-dead to fulfill a fantasy of endless return, a gesture which hints at horror of a different kind. It is not a fear not of persistence but of finality, of precisely that which *Super 8* and *Frankenweenie* appear to suggest but conspicuously avoid achieving: closure. The truly monstrous figure in Abrams' film is thus not the zombie but the mother who, as Joe's friend Cary (Ryan Lee) emphatically stresses during the wake, "is not a zombie" and therefore cannot return but can only be returned *to* as an image on the screen. If the train crash is *Super 8*'s spectacular center, the home movies of the mother are its emotional heart, fueling a desire for return which they are ultimately unable to bring to fruition. As the double screening of *Monsters from Beyond* suggests, the images cannot move forward (there can be no new footage) and all that Victor can do is to endlessly re-watch the same film. Yet, while both Joe and Victor learn to recognize the inevitability and irreparability of loss, *Super 8* and *Frankenweenie* both refuse to embrace the acceptance of closure they bestow on their characters. Abrams exorcises the figure of new media and refuses to move on from the image of the ruins of the past; Burton emphasizes his commitment to cyclicality by remaking his own film, and then using that remake to stage a defense of its own project. The contradictory messages conveyed by the films' finales signals an inability on the part of the filmmakers to fully renounce their attachment to the past and to embrace that times, and cinema, have changed.

Notes

1. The key difference between them was the size of the side perforations, the minimization of which allowed for a larger area for exposition.

2. *Frankenweenie* does not demarcate its temporal setting as precisely as *Super 8* (which superimposes a date onto its opening shot), opting instead for an imaginative recreation of the period. It is, however, possible to approximate *Frankenweenie*'s setting by its use of the characteristic props typically associated with 1950s prosperity—such as the television set, the rounded fridge, Chevrolet car, as well as through the costumes and hairstyles of the characters (particularly Mrs. Frankenstein's calf-length flared dresses and flip coiffure).

3. While Burton's dinosaurs similarly hint at issues of persistence, his depiction of the pre-historic creatures differs from the examples studied by Boym in a significant manner. As Boym points out in her analysis of *Jurassic Park* (Steven Spielberg, 1993) the depiction of the dinosaur is at once futuristic and prehistoric, and the recovery of the bygone involves the use of modern science and technology; in contrast, in Burton's film the creature is associated with an obsolete medium and its rendering betrays perceptibly of DIY quality, revealing rather than concealing the manner in which it had been produced (drawing attention to the dog beneath the dinosaur costume or the string from which the plastic pterodactyl is dangling).

4. As I was working on a draft of this essay, Kodak announced that it will be bringing back the Super 8, releasing a redesigned camera and stock. Unsurprisingly, the format is being endorsed by Abrams, who states that: "While any technology that allows for visual storytelling must be embraced, nothing beats film […]. The fact that Kodak is building a brand new Super 8 camera is a dream come true" (Pulver, 2016). Thus, if *Super 8*'s zombies can be read as a metaphor for nostalgia, the characterization of the living-dead as a virus can be perceived as alluding to the "infectious" spread of sentimental yearning to which the return of Kodak's Super 8 testifies.

5. *Sinister* follows a true crime writer Ellison Oswald (Ethan Hawke) who moves into the house of a murdered family in order to investigate the mystery of their deaths. In the attic of the property he finds a box of, what he first assumes to be, home movies.

The reels, however, are revealed to contain snuff films documenting the murders of several families including that of the previous occupants of the house. As the film progresses Ellison discovers that the 8 mm films are inhabited by a demon named Baghul who manipulates children into murdering their families.

6. Spielberg's influence on Super 8 is perceptible in the film's narrative—the interviewing of a family tragedy with an extra-terrestrial plot recalls Spielberg's *Close Encounters of the Third Kind* (1977) and *E.T.: Extra-Terrestrial* (1982)—as well as in the tone and style of the production, the frequent use of an expression of wonder which critic Kevin B. Lee (2011) has termed as "the Spielberg Face" and Abrams' signature lens flares.

7. The reading of *Frankenweenie* as a cinematic, or cinephillic, autobiography is further enhanced by Burton's admission that while Victor's classmates were partially based on real people they are also references to horror icons such as Boris Karloff and Peter Lorre, while the design for the science teacher Mr. Ryzuski bears a resemblance to Vincent Price (Gibson, 2013).

8. Once a domestic format, it is now mainly in professional pursuits: cinematic sequences such as those in Super 8, advertisements, music videos, and wedding photography.

9. In these films domestic moving images are presented not as a film-within-the-film (via a screening, as they are in *Super 8* and *Frankenweenie*) but as a texture deployed in the representation of the character's memories or, more generally, anteriority.

10. The directors' emphasis on the technology can also be perceived in the context of the contemporary proliferation of smartphone analog filter applications (which allow users to overlay their digital footage with small-gauge textures to make them appear as if they were shot on film) indicating a longing directed at the material culture of the past.

11. Kodak discontinued the production of KodaChrome Super 8 film in January 2011 following a steady decline of interest in the stock.

12. As Caetlin Benson-Allott (2011) points out in her study of Abrams' affective use of the lens flare, the setting of the accident serves to sharpen the sense of loss which the opening creates by hinting at the imminent decline of the U.S. steel industry.

13. The second screening also introduces Burton's interest in repetition which is central to *Frankenweenie*'s exploration of nostalgia.

14. The conversion of the DIY film studio into a laboratory can arguably be read as reflective of Burton's broader interest in the blurring between science and art. In an interview with Anthony Gibson the director admits: "I always treated science and art as quite similar, thematically" (Gibson, 2013).

15. The composition of the poster for *Close Encounters of the Third Kind*, depicting a road leading up to an illuminated sky.

16. The alien's unknowability and sophistication is foregrounded in the scientific films which depict the military researchers' incapability to comprehend either the mechanics of the alien spaceship nor the creature's biology, origin or culture.

17. The duality of *Super 8* can be traced to the genesis of the films which began as two separate projects which Abrams was struggling to get off the ground until Spielberg suggested that he should combine them (Boucher, 2011).

18. The film was granted a small release in the UK (alongside *Baby: Secret of a Lost Legend*) and was released on video in the U.S. alongside the release of *Batman Returns* (Burton and Salisbury, 2006).

19. Adams argues that returning to the studio 28 years later to direct the film

according to his initial vision "no doubt feels a little like a score finally settled" (Adams, 2012).

20. While the 1984 film is not animated, it nonetheless signals its interest in animation in the opening home movie. In both *Monsters from Long Ago* and *Monsters from Beyond*, Sparky is the only living presence; the supporting cast is made up of inanimate objects. While the manner in which Burton's protagonist brings them to life differ—in the 1984 version embellished potholders act as dinosaur puppets while in the 2012 Victor animates his toys using stop-motion—both opening sequences introduce Victor as an animator, a role which foreshadows his persona as a resurrectionist. The parallel between Victor's filmmaking with his revival of Sparky—a comparison which is further cemented as the boy converts his attic film studio into a laboratory—is, I believe, central to Burton's conception of filmmaking. The analogy suggests that the director's work is motivated not only by a desire to bring things to life, but also to reanimate, that is, to bring them back an interest which is perceptible in the dense nostalgic intertextuality of Burton's oeuvre.

21. The sequence also appears in Burton's 1984 film, except that it is the angry townsfolk and not Mr. Whiskers who pursue Sparky to the windmill on the mini golf course.

22. Burton's use of the car—an icon of the mobility and prosperity of 1950s America—to resurrect the film's metaphor for the attachment to the past, can be read as a reflection of *Frankenweenie*'s own commitment to explore nostalgia though bygone forms of filmmaking.

REFERENCES

Acland, C. (2007) *Residual Media*. Minneapolis: University of Minnesota Press.
Adams, T. (2012) Tim Burton: "The love and life and death stuff was stewing from the start." *The Observer*, October 7. http://www.theguardian.com/film/2012/oct/07/tim-burton-frankenweenie-interview. (Accessed May 22, 2015).
Benson-Allott, C. (2011) Slants of Light. *Film Quarterly* 65 (1), pp. 10–11.
Boucher, G. (2011) Steven Spielberg: "Super 8" is the first true J.J. Abrams film. *Los Angeles Times*, June 2. http://herocomplex.latimes.com/movies/steven-spielberg-super-8-is-the-first-true-j-j-abrams-film/. (Accessed May 22, 2015).
Boym, S. (2001) *The Future of Nostalgia*. New York: Basic Books.
Burton, T. and Salisbury, M. (2006) *Burton on Burton*. London: Faber & Faber.
Cavell S. (1981) *The Pursuits of Happiness: Hollywood Comedy of Remarriage*. Cambridge: Harvard University Press.
Cox, D. (2012) Stop Admiring *Frankenweenie*! Why Stop-motion Doesn't Move Me. *The Guardian*, October 15. http://www.theguardian.com/film/filmblog/2012/oct/15/frankenweenie-stop-motion-animation. (Accessed May 22, 2015).
Fischer, R. (2012) Film Exclusive: Tim Burton Discusses "Frankenweenie," Autobiography, and the Reliability of Memory. *Slash Film*, October 5. http://www.slashfilm.com/film-exclusive-tim-burton-discusses-frankenweenie-autobiography-and-the-reliability-of-memory/. (Accessed January 2, 2016).
Frankenweenie. (2012) [Film] Directed by Tim Burton. California: Walt Disney Studios Motion Pictures.
Gibson, A. (2013) Tim Burton: Disney was Brave to Let Me Make *Frankenweenie* in Black and White. *Metro*, 6 March. http://metro.co.uk/2013/03/06/tim-burton-disney-was-brave-to-let-me-make-frankenweenie-in-black-and-white-3526469/#ixzz3wxYwxhnl. (Accessed January 2, 2016).

Grainge, P. (2003) *Memory and Popular Film*. Manchester: Manchester University Press.
Gustini, R. (2011). Critics Divided Over How Nostalgic They Got During "Super 8." *The Wire,* June 10. http://www.thewire.com/entertainment/2011/06/film-critics-debate-how-nostalgic-they-got-during-super-8/38712/?. (Accessed May 22, 2015).
Heller-Nicholas, A. (2014) *Found Footage Horror Films*. Jefferson, NC: McFarland.
Hertz, G. and Parikka, J. (2012) Zombie Media: Circuit Bending Media Archaeology into an Art Method. *Leonardo* 45 (5), pp. 424–30.
Kattelle, A. (1986) The Evolution of Amateur Motion Picture Equipment 1895–1965. *Journal of Film and Video* 38 (3/4), pp. 47–57.
Kermode. M. (2012) Mark Kermode Reviews *Frankenweenie*. http://www.bbc.co.uk/programmes/p0100c31. (Accessed January 5, 2016).
Lee, K. B. (2011) The Spielberg Face. https://vimeo.com/33617207. (Accessed January 6, 2016).
Moran, J. (2002) *There's No Place Like Home Video*. Minneapolis: University of Minnesota Press.
Natale, S. and Balbi, G. (2014) Media and the Imaginary in History. *Media History* 20 (2), pp. 203–18.
Niemeyer, K. (2014) Introduction: Media and Nostalgia. In: Niemeyer, K. (ed.) *Media and Nostalgia: Yearning for the Past, Present and Future*. Basingstoke: Palgrave Macmillan, pp. 1–23.
Olivier, M. (2014) Sinister Celluloid in the Age of Instagram. *Refractory* 23. http://refractory.unimelb.edu.au/2014/06/26/instagram-olivier/. (Accessed January 6, 2016).
Orr, C. (2011) The Nostalgic Charms of "Super 8." *The Atlantic,* June 10. http://www.theatlantic.com/entertainment/archive/2011/06/the-nostalgic-charms-of-super-8/240231/. (Accessed May 22, 2015).
Papamichael, S. (2012). *Frankenweenie* Review—Tim Burton Revives a Dying Art, But is He Thinking of the Children? *Radio Times,* October 10. http://www.radiotimes.com/news/2012-10-10/frankenweenie-review—tim-burton-revives-a-dying-art-but-is-he-thinking-of-the-children. (Accessed May 22, 2015).
Pro8mm. (n.d.) Super 8 and Music Videos. https://web.archive.org/web/20150907074218/http://www.pro8mm.com/super-8-music.php. (Accessed May 22, 2015).
Puckrick, K. (2011) JJ Abrams: "I called Spielberg and he said yes." *The Guardian,* August 1. http://www.theguardian.com/film/2011/aug/01/jj-abrams-spielberg-super-8. (Accessed May 22, 2015).
Pulver, A. (2016) Kodak Launches New Super 8 Camera. *The Guardian,* January 6. http://www.theguardian.com/film/2016/jan/06/odak-launches-new-super-8-camera. (Accessed January 6, 2016).
Reynolds, S. (2011) *Retromania*. London: Faber & Faber.
Ross, M. (2012) *Frankenweenie*. Miriamruthross.wordpresswww, October 27. https://miriamruthross.wordpress.com/2012/10/27/frankenweenie/. (Accessed May 22, 2015).
Stasukevich, I. (2011) Monsters out of the Box. *American Cinematographer* 92 (7), pp. 24–34.
Super 8. (2011) [Film] Directed by J. J. Abrams. California: Paramount Pictures Corporation.
Weinstock J. A. (ed.) (2013) *The Works of Tim Burton: Margins to Mainstream*. Basingstoke: Palgrave Macmillan.
Zimmermann, P. (1995) *Reel Families*. Bloomington: Indiana University Press.
Zone, R. (2011) *3DIY: 3D Moviemaking on an Indy Budget*. Burlington: Focal Press.

Room 237

Cinephilia, History and Adaptation

LAURA MEE

Room 237 (Rodney Ascher, 2012) opens with a sequence which identifies it as a documentary about analysis, nostalgia, and cultural memory, but also as a film constructed from recycled and appropriated texts. Via voiceover, a man identified by subtitle as Bill Blakemore recounts the experience of his first viewing of *The Shining* (Stanley Kubrick, 1980) in a cinema in Leicester Square, soon after its release. On screen, a figure recognizable as Tom Cruise strolls down a neon-lit parade of cafés and clubs, and stops outside a cinema, taken with curiosity at the poster for *The Shining* and a set of lobby cards promoting "the wave of terror that swept across America." The scene is taken from Stanley Kubrick's final film *Eyes Wide Shut* (1999), where Cruise's character Bill Harford visits a jazz club upon noticing an old acquaintance is featured on the listings outside. In *Room 237*, however, the sequence is employed and adapted to represent Blakemore's cinema visit. The sign for the "Sonata Jazz Café" has been digitally altered to the "Sonata Cinema." The listings board does not detail the band, but instead shows the promotional material for Kubrick's film. Rather than watching Bill's growing sense of nostalgia as he remembers his friend and decides to go in and see him play, we see Cruise as Blakemore, transfixed by the images on display and the promise of the "wave of terror" offered by *The Shining*. "Blakemore" enters the now-cinema, and the scene is intercut with shots of dusty, red-velvet theater seats. An audience reverently watches the opening aerial shot of *The Shining*, following a yellow Volkswagen Beetle as it makes its way through winding mountain roads and across the big screen. When Blakemore leaves the cinema in a stunned daze to find his car, silently contemplating what he has just seen, it is no longer Cruise standing in for him, but Robert Redford in *All the President's Men* (Alan J. Pakula, 1976). These carefully constructed representations feature throughout *Room 237*, and the opportunity for the knowing audience member to identify its numerous cinematic sources are but one pleasure that Ascher's documentary offers.

Ostensibly, it is a film dedicated to uncovering the "true meaning" of *The Shining*, an adaptation of Stephen King's bestselling novel about an isolated hotel, its unstable caretaker Jack Torrance (Jack Nicholson) and his family, wife Wendy (Shelley Duvall) and telepathic son Danny (Danny Lloyd). Stranded over a particularly harsh winter, the family is haunted by the hotel's ghosts and the violent threat of Jack's unraveling sanity. As with many of Kubrick's films, *The Shining* became the subject of obsessive analysis and interpretation as its status grew. It is a film which raises more questions than it answers (and, perhaps, than Kubrick was inclined to address himself). Kubrick aficionados, confident in the knowledge that he never produced anything by accident, set out to find the hidden meanings and messages in *The Shining*, the secrets at play in the labyrinthine corridors of the film's Overlook Hotel. Years of debate, aided by the watching and re-watching, pausing and rewinding afforded by home video and, later, digital versions and internet discussion, saw fans poring over clues as to what *The Shining* was "really about." Bonus features and online discussions provide a wealth of information on Kubrick's perfectionism and deliberately cryptic style, and the DIY nature of contemporary cultural criticism means every opinion can be easily voiced through blogs, social media, and forums. Theories range from the commonly cited, such as one that reads it as an allegorical attack on Native American genocide (this is not a difficult conclusion to reach, and is supported by an Indian burial ground backstory recounted by The Overlook's manager as well as by the aboriginal art and portraits of Native Americans that fill the hotel's Colorado Lounge), through more awkwardly conceived ideas (it is about the Holocaust) to the totally outlandish (*The Shining* is Kubrick's confession and apology to his wife for supposedly assisting in faking the footage of the 1968 moon landing). In the digital age, everyone is a critic, and credentials are not essential for film analysis. It is this that *Room 237* simultaneously celebrates and gently mocks. On the one hand, it exemplifies the joy of looking below the surface, of searching beyond the obvious for hidden meaning, and the fascination over other people's observations, attention to detail, and understanding of things that we might ourselves have missed. On the other, it highlights the potentially problematic or even entertaining results of subjective scrutiny, of interpretative textual (and what some may think of as over-) analysis.

Subtitled "being an inquiry into *The Shining* in 9 parts" (likely a reference to the "Nadsat" speech of Alex and his "droogs" in another Kubrick adaptation, *A Clockwork Orange* [1971]), Ascher's film is, on the surface, concerned with the interpretations of five fans of the film who employ a mix of numerology, topography, historiography, conspiracy theory, and textual analysis in striving to explain *The Shining*. Yet *Room 237* itself offers no conclusive answer. It is a documentary with as many twists, turns, and layers as Kubrick's film itself, a "head-first plunge down the rabbit hole of Kubrickiana from which, for some, there is evidently no return" (McCarthy, 2012). Although most critics viewed the film favorably, its ambiguity infuriated some—Jonathan Rosenbaum (2012), for example, who criticized Ascher's refusal "to make distinctions between interpretations that are semi-plausible or psychotic, conceivable or ridiculous"—and a glance at viewers' comments online suggests similar frustrations. But I would argue that its lack of immediately identifiable agreement with or denial of any one of the five theories is one of *Room 237*'s strengths; after all, a film which deals with subjective interpretation has no real right to tell its audience what to think. While it is certainly possible to observe visual motifs and references to a number of the themes under discussion, to suggest in all seriousness that *The Shining* is wholly about any one of them would be to ignore the more prevalent meanings of Kubrick's film (a reflection on the horror genre and a puzzle film, as well as an interpretation of the patriarchal violence and isolation at the heart of King's book), and in places the analysis borders on being disingenuous.[1] David Bordwell (2013) and Girish Shambu (2012), among others, have written insightful pieces reflecting on the nature of the analysis in *Room 237*, and the potential problems of subscribing to such theories; not least, the reputation of film criticism in the face of an average audience encountering hermetic and, as Shambu terms it, "outré, freakish or crackpot" interpretation.[2]

The documentary itself is no more about the true meaning of Kubrick's film than *The Shining* is solely about telepathy. It is instead, as I have already suggested, a detailed, visually rich, and intricately woven story of the pleasures and pitfalls of cinematic analysis. But it is also a film about cinephilia and nostalgic re-appropriation. It is entirely assembled from the work of others: it carefully constructs a bricolage text of clips from films, adverts, photographs, newsreels and archival footage, poster art, animation, re-enactment, and graphics to visually represent the interviewees' narration. That the contributors remain unseen, that they are not filmed as per the traditional "talking heads" frequently seen in documentaries, is testament to *Room 237*'s apparent love of both *The Shining* and of cinema itself. Nearly every frame is instead devoted to the repetition or interpretation of the moving image, as created by Kubrick and beyond. *Room 237*, then, is built mostly from the work of others, a brilliantly spliced homage to cinematic analysis that is capable of eliciting our own memories of cinema and the films we have loved, as well as an examination of the ways in which subjective interests and personal circumstance can affect interpretation and "meaning." Rather than offer further interrogation of the theories in question when so much is already available,

I am instead interested in *Room 237*'s adaptive and appropriated construction, its portrayal of cinematic memory, and the way in which it re-appropriates footage from a range of sources to tell new stories, often in segments of nostalgic reminiscence from its commentators. Within *Room 237*, a number of nostalgic contexts are at play—nostalgia for *The Shining*, for the films and texts used, for cinema itself, and for the narrators' own histories. The rest of this essay explores the ways in which visual media are repurposed or adapted to create new meanings, and the part nostalgia and memory plays in this process.

Cinephilia and Cinematic Memory

Room 237 asserts itself early on as a film about cinematic memory as its narrators recall their first experiences of watching *The Shining*. Blakemore's cinematic encounter in Leicester Square matches his narration to the action on screen, Cruise's facial expressions registering familiarity as he takes in the details on the lobby card, curiosity as he makes his way into the Sonata, and pleasure as he begins to watch the movie. Both Blakemore's storytelling and Ascher's reconstruction of events here are highly detailed and synchronized. Blakemore describes sitting on the edge of his seat, how he gripped it "to try and control my terror" and "to keep from falling off" as the film unfolded and its "true" meaning became apparent to him. For him, Kubrick had made a film about Native American genocide, and the viewer watches Redford's stumbling, stunned exit as Blakemore, leaving the theater consumed by this revelation. The sequence not only elevates Blakemore's story to one more dramatic (and therefore worthy of cinematic retelling), but grounds the experience as a theatrical one.

Introductions to the other contributors and their theories are similarly framed as cinephiliac moments—even when the narrators make no reference to watching *The Shining* in a movie theater. Juli Kearns states that she saw the film twice on its release, but focuses on the details which led to her interpretations of references to Greek mythology and the Overlook's "impossible" physical layout, and unlike Blakemore, she does not discuss the actual experience of viewing it. Instead, her narration is visually represented using clips from *Demons* (Lamberto Bava, 1985) to reconstruct her watching the film: an usher checks the tickets of a distinctively Eighties-styled couple in a cinema lobby, light from the projector cuts through a haze of smoke, a shot from the front of the theater shows groups of young people scattered throughout the seats watching silently, a reverse shot shows the Warner Brothers logo and establishing shot of *The Shining* on the big screen. This sequence grounds Kearn's experience—which she otherwise omits—both temporally (the 1980s) and spatially (within the theater). Geoffrey Cocks (who expresses initial disinterest in the film before becoming intrigued by it during repeat viewings) and John Fell Ryan (whose work as a film archivist piqued his curiosity) have similar moments constructed to visualize their first viewings.

Ascher furthers this approach for Jay Weidner, who does not even discuss *The Shining* at this stage in the documentary. Instead, Weidner describes his "first religious experience" watching *2001: A Space Odyssey* (Stanley Kubrick, 1968). Identifying himself as a "smart kid" who appreciated art but considered films "substandard," especially during the "rather pathetic" 1960s period of *My Fair Lady* (George Cukor, 1964) and *Doctor Doolittle* (Richard Fleischer, 1967), he remembers being taken to see the film at the Cinerama Dome³ in Hollywood by his then-girlfriend. His narration is played over a montage of shots from *2001*, set to its soundtrack—the crescendo of Strauss' "Sunrise" fanfare—and culminating in Bowman (Keir Dullea) evolving into a "starchild," as Weidner describes his epiphany:

> I'd never in my life envisioned that a movie could do what this movie was doing, and it was showing me things that I'd never seen. It was intellectually challenging, an artistic masterpiece in every way, from the soundtrack to the visuals to the storyline. When it ended, I couldn't get out of my seat; I was frozen in the seat, completely paralyzed by what I had just witnessed. The usher had to come and get me out. I was the last person—me and her—and I staggered out of the movie theater completely changed as a human being and decided that at that moment the only thing I wanted to do for the rest of my life was to make films in one fashion or another. I owe Stanley Kubrick and his film *2001: A Space Odyssey* everything, for everything I have become in my life.

Within these opening sequences, *Room 237* foregrounds and romanticizes the specifically theatrical cinematic experience, likening it to a religious awakening, or deeply moving or all-consuming realization. The centrality of the cinematic space here is reflective of scholarly approaches to cinephilia, which historically understood film's "unique, unrepeatable, magic experiences" (Sontag, 1996, p. 61) to take place within the movie theater, the joy of watching film bound to where and how one watched it as much as what one watched. As Thomas Elsaesser (2005) writes, Susan Sontag's 1996 *New York Times* essay "The Decay of Cinema" lamented, rather than the demise of film itself,

> the decay of cinephilia, that is, the way New Yorkers watched movies, rather than what they watched and what was being made by studios and directors [...]. Cinephiles were always ready to give in to the anxiety of possible loss, to mourn the once sensuous-sensory pleasure of the celluloid image, and to insist on the irrecoverably fleeting nature of a film's experience [Elsaesser, 2005, pp. 27–8].

In re-presenting and strengthening (in the case of Blakemore and Weidner's accounts) or re-creating (for Kearns,' Cocks,' and Ryan's first-viewing stories) experiences as explicitly theatrical ones, *Room 237* captures this "sensory pleasure" within its construction—in the quiet of the auditorium, the projector's low hum and the whirring of the film reel, the dust and smoke highlighted by the beam of the projected image, hands gripping velvet-covered seats and running over wooden armrests, the gazing, awed faces of the viewers, and the sight of Kubrick's films up on the big screen. The centrality of the theater is also evident in the hierarchy allocated to the stories. Blakemore and Weidner are awarded longer sections to recount their cinema visits in detail and with a focus on the kinds of minutiae enabled by vivid, meaningful memories (at one point, Blakemore tells us, "I remember gripping my belt buckle with my … left hand, I think it was … yes, my left hand").

Since the turn of the 21st century, however, studies of cinephilia have reframed the concept, with an understanding of a "second generation" (Elsaesser, 2005, p. 36) cinephile characterized by online discussions, fan practices, textual poaching and obsessive rewatching, analysis, and interpretation afforded by DVD and (later) other digital formats[4]:

> At the forefront of cinephilia […] is a crisis of memory: filmic memory in the first instance, but our very idea of memory in the modern sense, as recall mediated by technologies of recording, storage and retrieval. […] Technology now allows the cinephile to re-create in and through the textual manipulations, but also through the choice of media and storage formats that sense of the unique, that sense of place, occasion, and moment so essential to all forms of cinephilia, even as it is caught in the compulsion to repeat [ibid., p. 40].

In the digital age, obsessive love of film is not located in a specific space or experience, necessarily, but rather is practiced and performed by more active viewers through the assimilation of knowledge (with cultural capital as indicative of "authentic" fandom) and the reading of a text in line with personal circumstance alongside such information. The subjects of *Room 237* exemplify this cinephile as active meaning-maker. Blakemore discusses how he hacked out the meaning with cinema-savvy friends, while Weidner describes his delight in confirming, after acquiring his new DVD copy of *The Shining*, everything he thought he had seen before. Engaged with their own histories, the ability to return to *The Shining* again and again, and in many cases armed with a good deal of knowledge of Kubrick's methodical, painstakingly detailed approach to filmmaking and the film's arduous and lengthy production, the documentary's narrators are not alone in their contemporary cinephiliac approach to analysis, nor the dialogue in which they are engaged with the film and its other fans.

Room 237 is both a film about cinephilia, and concerned with another film often subject to cinephiliac interpretation. But it is also framed *as* a cinephiliac text in its own right. It is intent on recreating the cinema-going experience, devoted to obsessive, detailed discussion of a cherished movie, and constructs new meanings by (digitally) utilizing clips and images from a wealth of additional sources, rewarding the knowing film-fan viewer with inside jokes, obscure references, and cinematic nostalgia. In addition to *The Shining*, many of Kubrick's other films, including *Barry Lyndon* (1975), *Spartacus* (1960), *A Clockwork Orange*, *2001: A Space Odyssey*, *Full Metal Jacket* (1987), *Paths of Glory* (1957) and *Dr. Strangelove* (1964), all feature. Scenes are also created from numerous additional films that span decades and genres, are from multiple countries, and range from expensive flops through popular drama to obscure horror and cult films—*Apocalypto* (Mel Gibson, 2006), *The White Buffalo* (J. Lee Thompson, 1977), *Schindler's List* (Steven Spielberg, 1993), *An American Werewolf in London* (John Landis, 1981), *Spellbound* (Alfred Hitchcock, 1945), *Fellini—Satyricon* (Federico Fellini, 1969), *Summer of '42* (Robert Mulligan, 1971), *The Beast in Heat* (Luigi Batzella, 1977), and so on. Finally, *Room 237* offers an appeal to *The Shining*'s fans by recreating its yellow poster and eerie, blood-filled trailer for the documentary's promotion, and aping the Warner Bros. ident which opens the film with the logo for Ascher's own production company Highland Park Classics. In this regard, the documentary can be seen as not only about *The Shining* but also as supplemental to it, offering a further appeal to viewers (specifically, fans) through these paratextual connections.

History and Historical Memory

On the surface, both King's novel and Kubrick's film locate their terror within personal memory and references to the past. Jack Torrance is an alcoholic with a history of violence[5] that has previously threatened the harmony of the family unit. While these themes are more explicit within the book (where past incidents are recounted in detail through Jack's recollections), they haunt the Torrance family in both narratives, and the tension that threatens them is largely built around Wendy's, Jack's, and Danny's memories and the threat of history repeating itself. The "shining" of the title refers to Danny's telepathy, which he visualizes as "traces of things that happened a long time ago." When Halloran (Scatman Crothers), who shares the ability, tells him "some places are like people—some shine and some don't," he is referring to the Overlook Hotel, its dark past, and its ghosts. Patterns are common throughout *The Shining* in its visual style and motifs, but also in the cyclical nature of the seasons, the repeated procedure for winter shutdown, the role of the caretaker, and especially in the way Jack is framed as fated to kill Danny and Wendy just as the former caretaker murdered his own family. All the terrors of the Overlook, of Jack's breakdown and his murderous intentions, and of Danny's shining, have their roots in pastness and the threat of repetition.

In the case of the hotel's ghosts, this is additionally shaded by a horrible 1920s nostalgia; flappers and well-heeled gentlemen attend a ball in the sickly decadent Gold Room, a tuxedoed spirit with a cracked skull raises a glass to Wendy, suggesting "great party, isn't it?" and the final shot, scored by an eerie Twenties song with crooning lyrics about midnight rendezvous, is a close-up of a photograph picturing elegantly dressed party goers in black and white and Jack at the very center, holding court, smiling to camera. The photograph is captioned "Overlook Hotel, July 4th Ball, 1921," suggesting that Jack, as earlier implied in a conversation with ghost Grady (Philip Stone), has indeed "always been" the hotel's caretaker.

It is not at all a stretch to suggest, then, as *Room 237* does, that *The Shining* is very much a film about history, ghosts, and how the past impinges upon the present. However, through the interpretation of possible meanings and messages, the documentary takes this argument further, connecting *The Shining* to important events and periods in American history—Native American genocide, World War II, and the moon landing—and lauding Kubrick as historiographer. The narrators describe how Stanley Kubrick himself "shined" to make movies "like the brain creates memories and dreams," and to make a movie about "the nightmare of history," "historical denial," and "the blood on which nations were built." Set to clips from *Paths of Glory*, the narrators describe Kubrick's methodical approach to detailed research, how he would spend hours on the telephone to the manager of the Stanley Hotel (King's inspiration for *The Shining*) and "unearthing Colorado history" in the State Archives. As Colonel Dax (Kirk Douglas) leads his men over the top of the trenches and into no man's land, the narration tells us how Kubrick sent a team of researchers out to the Stanley during development for a period of three months to document and photograph countless details. Here, the filmmaker and his researchers are presented as historiographical pioneers, heading into to the unknown to fight for accuracy and thoroughness, and to research the "full history and nature" of everything which Blakemore sees hidden within *The Shining*. Kubrick, he tells us, is thinking about the implications of "everything that exists," boiling down the traumatic "essence of history" and forcing *The Shining*'s viewers to subconsciously address the atrocities of American history through the nightmarish representations of pastness within the film. Only by acknowledging and facing up to the horrors of the past can we escape it, rewrite it, and "wake from the nightmare" of repetition, Blakemore argues. In this sense, if we are to buy in to his (or Cocks' or Weidner's) theories, *The Shining* encourages empathetic identification with (especially) Danny's and Wendy's terror, as a substitute for personal experience of the events the narrators see metaphorically hidden within the film. Blakemore quotes T.S. Eliot in his suggestion that "history has many cunning passages, contrived corridors," and that the passages and corridors of the Overlook are the ideal location to confront America's troubled past. *The Shining*, the narrators might claim, allows its audience "to experience the uncanny force of cinema as a parallel universe, peopled by a hundred years of un-dead presences, of ghosts more real than ourselves" (Elsaesser, 2005, p. 35).

In addition to their nostalgic recollections of cinema-going, the early sequences of *Room 237* feature an introduction to the interviewees' theories and to the circumstances and interests which influenced them. Cocks is a Professor who specializes in German history and has written a book on Holocaust themes in Kubrick's work, Ryan a former film archivist who runs a website dedicated to analysis of Kubrick's films, Weidner a Hermetic scholar and conspiracy theorist, Kearns a playwright and Blakemore a journalist and war correspondent who grew up by the Calumet harbor and spent his childhood digging up "bits of Indian pottery" in the sand dunes of Lake Michigan. Despite acknowledging the impact their backgrounds have on their analysis, they insist on their individual interpretations as accurate and singular—the only possible meaning. After asserting that *The Shining* is absolutely about the "genocide of the American Indians," Blakemore ponders why "only I saw this" while everyone around him seemed oblivious. He insinuates that his understanding was correct, that others had missed the (not so) subtle references to Calumet baking powder (a word used by colonialists for First Nations people's peace pipes), the Native American art and the brief story the hotel manager (Barry Nelson) tells the Torrances about the Overlook's foundations being laid on a burial ground, when builders had to "repel a few Indian attacks" in the process.

Most critical or scholarly analysis would (or should) propose a theory as merely one possible interpretation rather than as the only one. Yet this highlights a broader, obvious issue with textual analysis—namely, that it is impossible to watch in a vacuum because subjectivity is furthered by familiarity with other films, or by knowledge of historical events, or by the recollection of personal memories. Every viewer will be influenced in some way, and a horror fan, a Kubrick aficionado, a historian, an artist, a King reader, are all likely to take different meanings from *The Shining*. Even if an official record of Kubrick's intentions existed, this would not detract from the messages seen by each viewer. Writing on memory and history in film, Pam Cook suggests that "the authority assumed to reside in the text as the location of official meanings and ideologies has shifted to the viewer, perceived as a kind of scavenger, engaged in a process of appropriating the text and rewriting it to suit their own purposes" (2005, p. 1). This scavenging, appropriation and rewriting is evident throughout *Room 237* in its search for clues within *The Shining*, and its reconstruction of event and experience through the appropriation of existing texts.

Adaptation, Appropriation and Meaning

Using existing material to visualize the narration in *Room 237* changes the meanings of both the films from which it is borrowed and *The Shining* itself. Appropriating sequences from, for example, *Paths of Glory*, *2001* or *Eyes Wide Shut* removes scenes and characters from their original contexts and places them not only within *Room 237* but also alongside *The Shining* and other films with which they might otherwise have little reason to be associated. In these instances, Kubrick is obviously the thread which connects the texts. Still, footage from *The Shining* and films within Kubrick's broader oeuvre is frequently shown alongside that from various unconnected films and filmmakers, seemingly randomly and with only the purpose of constructing an aesthetic representation of the interviews. In this appropriation, the intended meaning of the original sequence is adapted to instead support the narrators' theories. *Wolf* (Mike Nichols, 1994) and *An American Werewolf in London* become associated closely with anti–Semitism and the Holocaust, *All the President's Men* and *Demons* are used to evoke movie-going and audience affect, and multiple Westerns are suggested as documentary footage of Native American genocide.

In most instances, these constructions are clearly intended to help the audience visualize the arguments by the film's narrators. Talking heads without demonstration would likely be not only unconvincing, but also perhaps not very entertaining, and *Room 237*'s montages help to create meaning and provide a more enjoyable viewing experience by dramatizing the often bizarre and sometimes banal observations of its subjects. In places, however, they add further weight to those observations. Taking moments and shots from *The Shining* and repeating them, freezing them, highlighting or circling areas of the screen draws the viewer's attention and makes the reason for such arguments apparent. Using two shots alongside each other in split screen often furthers this, supporting the narrators' suggestions and reframing the meaning of the original text. So, in arguing that NASA's moon landing footage was faked, and that Kubrick was responsible, that footage is shown alongside similar shots from *2001: A Space Odyssey*. A resemblance, understandable given science fiction's generic iconography and the time of its making, becomes uncannily notable as Weidner's voiceover explains how the footage appears faked because of the "obvious" visible distinction between back projection and soundstage.

This appropriation has a dual purpose in Ascher's film, however, and moments which may fascinate or thrill the audience (largely in response to obsessive, detail-oriented observations, or moments fans of *The Shining* may themselves have originally missed) are at least equaled by subtle, wry suggestions that we should not take the narrators' theories at face value. Ascher does this primarily through repetition. In a well-known sequence in Kubrick's film, Wendy responds with horror to the hundreds of typed pages her husband has churned out under the guise of writing a novel, which repeat the phrase "All work and no play makes Jack a dull boy," confirming her suspicion that Jack is losing his mind and has become a serious threat to her and her son's safety. In *Room 237*, these moments are appropriated to show Wendy as Kubrick's wife, shocked at realizing his part in faking the Apollo footage. But the same sequence is used to construct alternative meanings elsewhere, in discussion of the Holocaust, where Wendy reacts to the typed pages in horror as Cocks describes the importance of the typewriter to Nazi history, and the scene is intercut and underlined with shots from *Schindler's List*. Using the same scenes to support varied interpretations outlines the subjective nature of critical analysis and the way in which personal interest shapes that interpretation, and challenges the implied singularity of the narrators' analyses.

In addition to these moments of repetition, Ascher is not averse to gently mocking his interviewees. He is as likely to show us a digitally altered, frame-by-frame slow motion sequence which supports the analysis at hand as he is to ironically distance us from the theorizing and encourage us to ourselves analyze and interpret what we are shown. He does this by again repurposing clips from *The Shining* itself. In response to the suggestion that Kubrick packed the film with sexual symbolism after becoming fascinated by the use of subliminal advertising techniques, the film cuts to Torrance, raising his glass directly to camera and proclaiming with a sly grin: "anything you say, Lloyd, anything you say…." The purpose of these moments is twofold. Firstly, they assure the audience that the filmmaker is in on the joke, that he realizes the outlandishness of some of the claims, and that he too is approaching *The Shining*'s deconstruction with the proverbial pinch of salt. Secondly, it serves as a reminder that, rather than being a film directly (or solely) about *The Shining*'s conspiracy theories, it is instead concerned with obsessive analysis, and the roles that cinematic nostalgia and personal history play in that.

The use of appropriated media within *Room 237* provides opportunities for audiences, when faced with multiple possible meanings, to construct their own. A viewer who chooses not to see Ascher's ironic reflections might instead find value within the documentary as fan-object, or take pleasure in recognizing the various aspects of its construction, or perhaps be fascinated with the theories on display—or, indeed, feel vindicated should they subscribe to any one of the interpretations on offer. Writing about the opportunities offered by cinephilia to adaptation studies, David T. Johnson suggests that "cinephilia reminds us of the porosity of media, especially cinema, for the 'migration of meanings,' in Barthes' words, so that adaptation is not a one-way conduit but rather a constantly ongoing process in every reception experience" (2012, p.

36). Just as we might see *Room 237* as adapting the meaning of *The Shining*, and appropriating other texts in the process, so too should we consider the part the narrators play in shaping the meaning of the documentary, and ultimately, the role of the audience in the creation of meaning: "the [cinephiliac] moment's very instability leading both inward, toward its originating context, and outward toward other texts brought to bear on it by the viewer" (ibid.).

Conclusion

Room 237, I have suggested in this essay, is a film about film analysis, history, and cinematic memory. Moreover, in its bricolage nature and appropriated construction, it is a film well suited to the contemporary nature of cinephilia. Digital techniques allow the recreation of personal memory or historical moments, the creation of new meaning and the possibility for alternative interpretations. Work on cinephilia and, more broadly, nostalgia and memory in film, has often focused on the re-presentation of the past in cinema, concerned with either the attempts at accuracy and authority in representing historical events or the application of retro style to fictional narratives. Ascher's film may not be attempting either, exactly, but rather it is exemplary of that desire to re-create and re-present, and to connect the past (in its film clips, recollections and discussions of historical events) to the present (in its digital construction and creation of new meaning).

In "addressing audiences as nostalgic spectators," Pam Cook argues, "the media invites exploration and interrogation of the limits of its engagement with history" (2005, p. 2). An adaptive, appropriated text which mediates not only history but also memory, *Room 237* invites its audience to revel in its nostalgia for the cinema, its reverence for *The Shining* and Kubrick's work, and the fascinating/outrageous theories at its heart. Simultaneously, it asks us to adopt a critical position in questioning the legitimacy of its presentation and to what extent it supports the analyses of its subjects. *Room 237*, much like the film over which its narrators obsess, is left open to interpretation with regard to its "true meaning," but provides plenty of cinephiliac pleasure in any attempt to figure that out.

NOTES

1. The Overlook's most haunted room, 237, was supposedly changed from the novel's room 217 to avoid scaring away potential guests at the Timberline Lodge, which stood in for the Overlook in exterior shots. Jay Weidner claims that Timberline has no room 217, that the story is not true, and that Kubrick changed it to 237 to indicate the c. 237,000 miles between the Earth and the moon, to symbolize the "moon room" soundstage where the director constructed NASA's landing footage.

The Timberline's website confirms the existing story, noting that "ironically, room #217 is requested more often than any other room at Timberline" (http://www.timber linelodge.com/the-shining/).

 2. I.Q. Hunter's chapter on *The Shining*'s conspiracy theories in his book *Cult Film as a Guide to Life: Fandom, Adaptation and Identity* (2016) provides a more detailed account of the obsessions of *Room 237*'s interviewees, and offers a useful approach to considering such zealous analysis as fan practice indicative of a film's cult status.

 3. This theater, with its iconic design, Sunset Boulevard location, and historical significance as one of the few remaining Cinerama screens, could be argued as a site of cinematic nostalgia itself.

 4. Collections by Marijke de Valck and Malte Hagener (2005) and Scott Balcerzak and Jason Sperb (2012) deal with the relationship between cinephilia and advanced digital technologies.

 5. The scene between Wendy and a doctor discussing Jack breaking Danny's arm, and parts of Jack's later monologue at the bar where he reflects on the "accident," are missing from some versions seen outside of the U.S., although Jack's existing violent nature is still implied.

REFERENCES

Balcerzak, S. and Sperb, J. (2012) Introduction: Remapping Cinephilia. In: Balcerzak, S. and Sperb, J. (eds.) *Cinephilia in the Age of Digital Reproduction: Film Pleasure and Digital Culture Vol. 2*. New York: Wallflower.

Bordwell, D. (2013) All play and no work? ROOM 237, April 7. http://www.davidbordwell.net/blog/2013/04/07/all-play-and-no-work-room-237/. (Accessed December 12, 2015).

Cook, P. (2005) *Screening the Past: Memory and Nostalgia in Cinema*. Abingdon: Routledge.

de Valck, M. and Hagener, M. (2005) Down with Cinephilia? Long Live Cinephilia? And Other Videosyncratic Pleasures. In: de Valck, M. and Hagener, M. (eds.) *Cinephilia: Movies, Love and Memory*. Amsterdam: Amsterdam University Press, pp. 11–24.

Elsaesser, T. (2005) Cinephilia or the Uses of Disenchantment. In de Valck, M. and Hagener, M. (eds.) *Cinephilia: Movies, Love and Memory*. Amsterdam: Amsterdam University Press, pp. 27–43.

Hunter, I. Q. (2016) *Cult Film as a Guide to Life: Fandom, Adaptation and Identity*. London: Bloomsbury.

Johnson, D. T. (2012) The "Flashing Glimpse" of Cinephilia: What an Unusual Methodology Might Offer Adaptation Studies. *Adaptation* 6 (1), pp. 25–42.

McCarthy, T. (2012) Room 237: Sundance Film Review. *Hollywood Reporter*, January 26. http://www.hollywoodreporter.com/review/sundance-room-237-review-285173. (Accessed April 1, 2013).

Room 237. (2012) [Film] Directed by Rodney Ascher. New York: IFC Films and IFC Films Midnight.

Rosenbaum, J. (2012) ROOM 237 (and a Few Other Encounters) at the Toronto International Film Festival, 2012. September 14. http://www.jonathanrosenbaum.net/2012/09/room-237-and-a-few-other-encounters-at-the-toronto-international-film-festival-2012/. (Accessed April 3, 2013).

Shambu, G. (2012) On "Room 237." Criticism and Theory, October 10. http://girish

shambu.blogspot.co.uk/2012/10/on-room-237-criticism-and-theory.html. (Accessed April 1, 2013).

Sontag, S. (1996) The Decay of Cinema. *New York Times Magazine*, February 26, pp. 60–61.

The Shining. (1980) [Film] Directed by Stanley Kubrick. USA: Warner Bros. Inc.

Thomson, D. and Atkinson, M. (2012) Things Overlooked. *Sight & Sound* 22, 11, pp. 48–49.

Totaro, D. (2015) Room 237: Experimenting with Documentary and Film Criticism. *Offscreen* 19 (6). Available at: http://offscreen.com/view/room-237-documentary-and-criticism. (Accessed December 12, 2015).

PART IV

Sites of Memory:
Mediating Iconic Spaces,
Objects and Ephemera

The BBC Archive
Post–Jimmy Savile
Irreparable Damage or Recoverable Ground?

ROWAN AUST *and* AMY HOLDSWORTH

Clad in a gold-lamé tracksuit, jacket unzipped to reveal a blue T-shirt emblazoned with the broadcast dates of the BBC's long-running pop music show *Top of the Pops* (1964–2006), presenter Jimmy Savile returned, aged 80, to co-host its final installment. So iconic was his relationship with the show that he was given the honor of symbolically turning off the studio lights for the final time. Behind the stage, walking past electrical rigging, the veteran broadcaster sighed and gently shook his head with sadness as he flipped the switch; the studio lights shut down in sequence and the scene went to black. Five years later, following Savile's death in 2011, this scene was revisited to symbolize another ending. Layered against the celestial yet celebratory tone of contemporary pop act Florence and the Machine's "Cosmic Love" (complete with sections of harp glissando) the sequence formed part of the concluding section of the tribute program *Sir Jimmy Savile: As It Happened* (2011). Part of a series of televised memorials and deftly employing 60 years' worth of BBC television archive content alongside testimonials from Savile's colleagues, peers and fans, the program worked to remind the viewer of the centrality of Savile to both the BBC and British popular culture. Broadcaster Chris Evans' voice-over reminded us that "for six decades, *Sir* Jimmy Savile was part of the fabric of British life" and concluded with the line "Now, Sir Jimmy has gone, but undoubtedly his legend will live on." Less than a year later, this line is infused with dark irony: in 2012 Jimmy Savile is exposed as having been a voracious sexual predator and is at the heart of the biggest sexual abuse scandal in British history.

This essay is concerned with what is now a cavity at the heart of the BBC archive: the space the broadcaster Jimmy Savile once occupied and the connection that the BBC once celebrated. It aims to demonstrate that, despite efforts by the BBC to eradicate Savile from its televised (and online) archive, specifically in relation to *Top of the Pops*, full removal is impossible. Savile was too significant a presence within the light entertainment and popular music culture of the late 20th century BBC—and therefore of Britain—to ever be forgotten. His prominence in shared British cultural memory is evident in the importance the BBC placed upon Savile in the years leading to his death. Post-scandal, as the BBC has attempted this eradication, Savile's place within both criminal and broadcasting history is more assured than ever, most ironically due to the BBC's obligation to report one of the most extensive criminal investigations ever undertaken.

Opening with a discussion of the BBC's relationship with Jimmy Savile and the broadcaster's response to both Savile's death and the emerging scandal (which is situated within a history of crisis at the BBC) this essay continues by paying specific attention to Savile's legacy in relation to the *Top of the Pops* brand and archive. Despite turning off the lights on the live show in 2006, both Savile and *Top of the Pops* have found a perennial home on both BBC2 and BBC4 through cycles of both nostalgic and historical programming. We examine the shift in the framing of this programming as the scandal irrupts and Savile is excised from the show's history. Finally, we reflect on the re-encounter with images from the Savile archive post-scandal and how the changing meanings and interpretations impact on the British public's and the BBC's senses of culpability.

The Life, Death and Afterlife of Jimmy Savile

Jimmy Savile died in October 2011, at the age of 84. His career had been both stellar and unique, with innumerable hours of airtime over both television and radio.[1] Described as "the country's first pop disc jockey" ("Obituary: Sir Jimmy Savile," 2011), Savile's flagship pop music program *Top of the Pops* premiered on New Year's Day, 1964. He remained a regular presenter well into the 1980s and returned in 2006 for the final live show. He was also widely known for his charity work, raising an estimated £40 million for various causes over the decades ("Sir Jimmy Savile," 2011). Television and charity were intertwined; in 1971 he fronted the road safety campaign *Clunk Click Every Trip*, while from 1973 to 1975 he hosted the BBC1 entertainment show *Clunk Click*. His image was carefully cultivated: the platinum silver hair, the cigar smoking, the gold chains, perennially costumed in a (often customized) tracksuit both on screen and while running his prolific money-raising marathons. He was closely associated with Stoke Mandeville and Broadmoor Hospitals, while also working as a porter in Leeds General Infirmary. His catchphrases "Now then, now then" and "As it happens" cemented him among those few known purely by the swiftest of references. Savile's eccentric benevolence bled back into TV: from 1975 to 1994 he presented *Jim'll Fix It*, a BBC1 Saturday night primetime entertainment show in which Savile "fixed" requests sent in by children for such televisual deeds as visiting a forest with trees festooned with sweets or seeing the reverse face of Big Ben. Savile's longevity within BBC and *Top of the Pops* heritage ensured he was caught within cycles of nostalgia, recreating the first edition of the pop program for its 25th anniversary and fronting its final installment, while *Fix It* itself returned for a 2007 special in *Jim'll Fix It Strikes Again*. Among numerous honors, he received an OBE in 1971 and both a knighthood and Papal knighthood in 1990. Establishment celebrity was further weaved into Savile's fame via publicized friendships with Margaret Thatcher, Prince Charles, and Princess Diana ("Jimmy Savile's Public Persona," 2011). Savile's achievements and recognitions were legion; he was a national figure and he was at the center of the BBC.

In the wake of Savile's death, the then BBC Director General Mark Thompson commented, "From *Top of the Pops* to *Jim'll Fix It*, Jimmy's unique style entertained generations of BBC audiences. Like millions of viewers and listeners we shall miss him greatly" ("Jimmy Savile: Tributes Flood In," 2011). Multiple tributes were aired: *Sir Jimmy Savile: As it Happened*; the Christmas specials *Sir Jimmy Savile: In His Own Words* (2011); and the Boxing Day reimagining of *Jim'll Fix It* (2011), in which *EastEnders* actor Shane Richie stood in for the late Savile. Lines of popular entertainment converged within this show—of soap opera in the body of Ritchie, of BBC archive and history in the reiteration of *Jim'll Fix It*—while the heady mix of nostalgia and cultural memory, always so acute among the many rituals of Christmas, was eagerly prompted in the programming. Two days later, BBC2 broadcast an hour-long archive special, *Sir Jimmy Savile at the BBC* (2011). This laid additional claim that the BBC would remain as the repository for the televisual memories of this much-loved, recently passed figure.

The revelations that emerged in the aftermath of Savile's death caused one of the biggest crises in the corporation's history. Immediately after he died, *Newsnight*, BBC television's weekday news and current affairs program, commenced an investigation into allegations that Savile was a pedophile. In December, the resulting report was pulled shortly before the Christmas specials were aired. Eight months later, in October 2012, and after months of speculation over Savile's proclivities in the printed press, ITV (the BBC's commercial competitor) broadcast the allegations in an edition of their own current affairs strand, *Exposure*. The BBC stood accused of protecting its own, a fact made ironically most explicit when Peter Rippon, the editor of *Newsnight*, went on the offensive and wrote in his BBC blog, "It has been suggested I was ordered to […] [pull the Savile investigation] by my bosses as part of a BBC cover-up" (Rippon, 2012).

The ensuing panic on *Newsnight* allowed a second piece around pedophilia to be broadcast without the proper verifications. The piece implicated an establishment figure in institutional child abuse, and while he was not named in the report, he was subsequently named on the internet as former Tory minister Lord McAlpine. The BBC paid damages for libel, various members of *Newsnight* and the BBC News management team were fired, and the Director General George Entwistle resigned after just 54 days in office (Marsh, 2012). The Pollard Review, a BBC investigation into the events surrounding the dropping of the *Newsnight* report on Savile,[2] concluded, "In my view, the most worrying aspect of the Jimmy Savile story for the BBC was not the decision to drop the story itself. It was the complete inability to deal with the events that followed" (Pollard, 2012, p. 22). In their article on the Savile scandal, Chris Greer and Eugene McLaughlin note both the "symbiotic relationship between Savile and the BBC" (2013, p. 250), and the BBC's own role in the obscuration of events as being central to the confusion that followed the initial revelations. More than three years on, Savile continues to be investigated by both the Metropolitan Police and through the Smith Review.[3] However, his guilt is fully recognized; in January 2013, Peter Watt of the NSPCC referred to Savile as "without doubt one of the most prolific sex offenders we have ever come across" ("Jimmy Savile Scandal: Report Reveals Decades of Abuse," 2013).

A History of Crisis

Crisis has long been part of the BBC's being and it has been shaped by its responses to the continual waves of criticism. Historically, crises have been catalyzed by political figures such as Winston Churchill and Margaret Thatcher, or from public bodies such as the National Viewers and Listeners Association. This was headed by the formidable Mary Whitehouse, who battled from the 1960s against what she saw as the BBC's responsibility for Britain's moral decline. The 1980s saw sustained governmental attacks on the BBC. In 1984, the corporation was sued for slander over the *Panorama* episode *Maggie's Militant Tendency*; the case went on for two years until the BBC withdrew and awarded the MP Neil Hamilton £20,000 in damages. In 1986, Special Branch raided BBC Scotland, concerned that a program about a secret satellite system would constitute a security breach, and this was not shown until two years later. From 1988 to 1994, there was a broadcast ban of all voices of Irish Republican or Loyalist paramilitaries in an attempt to censor the reporting of the Troubles. All of these elements are broadsides on the purpose of the BBC. While Mary Whitehouse may have been making moral claims for what was "right" to broadcast and demonstrating a worry about the power television has on the community, governmental intrusions are attacks on the key BBC tenet of journalistic impartiality and how the news should operate in differing political contexts. If this principle is placed under doubt, it undermines trust in the BBC as a body worthy of delivering news: the information which contextualizes and defines our place in the world. Without trust underpinning its purpose, the BBC can make no claim to function as the public's (all notions of the Broadcasting Corporation are proprietary) primary broadcaster.

The 2003 Hutton Inquiry delivered a stinging blow to this crucial notion of trust, recent enough to still be fresh in the minds of senior corporation figures. Convened after the death of David Kelly, who had been revealed as a source of a report by journalist Andrew Gilligan, the inquiry resulted in both Gilligan's resignation and that of Director General Greg Dyke. It was not concluded there, however; the Kelly affair also revealed a process of obscuration and counter-obscuration by the BBC and the government—an inconclusive "he said, she said" that was still being played out in the press some six years later by Gilligan and *The Observer*'s Nick Cohen (Cohen, 2010; Gilligan and Hoon, 2010). In this age of supposed transparency and accountability, processes of media and government can still be willfully unrevealed. Hutton found the BBC culpable of enabling Gilligan to present the most serious of allegations against the government while "the editorial system which the BBC permitted was defective" (Hutton, 2004); this cut so deeply into the heart of the BBC's news culture that it cost the Director General his job. While previous governmental attacks may have been repeated attempts to undermine the editorial principles of the BBC, Hutton confirmed them as defective. Therefore, while crisis can be seen as part of the BBC's being, always the crises were a battle with external forces: battles over what the BBC should and could do. This changed with Hutton, a crisis characterized by disorganization and misinformation from within. Savile reveals something far more insidious: the fact of a BBC broadcasting legend being unutterably different from his actual person, and the possibility that the BBC enabled this. The Savile scandal eroded trust in the BBC, not just in the delivery of news but as evidence of a systemic failure in its "duty of care" as a public service institution.

Given his prominence and longevity within the corporation, Savile therefore presents a psychic horror of an unprecedented scale. He destabilized the BBC from within, while public trust plummeted in the wake of the revelations. A survey in November 2012 showed that trust in BBC journalists had dropped by 37 percent since Hutton (Kellner, 2012), while a month later, another reported that 49 percent of people trusted the BBC less than before the Savile revelations ("Staring into the Abyss," 2012, p. 2). By June 2013, a third survey found that only 30 percent of people considered the BBC "reliable" (Fildes, 2013). With the delay of the Smith report and the BBC entering another period of charter renewal negotiations, the Savile scandal continues to reverberate through the institution simply through its lack of conclusion. While we do not wish to speculate on these unknown futures, we want to question, given the BBC's history of crisis, both what makes the Savile scandal so peculiarly damaging for the BBC and how the institution continues to evolve and adapt. These questions are considered through an analysis of the BBC's attempts to re-contextualize and de-contaminate the *Top of the Pops* archive.

A Crisis of History

Jimmy Savile presents a point where the history and memory *of* the BBC, popular history *on* the BBC and crisis *within* the BBC converge. As has been discussed, Savile's presence in British popular culture across the decades until his death in 2011 was as prominent as anyone's. The need to fill hours in the wake of digital multiplication meant that Savile's shelf-life as a television personality even outran his broadcasting career, with his presenting regularly being repeated in *Top of the Pops* reruns and in compilations of the show on *Top of the Pops 2* (BBC2, 1994–present). Further programming around the show includes one-off documentaries such as *Top of the Pops: The True Story* (2001 and re-versioned in 2006), first shown as part of a themed evening on BBC2, *I Love Top of the Pops*, hosted across its 145-minute transmission by Jimmy Savile himself; *Top of the Pops: The Story of 1976–1980* (2011–14) and 2015's *Big Hits: TOTP 1964 to 1975*, itself an iteration of a special of the same name shown in 2011. These repeats and re-versions are firstly examples of the BBC's dependence on its archive as a source of cheap programming. They also present *Top of the Pops* as demonstrative of the variances and possibilities of history, memory, and nostalgia on television—of television production culture, of pop music on television, of fashion, of the DJs who presented it— and re-present the renewal of the BBC's cultural identity and its construction of a specific cultural memory. Astrid Erll states that cultural memory "requires the continuation of meaning through established, stable forms of expression" (Erll, 2011, p. 29). Anyone who danced to *Top of the Pops* as a child, and in the '70s there were 19 million viewers ("Top of the Pops Through the Decades," 2004), will both recall the comfort of this expression while retaining and inhabiting these cultural memories to which Savile, while acknowledging an unease with his persona, was central. Hazel Collie and Mary Irwin identify this unease among their research subjects, stating that *Top of the Pops'* "middle-aged male presenters were perceived as 'cheesy' and even sexually predatory" (Collie and Irwin, 2013). But still, the show continued in its original form from 1964 to 2006 and bled across into the newer channels, creating new memories for new audiences and layering older memories for those already existing, persistently engaging new audiences in repeated cycles of iterative programming, always with Savile at its center.

The longevity of *Top of the Pops* and its centrality to nostalgic re-contextualizations of British popular (music) culture operated as a specific example of both the reassurance and the intimacy of television. It was part of the everyday rituals and routines of its viewers and was danced to in a million teenage bedrooms. Savile's posthumous transformation from eccentric national treasure to notorious pedophile has the potential to utterly rupture these memories. Patterns of scandal behave in a similarly iterative way, looming repeatedly with each new revelation, inquiry, and report, as well as in this case with allegations about other celebrities such as Stuart Hall, Rolf Harris, Gary Glitter or Dave Lee Travis (although all were convicted of smaller-scale crimes than Savile's) and in the U.S. context, Bill Cosby. Savile, therefore, represents a rupture of the safe iterative pattern to be replaced by something quite ghoulish: a recurring nightmare. But the archive body that is *Top of the Pops* is too important to cease on the BBC altogether. From even within the throes of the original crisis in 2012–13, Richard Klein, then controller of BBC4, stated that repeats of the show would continue on a "case-by-case" basis ("Top of the Pops Reruns Continue," 2013). While this could be seen as indicative of simple indecision on the part of the BBC, it also suggests an archive body too important to dismiss. Repeats continue to be shown, from which Savile has—mostly—been excised: when a clip of him presenting was shown in September of 2014, the BBC duly apologized for its mistake ("BBC Apologises for Airing Jimmy Savile Appearance," 2014). This accidental appearance came some 18 months after a character appeared dressed as Savile and uttered his catchphrase "Now then, guys and gals" within a repeated episode of the preschool children's show *The Tweenies,* for which the BBC received 216 complaints ("BBC Receives 216 Complaints for Tweenies Jimmy Savile Spoof," 2013). Of course, Savile still appears in news reports as the investigation into his and others' alleged and convicted crimes continues.

The New (Old) Top of the Pops

The re-contextualization of the television archive allows program-makers to position content "within new frames and contexts that hold the past at a distance and reframe it in relation to the present" (Holdsworth, 2011, p. 98). The *Top of the Pops* archive is now being repositioned to both bound the appearances of Savile and alter the viewer response to the show, essentially repackaged to retain elements of nostalgia while negating the presence of Savile. Firstly, and most obviously, is the post-scandal removal of Savile from the documentaries around *Top of the Pops*. A comparison of the program *Top of the Pops: The True Story* (2001 and 2006) and the series *TOTP: The Story of 1976, 77, 78, 79, 80* (2011–present) demonstrates the way in which Savile has been extracted from the newer televisual histories of the show and the impossible conundrum faced by the BBC in its archival treatment of Savile. As mentioned, *Top of the Pops: The True Story* first aired on December 8, 2001, as part of a BBC2 evening hosted by Savile and devoted to the show. It was re-versioned after *Top of the Pops* was axed in 2006 and shown in that version on July 30 of that year as part of the BBC2 evening *Top of the Pops: The Final Countdown*; it was broadcast again on BBC4 on January 7, 2008, and April 1, 2011. Using a combination of presenter links, archive, and talking heads, themselves a mix of starry—Kylie Minogue and Keith Richards among them—and authoritative, Savile is present throughout. He is there in the archive, presenting in excerpts from the 1960s and '70s, while also serving as a talking head, commenting on the significance of the show as a boost to acts' record sales and on the changing style and production culture over the years. His tone is not always complimentary; at one point, he sneeringly says that "it became like an American political convention." This underlines his prominence as an associated figure: he can say whatever he likes. The final shot of the documentary is culled from the final episode of *Top of the Pops* itself: Jimmy Savile turning off the studio lights.

Top of the Pops: The Story of 1976 (2011) contains archive of Savile in the introduction and then features him prominently in the back story commentary: the recollection of the early years of the series. This is partly explicable because of the introductory nature of this episode within the strand, but the prominence of Savile throughout the show demonstrates his continuing centrality. *Top of the Pops: The Story of 1977* (2012) is differently problematic in the emerging landscape of the scandal. The inherently lewd nature of the show is foregrounded with frequent shots of wiggling female bottoms, and is explicitly addressed in the segment on the ageing DJs surrounded by, enjoying, and ogling the much younger female company. The DJs, including Savile, are presented as an outdated precursor to the coming of punk, but essentially harmless given the cultural norms of the time. This episode also contains footage of Gary Glitter. Glitter had been convicted in 1999 of possession of indecent images, serving two months and jailed in Vietnam in 2006 for child abuse. How was it acceptable for him to appear? One can conclude that Glitter's crimes were separate enough from the BBC as to be deemed undamaging to the corporation should he be shown in archive. The two episodes for 1978 and 1979, produced post-scandal in 2013 and 2014, respectively, are a notable shift away from the previous analyses. Despite voiceover lines such as "the DJs were the real stars" (from 1978), the first episode emphasizes production, performers, and audience, while the latter moves into contextualizing the show within music history in its discussion of the punk/disco dichotomy and *Top of the Pops* as a showcase for reggae and 2 Tone. Both episodes make heavy use of the late '70s context of significant social unrest and how the show functioned as escapism in troubled times. Neither episode mentions Savile. It may be arguable that the later episodes in this series, continuing into *The Story of 1980* (2015), reflect the changing emphasis of the show itself. However, this is contradicted by the fact that all the documentaries produced pre-scandal celebrating both *Top of the Pops* and Savile place him as central to the show throughout its lifespan. For example, *Sir Jimmy Savile at the BBC* uses *Top of the Pops* performances throughout the decades—the Rolling Stones for the '60s, Sweet for the '70s and the Human League for the '80s— as a spine to demonstrate Savile's longevity.

What, however, is the BBC to do? It is clear that the *Top of the Pops* archive remains too important a source to be abandoned, so the BBC must eliminate Savile from its iterations of the show and in doing so stand accused of attempting suddenly and retroactively to reposition one of the most important cultural products it has produced. Is it the suddenness of this repositioning that retains a quality of distastefulness, as if a period of mourning has gone ignored? Should the BBC have suspended all programming associated with Savile during the period of investigation, or would this have left it open to seeming culpability? Certainly, including Savile in post-scandal programming could only have allowed and even prompted further scrutiny through what Frank Furedi calls "the project of re-examining the past for clues" (Furedi, 2013 p. 16). This might entail a search for evidence of Savile's crimes, in particular by the printed press, within the BBC archive: grainy images from Savile's teleography re-printed in close-up and images and details pored over, annotated, ringed, and highlighted as journalists and investigators "seek out" and sensationalize alleged incriminating behavior.

Re-Encountering the Savile Archive

The shift, within less than a year, from a context of memorialization and celebration to one of controversy and scandal has left the BBC with an archive suffused with alternate meanings and interpretations. The programs produced in the immediate context of Savile's death and then in the irruption of the posthumous scandal reveal much about the ways in which archival images and sounds are managed and shaped through their re-contextualization. The re-framing of images used in the 2011 tribute programs *Sir Jimmy Savile: As It Happened* and *Sir Jimmy Savile at the BBC* to their use in 2012's *Panorama* special, "Jimmy Savile—What the BBC Knew" (2012) produce an unpleasant affective change in response—from familiar nostalgic feeling to the suspicion of culpability just by the act of viewing. For example, the caravan, which toured with Savile during his BBC roadshows and charity marathons, is featured prominently in *Sir Jimmy Savile at the BBC* as a focus for the crowds of girls drawn towards the celebrity (with Savile hemmed in as they clamor for autographs). In the *Panorama* episode the same footage is used to accompany the description of the caravan as a place in which Savile would assault underage girls. There is repeated use of a clip where Savile strides, in long shot, in a red tracksuit across a courtyard at Broadmoor Hospital; the shift in focus moves him from eccentrically attired kindness to something inhumanly predatory. *Sir Jimmy Savile at the BBC* even makes central Savile's pursuance of women, with now-revealing clips of him on *Parkinson*, in an interview with Uri Geller and a clip of Savile with a bedbound woman in a hospital, within which Savile's "playful" attitude towards sex is emphasized. The final shot of this archive hour seems horribly prescient as he stands with a pubescent girl and says straight to camera, "As it happens, see you later," as she glances over to him.

Here, we recognize two particular modes of re-contextualization: the first produced by the program-maker through the new framing of familiar images and the second "felt" or "read" by the viewer in their re-encounter with images within a dramatically new context.[4] Images of a contemplative Savile are re-read as ominous, his famed eccentricity or oddness re-interpreted as criminal deviance; images and words are flooded by a dramatic irony. Martin Jay defines dramatic irony as occurring when "hindsight provides some purchase on a truth denied actors at the time history is made" (2013, p. 32). This irony is read as particularly cruel by the continual assertion that Savile was "hiding in plain sight." This appears "confirmed" by the re-encounter with the archive. From Mohammed Ali's amusing and bemused dismissal of Savile's eccentricity (signaling to camera through silent comic asides that Savile is not mentally well) during his appearance on *Jim'll Fix It* in 1976 to documentary maker Louis Theroux's direct confrontation of Savile (and the veteran's rebuff) with the perennial tabloid accusation that, given his "odd" persona and his high-profile work with children on TV and for charity, he might be a pedophile ("When Louis Met…. Jimmy," 2000). The portentous quality of the image (as famously discussed in relation to photography by both Walter Benjamin [1931] and Roland Barthes [1980]) offers a fantasy in which we can read our knowledge of the future into the archival image. From the vantage point of the present, it is the now apparent "obviousness" of Savile's crimes, articulated through this imaginative encounter with the archive, that further condemns the BBC and other institutions (e.g., the NHS) wrapped up in the scandal.

Jimmy Savile has lingered, unresolved, as a toxic asset within the corporation and the television archive since the scandal broke in 2012. How can such damage to the archive be remedied? If a library is burnt to the ground, with papers and irreplaceable books turned to ashes, it can be mourned, while work can be done to repair what has been lost. But a cavity such as the one Savile has left is irreparable. His crimes are contaminatory to those brands associated with the celebrity and to the BBC. His image and archival presence is akin to a tumor that must apparently, given the BBC's actions, be excised. But bounding Savile is impossible. While Savile presents, in Greer and McLaughlin's terms, a "scandal without end," enabled and maintained by myriad media platforms and digital archives (2012, p. 247), his role as a presenter ties him to certain facets of the programs he fronted and the values of the institution. Ann Gray and Erin Bell demonstrate how presenters of history documentaries are the personification of the BBC as a "knowledge brand," where persona and authority converge for a particular style and tone of delivery (2013, p. 74), while Jean Seaton characterizes Sir David Attenborough as a "proportionate human measure" against which audiences could judge the majesty of the natural world (2015, p. 107). Savile was the "other," the anti–Reithian eccentric everyman who looked and sounded like nothing else and was used to introduce ideas of youth and difference to a BBC which needed, in the early '60s, to respond to both the challenge of the television duopoly and to reach a recently cohered youth audience. The journalist and critic Dave Haslam, talking in *Top of the Pops: The Story of 1976*, defines Savile as a "DJ pioneer" and "genuine music lover." Savile represented new possibilities for television in both his bringing of pop music and the sense of a new order; the unique personality, look, sound, and attitude; the working class ex–miner–turned–DJ plucked from Radio Caroline; and at the vanguard of the new aristocracy, celebrity.

In the tribute program *Sir Jimmy Savile: As It Happened*, this collapse of the old order is made explicit in the segment detailing Savile's relationships with the highest of establishment figures that include Margaret Thatcher and Prince Charles. His creation by the BBC is explicitly articulated. Using the voiceover of Chris Evans, an arguable successor to the anarchic presentation style of Savile, the script states, "*Top of the Pops* had provided Jim with a platform and now the whole world was his stage," and takes credit for making Savile a star, while singer Lulu, as a talking head, elaborates on Savile's subsequent level of celebrity, saying, "He was pretty famous, yeah he was huge," while still images of Savile with iconic bands such as the Beatles and the Rolling Stones are flashed up on the screen. It is precisely his celebrity that is commonly seen as enabling both Savile's crimes and the reason his victims felt unable to speak out.

While Savile's complete exorcism from both the archive and cultural memory remains an impossibility, we want to conclude with a series of questions and possible ramifications that arise in response to his attempted removal. Firstly, at what point do the attempts at such excision continue to deny the victims' rights to have their suffering acknowledged? The BBC did not acknowledge the victims as its first response; it attempted to deny all responsibility, nullifying subsequent admissions of sympathy. In the context of the victims' needs, the BBC's association with Savile continues to be minimized. If Savile's modus operandi, as it has been repeatedly described, was to "hide in plain sight," does the British public simply shut down the part of its collective (popular cultural) consciousness that serves as a witness? While the legacy and history of *Top of the Pops* is re-shaped and made safe for consumption, there are the more difficult, problematic, and unpredictable histories and memories that are contained and silenced. What, for example, might the television archive reveal about the cultures and attitudes towards young women and children that enabled such widespread sexual abuse to occur? How do they continue or connect with the present? The Savile scandal places the BBC within a particular tension, caught by the need to preserve the trust of its audience but to also uphold the values of transparency. The extent to which the BBC can turn the studio lights back on and illuminate its role in these difficult histories and memories remains to be seen.

NOTES

1. On radio, Savile presented *Savile's Travels* (Radio 1, 1968–77), *Speakeasy* (Radio 1, 1975–77) and *Jimmy Savile's Old Record Club* (Radio 1, 1978–87), as well as regular appearances across other shows. Source: BBC Genome Project, http://genome.ch.bbc.co.uk.

2. Nick Pollard was engaged by the BBC to investigate events around the dropping of the *Newsnight* report into Savile. His findings were published on December 18, 2012.

3. An inquiry led by Dame Janet Smith was established by the BBC in October, 2012, to conduct an "impartial, thorough and independent review of the culture and practices of the BBC during the years that Jimmy Savile worked there" (Dame Janet Smith Review, 2015). At the time of writing, the findings of the Smith Review are yet to be released at the request of the Metropolitan Police who are concerned that the report could prejudice ongoing investigations ("BBC Jimmy Savile Abuse Report," 2015).

4. Linda Hutcheon's writing on nostalgia and irony is particularly revealing here as she emphasizes the similarity between the two as modes of engagement with or felt responses to the moment of encounter between past and present. She writes: "I want to argue that to call something ironic or nostalgic is, in fact, less a *description* of the ENTITY ITSELF than an *attribution* of a quality of RESPONSE. Irony is not something in an object that you either 'get' or fail to 'get': irony 'happens' for you (or,

better, you *make* it 'happen') when two meanings, one said and the other unsaid, come together, usually with a certain critical edge. Likewise, nostalgia is not something you 'perceive' *in* an object; it is what you 'feel' when two different temporal moments, past and present, come together for you and, often, carry considerable emotional weight. In both cases, it is the element of response—of active participation, both intellectual and affective—that makes for the power" (1998, paragraph 15).

REFERENCES

Anonymous. (2004) Top of the Pops Through the Decades. *The Guardian*, November 29. http://www.theguardian.com/music/2004/nov/29/popandrock.television. (Accessed June 6, 2015).

Anonymous. (2011) Jimmy Savile: Tributes Flood In. *BBC News*, October 30. http://www.bbc.co.uk/news/uk-15507826. (Accessed June 30, 2015).

Anonymous. (2011) Jimmy Savile's Public Persona. *BBC News*, October 22. http://www.bbc.co.uk/news/uk-20027996. (Accessed May 6, 2015).

Anonymous. (2011) Obituary: Sir Jimmy Savile. *BBC News*, October 29. http://www.bbc.co.uk/news/entertainment-arts-15053431. (Accessed May 6, 2015).

Anonymous. (2011) Sir Jimmy Savile. [Obituary] *The Telegraph,* October 29. http://www.telegraph.co.uk/news/obituaries/8857428/Sir-Jimmy-Savile.html. (Accessed May 6, 2015).

Anonymous. (2012) "Staring into the Abyss": The BBC, Trust and Jimmy Savile. Survey Results Published by Conquest Research & Consultancy for *The Guardian*, December 17. http://www.theguardian.com/media/interactive/2012/dec/17/bbc-trust-jimmy-savile-survey. (Accessed May 6, 2015).

Anonymous. (2013) BBC Receives 216 Complaints for Tweenies Jimmy Savile Spoof. *BBC News*, January 21. http://www.bbc.co.uk/news/entertainment-arts-21108337. (Accessed June 24, 2015).

Anonymous. (2013) Jimmy Savile Scandal: Report Reveals Decades of Abuse. *BBC News*, January 11. http://www.bbc.co.uk/news/uk-20981611. (Accessed June 30, 2015).

Anonymous. (2013) Top of the Pops Reruns to Continue. *BBC News*, January 10. http://www.bbc.co.uk/news/entertainment-arts-20969876. (Accessed May 19, 2015).

Anonymous. (2014) BBC Apologises for Airing Jimmy Savile Appearance. *BBC News*, September 22. http://www.bbc.co.uk/news/entertainment-arts-29308337. (Accessed July 20, 2015).

Anonymous. (2015) BBC Jimmy Savile Abuse Report Delayed at Police Request. *The Guardian*, May 1. http://www.theguardian.com/media/2015/may/01/bbc-jimmy-savile-abuse-report-police-dame-janet-smith. (Accessed July 30, 2015).

Barker, D. (2001) Mary Whitehouse. [Obituary] *The Guardian*, November 24. http://www.theguardian.com/media/2001/nov/24/guardianobituaries.obituaries. (Accessed August 1, 2015).

Barthes, R. (2000 [1980]) *Camera Lucida*. London: Vintage.

Benjamin, W. (1999 [1931]) A Little History of Photography. In: *Selected Writings Volume 2: 1927–1934*. Trans. Rodney Livingstone. Cambridge: Harvard University Press, pp. 1931–934.

Born, G. (2005) *Uncertain Vision: Birt, Dyke and the Reinvention of the BBC*. London: Vintage.

Cohen, N. (2010) The Media's Part in the Death of David Kelly. *The Guardian*, August 22. http://www.theguardian.com/commentisfree/2010/aug/22/david-kelly-tony-blair-iraq-wmd. (Accessed June 1, 2014).

Collie, H. and Irwin, M. (2013) "The Weekend Starts Here": Young Women, Pop Music Television and Identity. *Screen* 54 (2), pp. 262–69.

Dame Janet Smith Review. (2015) *The Dame Janet Smith Review.* http://www.dame janetsmithreview.com/. (Accessed August 30, 2015).

Erll, A. (2011) *Memory in Culture.* New York: Palgrave Macmillan.

Fildes, N. (2013) BBC's Credibility Dives After Savile. *The Times,* June 28. http://www.thetimes.co.uk/tto/business/industries/media/article3802468.ece. (Accessed July 30, 2015).

Furedi, F. (2013) *Moral Crusades in an Age of Mistrust: The Jimmy Savile Scandal.* Basingstoke: Palgrave Macmillan.

Gilligan, A. and Hoon, G. (2010) Andrew Gilligan: I Did Not Betray David Kelly or Reveal Him as My Source. *The Observer,* August 29. http://www.theguardian.com/theobserver/2010/aug/29/david-kelly-nick-cohen-andrew-gilligan. (Accessed May 18, 2015).

Gray, A. and Bell, E. (2013) *History on Television.* London: Routledge.

Greer, C. and McLaughlin, E. (2013) The Sir Jimmy Savile Scandal: Child Sexual Abuse and Institutional Denial at the BBC. *Crime, Media, Culture* 9 (3), pp. 243–63.

Holdsworth, A. (2011) *Television, Memory and Nostalgia.* Basingstoke: Palgrave Mac-Millan.

Hutcheon, L. (1998) Irony, Nostalgia, and the Postmodern. http://www.library.utoronto.ca/utel/criticism/hutchinp.html. (Accessed July 30, 2015).

Hutton, L. (2004) Hutton Inquiry—Report by Lord Hutton. Chapter 12, 467 (3, ii). http://webarchive.nationalarchives.gov.uk/20090128221546/http://www.the-hutton-inquiry.org.uk/content/report/chapter12.htm-a90. (Accessed May 18, 2015).

Jay, M. (2013) Intention and Irony: The Missed Encounter Between Hayden White and Quentin Skinner. *History and Theory* 52 (1), pp. 32–48.

Kellner, P. (2012) The Problem of Trust. *YouGov,* November 13. http://yougov.co.uk/news/2012/11/13/problem-trust/. (Accessed May 6, 2015).

Marsh, K. (2012) Why the BBC's Boss Had to Go. *British Journalism Review* 23 (4), pp. 19–28.

Panorama. (2012) [TV] Jimmy Savile—What the BBC Knew. United Kingdom: BBC1. October 22.

Pollard, N. (2012) The Pollard Review. *BBC Trust,* December 16. http://www.bbc.co.uk/bbctrust/our_work/editorial_standards/pollard_review.html. (Accessed July 30, 2015).

Rippon, P. (2012) Newsnight and Jimmy Savile. *BBC Online,* October 2. http://www.bbc.co.uk/blogs/theeditors/2012/10/newsnight_and_jimmy_savile.html (Accessed July 30, 2015).

Scannell, P. and Cardiff, D. (1990) *A Social History of British Broadcasting. Vol. 1, 1922–1939: Serving the Nation.* Oxford: Blackwell.

Seaton, J. (2015) *"Pinkoes and Traitors": The BBC and the Nation, 1974–1987.* London: Profile Books.

Sir Jimmy Savile: As It Happened. (2011) [TV] United Kingdom: BBC1. November 11.

Sir Jimmy Savile: In His Own Words. (2011) [Radio] United Kingdom: BBC Radio 2. December 25.

Sir Jimmy Savile at the BBC. (2011) [TV] United Kingdom: BBC2. December 28.

Top of the Pops. (2006) [TV] Final episode. United Kingdom: BBC2. July 30.

Top of the Pops: The Story of 1976. (2011) [TV] United Kingdom: BBC4. April 1.

Top of the Pops: The Story of 1977. (2012) [TV] United Kingdom: BBC4. January 6.
Top of the Pops: The Story of 1978. (2013) [TV] United Kingdom: BBC4. January 4.
Top of the Pops: The Story of 1979. (2014) [TV] United Kingdom: BBC4. January 3.
Top of the Pops: The Story of 1980. (2015) [TV] United Kingdom: BBC4. January 2.
Top of the Pops: The True Story. (2001; 2006) [TV] United Kingdom: BBC1, January 1, 2001; July 30, 2006.
When Louis Met… (2000) When Louis Met…. Jimmy. [TV] United Kingdom: BBC2. April 13.

A Psychoanalytic Perspective on Childhood Television Memories

Jo Whitehouse-Hart

"Mother didn't understand that children aren't frightened by stories; that their lives are full of far more frightening things than those contained in fairy tales."—Kate Morton, *The Forgotten Garden*[1]

Television Memories and Psychoanalysis

If we ask audiences about their "favorite" films and television programs we are likely to learn something of the viewer's tastes. However, this seemingly benign category frequently generates discussion about the particular texts to which viewers feel a strong and enduring emotional attachment, and which often transcends current "likes" and "dislikes." In particular, "favorites" often act like mnemonic devices or as aide-memoirs, stimulating biographical memories of life events which are often linked to childhood viewing in the home. Thus any examination of favorites in childhood inevitably takes us into the terrain of memory and the life story, which this essay explores from a *psychoanalytic* perspective. I offer this to illustrate that psychoanalysis has a place in empirical audience research. Previously, psychoanalysis has been mainly associated with text-based approaches (see Modleski, 1982; and for a basic introduction Lapsley and Westlake, 1988; also Cowie, 1997). Psychoanalysis is particularly pertinent for any research where memories are concerned, as memory is a central strand present in all branches of psychoanalytic thought. Psychoanalysis offers compelling and persuasive concepts and theories with which we can understand both the nature of viewing memories and their emotional and unconscious significance for the viewer. One such concept is the "Screen Memory," which as a linguistic term seems apt for a study of television and film memories, but is actually a concept devised by Freud (1899) to understand the role of memory in emotional difficulties and trauma. Media research has been interested in both the "effects" of media texts and in how audiences "use" television. This has largely been focused on social and very poorly defined "psychological" needs captured in approaches such as uses and gratifications (Elliott, 1974).

This essay will introduce the reader to some psychoanalytic theories and concepts with the aim of illustrating that there is a place for psychoanalysis in audience studies, particularly in relation to the areas of emotion, identity, and memory, which purely sociological approaches are unable to fully capture. However, it does not promote psychoanalysis as superior to other forms of analysis, but rather as an enhancement to existing approaches. Thus the essay proposes that we view the study of audiences psychosocially, attending to both unconscious and "psychic" processes as well as those that are social; that is to say, attending to the mutually constitutive relationships between inner and outer worlds. The essay will begin by introducing the study on which the discussion is based and then closely examining interview data to show that "effects" and "uses" are related to complex meaning-making processes that contain some highly personalized features.

This essay explores childhood viewing memories which emerged from a psychoanalytically informed[2] interview-based piece of audience research[3] examining the psychosocial significance of "favorites." This research used Wendy Hollway and Tony Jefferson's (2000) Free Association Narrative Interview Method (FANI)[4] which is designed to elicit narratives that demonstrate the emotional significance for the interviewee of the topic in question, rather than intellectualized cognitive responses (see Whitehouse-Hart, 2014). The approach that was used took individual biography into account while acknowledging that "universal" experiences such as the Oedipus complex, through which the child acquires their sexual identity, take place in sets of historically and socially specific circumstances that are unique to each "family" and individual biography; thus the individual's journey is always *unique*. The essay makes use of the clinical vignette or case study to explore this journey and the imaginative role played by television. The method follows Freud's logic of free association, which, along with dreams (which in psychoanalysis are frequently associated with film), are part of the "royal road to the unconscious" (Freud, 1900). The interviewer allows the subject to "talk" about anything that comes to mind in relation to the topic (favorite films and television programs), rather than impose an agenda which follows the interviewer's interests. The material is analyzed as a "whole" rather than in sequence, taking account of material which might seem to be illogical and anti-contextual.

Psychoanalytic film theory has proposed that cinema is a *uniquely psychic experience* (Cowie, 1997; Hawke and Alister, 2001). Cinema is said to create dream-like states and provoke unconscious processes associated with foundational moments in identity acquisition, such as the Oedipus complex and Mirror Phase narrated by Freud and Lacan. One difficulty with psychoanalytic film theory concerns its claim to the superiority and psychic intensity of the cinematic experience. My research found the domestic setting or the "home" to be a far more powerfully psychic setting. It seems strange to place so much emphasis on the cinematic setting to understand films, when watching films has always been a central feature of watching TV *in the home*. In fact, as one viewer stated: "I don't know why but the films that have had the most powerful effect on me are the ones I've watched at home." The "effect" they refer to relates to what I have called "Impact Texts" (Whitehouse-Hart, 2014), or texts that leave a strong affective impression and that are *unforgettable*. Definitions of the word "impact" include the effect or impression of one thing on another; and the power of making a strong immediate impression (Webster's Dictionary). These phrases capture some of the significant viewing experiences this essay is concerned with, such as the shock and unexpectedly strong reaction viewers can have to a text. Often what impacts on the viewer are mere *moments* from a film or program, perhaps a visual image or a particular instance of plot development. This moment is often stored as a memory and is distinguished by an association with an ill-defined, unexamined, and often surprising emotional impact at the time of viewing. The memories are often not understood ("I don't understand it," "I don't know why this keeps coming to mind"). A psychoanalytic perspective would see the emergence of such memories as indicative of its *emotional significance*. This essay focuses on the durability of the profoundly mnemonic features of impact texts.

The home as a viewing setting represents many things: it is a place of relaxation and safety, of joy and intimacy, and at the same time it may be an intense and oppressive place. In childhood, home is the canvas where identity is painted through experiences such as the Oedipus complex, or where the outer social world of discourse is represented to us, for instance through TV. The acquisition of sexual and gender identity involves the individual moving through "normal" stages; however, the journey is not always easy, and in specific sets of circumstances they can also have "traumatic" features which will be explored below. Homes are associated in infancy with families, and in all branches of psychoanalytic theory our earliest experiences, in particular with our primary carers (parents) and others such as siblings, have a profound and on-going effect on our identity formation and emotional lives. As psychoanalyst Christopher Bollas (1992, p. 59) writes, significant relationships and encounters with others in earliest life leave their traces as "psychic textures";

these can be activated as memories and affect by certain "psychic keys," in this case childhood television memories. The home is also a highly personalized setting containing our private "objects" which are imbued with personal significance, making the home a more profound psychic setting for viewing than the cinema, where despite the darkened auditorium spectators are conscious of social protocols and the presence of strangers.

It has been argued that out of the individual's innumerable early life experiences a small number of powerful childhood memories are retained. These memories play a pivotal role in the life story (Freud, 1899; Rosenbaum, 1998). In keeping with Freud's analysis of dreams, psychoanalytic theories of memory are alert to the significance of both what is "revealed" (manifest meaning) *and* what is "hidden" (latent meaning). The *accuracy* or the "facts" of childhood memories, such as those presented in the case study below, are less important than the *affect* and emotional significance of the event (Rosenbaum, 1998, p. 69). Indeed, when analyzing memories, factual inaccuracies might be more productively identified as forms of parapraxes, a collective noun used by Freud for all slips and "errors" such as mispronunciation which have *unconscious* significance (Kegan, 2002, p. ix). For Freud (1901) "getting it wrong" is always of interest, as parapraxes are indicative of unconscious content and processes, such as repression and repetition which are also linked to trauma. Milton Rosenbaum (1998) argues that some childhood memories are "Screen Memories": those which are associated with unconscious processes such as repression, and which are most likely to repeat, reappear, and be unforgettable. Some memories from childhood often seem factually "trivial and unimportant" (such as memories of watching television); others, as I will show below, may not be fully understood by the individual and are usually associated with powerful affective responses. Freud (1901, p. 45) explained this as a process of displacement, where "genuinely significant impressions" and traumatic events have been repressed. In fact, Freud was skeptical about the ability to distinguish between truth (memory) and fiction (fantasy) as *both* are charged with affect and fantasy. I want to examine these ideas in relation to the childhood memories of Mary, a middle-aged working class woman, by asking specific questions about the role played by television.

On analyzing the many hours of interview material with Mary, it was found that three temporal periods dominated: a time in her life when she was "seven or eight"; her teenage years; and current times surrounding the impending marriage of her much adored only son. In fact, she was "dreading" him leaving home and getting married. She was worried about what life would be like without him, and was thus entering a period where her identity as a mother was in transition, which Erik Erikson (1959) has pointed to as being difficult and anxiety provoking. Similarly, "seven or eight" was also a key moment in Mary's identity as it is associated with a change in status and identity instigated by the birth of siblings after what in the 1960s and 1970s would have been an unusually long period of being an only child. Her first sister was born, closely followed by another sister a year later. This was traumatic for Mary, as she went from being her father's "princess" to being "lonely," and in her teenage years she felt "very much one on my own out of five." Her memories were not discussed chronologically; Mary moved in and out of these three time periods across the interviews. This demonstrated the three notions of time outlined by Rosine Perelberg (2008, p. 24): "repetition, irreversibility and oscillation," which are present in Freud's theory of memory and time. These time periods are also significant, because, as I will show, the birth of siblings is a momentous and, in this case, traumatic moment in the formation of identity, and one that has often been neglected in psychoanalytic theory in favor of prioritizing the Oedipus Complex (Mitchell, 2003).

It has been argued that cinema spectators (or television viewers) carry a "cinema"/"viewing" history which is returned to and re-translated in the light of biographical experiences and events (Sutton, 2004). When spectators return to a text in viewing or in memory their history is expressed in both diachronic and synchronic terms, in relation to the moment of the event and of the view of the memory from the *current* position. Freud's notion of Nachtraglich or "deferred action" refers to experiences, "impressions and memory traces which may be revised at a later date when the individual reaches a new stage of maturation" (Perelberg, 2008, p. 26), most significantly puberty in teenage years (Freud, 2011). For Freud the first originary scene is of parental intercourse (the primal scene where the child becomes aware of parental sexuality) directly witnessed, overheard or imagined. Primal encounters either in reality or fantasy usually result in repression of the memory. Primal fantasies and Screen Memories are often produced with a defensive function to prevent the child being overwhelmed by accessing the actual scene which it does not have the capabilities to "translate"; or they are produced at a later time in life when the child has matured and then fully recognizes the significance of what they have seen. In both cases the function of the fantasy or memory is to "screen" the subject from the realities of the primal scene. Jean Laplanche (1992, 1999), building on Freud, developed the concept of après-coup; he thought this initial moment was not in and of itself traumatic, but that it is only perceived so at a later stage of maturation when the older child recognizes the sexual significance of what it saw and thus becomes able to "translate" the significance of the event. For Freud, memories are supplemented over time by a series of rearrangements and auxiliary scenes, meaning memories are not present only once but several times over (Perelberg, 2008).

Thus psychoanalysis does not propose a simple cause-effect model which traces everything back to the repressed memory of a traumatic event, but rather offers a "more complex temporal structure in which the initial traumatic scene is supplemented by a series of later auxiliary scenes" (Fletcher, 2013, p. 126); it therefore takes two or more scenes to make a trauma, with the key factor being the time lag between them. It is usually puberty which brings about the translation whereby previously innocuous or misunderstood scenes are given new significance. If the significance still provokes anxiety it may remain subject to further repression or refusal to bring to consciousness the significance. The principle of après-coup suggests that memories are changed in the light of later life experiences; they may be remembered differently and are reinterpreted. For this reason, in psychoanalysis the present is always relevant when reinterpreting the past; thus, in my research, Mary's dread of the imminent loss of her son will be significant because it forces a change to her identity as a mother and forces her to confront her son's identity as a sexually mature being. Therefore, what we are dealing with is a complex double logic of après-coup involving deferral and retrospection (Fletcher, 2013, p. 126).

In this study, I follow Freud who placed the analysis of memory "scenes" as central to his theoretical development[5] (see Fletcher, 2013). I want to argue that images from television—precisely because the medium is so central to the home—provide symbolic raw material which children appropriate and incorporate into their own unique signification system. To explore this further I will examine Mary's viewing memories to show how the "scenes" she recalled can be thought of as defensive Screen Memories produced to ward against unconscious anxiety associated with traumatic events such as sibling birth.

Time and Memory: The Birds

The period of being "seven or eight" is associated with a number of scenarios relating to television viewing which Mary remembers as "upsetting" and "frightening." Characters and scenes from television often featured in Mary's frequent childhood "nightmares." Mary placed the memory scenes in the context of having a "vivid imagination" as a child and being prone to "sleepwalking," "nightmares," and "crying a lot," so it is not always clear if what Mary recounts are from waking or dreaming states, as the extract below suggests. I want to explore an enduring and disturbing memory from the time she was "seven or eight" of Hitchcock's *The Birds* (Alfred Hitchcock, 1963):

> I remember coming downstairs in the middle of the night.[6] I don't know whether I was upset and I couldn't sleep and I walked in on my Mum and Dad who were watching Alfred Hitchcock's *The Birds. And it was the bit where the lady sat at the bottom of her bed and had her eyes pecked out* [author emphasis]. And that gave me nightmares for years and years. I have to say by then the damage was done. It was a film they were enjoying and they were quite engrossed in. And I wandered in and I don't quite know why I wandered in. I used to do a lot of wandering when I was little. I did a lot of sleepwalking but I was definitely awake at this point. I'm guessing I was *nearly eight* [author emphasis]. And I

walked into the room and in the time it took for them to realize I was in the room and obviously there was no remote control, you'd have had to jump out of your seat and run over and turn it off. And in the time that any of that may or may not have happened, I'd been turned round and ushered out of the room, I'd walked right in at the bit where the lady is sitting on the floor at the end of the bed and the birds are pecking her eyes out and that was enough. [...] I had nightmares for a long time after that. I can remember asking my Mum about it, asking her why the birds were attacking the lady.

The repetitive nature of the memory coupled with powerful affect is suggestive in psychoanalytic terms of something traumatic. Therefore, it is worth exploring what the "damage" might be that haunted Mary for years. For Freud some memories operate like dreams, particularly where trauma is concerned. What is presented is likely to be factually inaccurate and the result of processes of displacement, condensation, substitution, and symbolization as Freud (1900) outlined in *The Interpretation of Dreams.*

The scene Mary describes is unclear; if we look at the text of *The Birds* it suggests that there has been some conflation and rearrangement. It is not clear if she has seen the film subsequently, and how that might have affected the memory scene reproduced. There are various scenes in the film where women, men, and children are attacked by birds. However, as emphasized above, the part that gave Mary "nightmares for years and years" was the "bit where the lady *sat at the bottom of her bed and had her eyes pecked out.*" This, however, is an inaccurate memory. I would argue that the error points to the way in which the memory has been personalized by Mary, which I will discuss below in relation to the primal scene. The final scene of the film where the female protagonist Melanie Daniels (Tippi Hedren) is attacked by the birds takes place in a bedroom (a location that is associated with parental intimacy and from which children are often excluded). However, in the film Melanie is against a door, and not at the end of a bed as Mary recalls. Furthermore, while in the scene all parts of her body including her face are attacked, her eyes are in fact spared.

The most famous scene in the film involving eyes being attacked features a man—a farmer named Dan Fawcett. Melanie Daniels discovers this man beside his bed—he is already dead, surrounded by dead birds and with blood streaming from his eyes. The gore in this scene is reminiscent of the Oedipus Myth.

The extract ends with Mary's request for "translation" from her mother, which unfortunately was inadequate as she was unable to assuage her fears; she tried to "rationally explain" it to Mary in a "very adult way ... in quite a lot of detail." Even though she was very young Mary remembers "it would've been very much taught to me as a grown up even at that age." Mary explained her response to this experience (and other similar occasions): "I remember what I did a lot of was to actually make up the rest of the story because I was quite shocked" (at both the event and her mother's explanation). So from an early age Mary was being treated as more mature than she was, and this in itself was problematic; she was reliant on her own ability to "translate" her experiences. She explained her experience of this television memory as "children feeling the vibe of emotion but not understanding what is going on."

Memories that repeat and are associated with a strong emotional reaction, and where the reason for this reaction is not fully understood, are indicative of what Freud (1899, 1901) called "Screen Memories." These memories serve defensive functions as they "cover over and repress disturbing and compelling infantile experiences for which it stands" (Fletcher, 2013, p. 120). They are "substitutes for genuinely significant impressions […] since they owe their retention in their mind not to their own content but to its associative connection with another repressed subject" (Freud, 1901, p. 45). The memory is produced out of processes of displacement whereby significant threatening impressions and traumatic events have been repressed (Freud, 1901). "Memory-work," then, is similar to the work of dreams where events are worked upon, displaced, rearranged, and worked into a personal signification system, which is provided in this case by the television. Laplanche (1999) argues that childhood "trauma" results from "wounds" experienced in the child's encounter with the *unconscious* sexuality of the adult other. In the *normal* manifestations of childcare and nurture, "enigmatic signifiers" or messages about sexuality are transmitted to the child via verbal and non-verbal forms, and their implantation is wounding to the child although this might not be recognized until later periods in their life.

But how do these experiences wound? In Mary's case there is clearly something problematic about her being given information and explanations that she was not mature enough to understand. This continued into her teenage years where she played an important role for her mother, standing in for her frequently absent father, and one that she was not entirely comfortable with:

> I was kind of a bit of a confidante to my Mum quite a lot of the time. I realize now growing up she'd told me quite a lot of things that really weren't for *young children* [interviewee emphasis] to hear to be honest. I think I was her company when my Dad wasn't there. She would take me into her confidence she'd chat to me about the things that *she really should've talked to her friend about* [author emphasis]. By the time I was fourteen I knew a lot of things probably fourteen year olds shouldn't know or should *ever* [interviewee emphasis] know really.

Mary doesn't specify what these things are, but it is clear that she was privy to information she was not mature enough to manage in her teenage years; this might also point to Laplanche's concerns about the unconscious messages about adult sexuality that are passed onto children in the normal routines of life and care (ibid.). Additionally, Mary states that her mother told her things as a "*young child*," suggesting that this adult information was being given to her much earlier. Information that should not "*ever* be known" might suggest a discomfort about knowledge of private details of the parental relationship, as this is unlikely to be shared with most children even as adults. As I have noted, this could also have emerged out of processes of fantasy about the inferred "facts" of parental sexuality, which would be suggestive of the need for the production of Screen Memories.

If we examine the language and tone of the memory of the scene from *The Birds* we can observe some of the characteristics of a Screen Memory against the primal scene. Mary walked in on her parents who were "engrossed" in something. It took them a few moments to realize she was there, and for them to then react by quickly jumping up and stopping what they were doing. This is strikingly similar to what would happen if a child walked in on its parents having sex. In Mary's case this is reinforced by the fact that she says she was "seven or eight," which would mean that one sister had already been born and the next had probably already been conceived. Curiosity about origins (put simply, "where babies come from") would have been significant for Mary at this time. She also notes that she had often been "sleepwalking" and had "done some strange wandering about at night" when she was a child. It is quite possible that there had been other occasions where she had become aware of her parents' sexuality, perhaps walking in on them having sex or hearing something in this regard, and the film moment becomes a Screen Memory for this. Within the Kleinian psychoanalytic tradition[7] it has been argued that children have instinctual knowledge of sexuality, and of a penis and vagina meeting, without the "actual witnessing of the primal scene" (Hinshelwood, 1989, p. 297). The memory produced infers something sexual and is often a combination of "things seen and heard but not understood" (Fletcher, 2013, p. 91). This is captured in Mary's statement that she *sensed* something without being able to fully comprehend or articulate its significance, and is suggestive of the need to return to the scene for translation (Laplanche, 1999). If we follow the psychoanalytic definition of trauma as "rupture"—creating a wound which affects the whole psychic organization (Fletcher, 2013, p. 127)—then it is clear that the result of parental sexuality (the birth of siblings) was traumatic for Mary, as she was displaced and a new family dynamic was created. A separation occurred which she did not fully come to terms with.

Lucy LaFarge (2015, p. 42) explains that "childhood trauma is often *visual*—the experience of something that is frightening that is seen." In Mary's memory of *The Birds* the acts of seeing and blinding are significant. Voyeurism in the cinema is theorized as a form of pleasurable looking which allows the spectator to engage safely in forms of *prohibited* looking. If this is a form of Screen Memory for Mary, then the image of the "woman" with her "pecked out" eyes signifies that she had seen (in reality or fantasy)—something that was forbidden and thus anxiety provoking; this might explain her "error" in remembering the details of the scene. This is based on the assumption that Mary identifies with the "lady" in the scene. Furthermore, it is significant that in Mary's particular narration of the scene the consequences of prohibited looking are that the viewer/ Mary herself has been punished with damage to the eyes. Freud (1919a, p. 139) notes that in children the fear of damage to or loss of the eyes is prevalent. He also notes "the study of dreams, fantasies and myths has taught us that anxiety about one's eyes and fear of going blind is quite often a substitute for the fear of castration" (ibid.). The quest for pro-scribed knowledge of origins and punishment for curiosity are central features of the Garden of Eden, Tower of Babel, and Oedipus myths, with blindness as the specific punishment in the latter (Grinberg, Sor, and Tabak de Bian-chedi, 1993). However, identification is more complex than straightforward gender correspondence. A reading of "A Child Is Being Beaten" (Freud, 1919b) shows that is it possible to have multiple identifications with characters and objects in a film scene (see also Cowie, 1997).

In this particular rearrangement of the scene, identification might also be with the attacking birds. In unconscious fantasy the "lady" might also be her mother, thereby acting as a form of wish fulfillment to kill and replace her mother in the Oedipal drama, which is not an uncommon fantasy. This re-narration of events, particularly the child ridding itself of a parent, is also common. It is a form of wish fulfillment emerging in relation to the common disappointments of childhood, such as perceived slights against the child by parents, and in particular having to share parents with siblings. The purpose of aggressive wish fulfillment is normal; it is an attempt in fantasy to "correct" real life, and is not a consequence of malevolent but rather of loving forces in the child (Freud 1909, pp. 38–39).

However, in this case the distress is also linked to the poor explanation of events by Mary's mother. It is possible to understand this with reference to the work of Wilfred Bion (1962) who has been instrumental in pointing to the "*two* person origin of the capacity to think and represent" (LaFarge 2015, p. 43, original emphasis). Bion points to the child's capacity for thought as a product of the way in which the emotional experiences of the child are man-aged by the mother/primary carer. Lafarge (2015, p. 43) adds that "the two-person quality of thinking is particularly important in traumatic experience as in trauma we lose the sense of being witnesses and along with that the sense that our experience has meaning." As we have seen in response to her fear, and to help her make sense of the film, Mary sought reassurance from her mother. For Bion (1962) the mother functions as a container for intoler-able feelings, fears, and frustrations which are projected onto her by the infant. Significantly, she not only *contains* them for the child but *mollifies* them and *returns* them back to the infant in a manageable form. As Mary explained, her mother was unable to contain or assuage her fears on this and also other occasions, often explaining things to her in adult terms. Mary explains how she coped with this: "what I did a lot of was to actually make up the rest of the story myself because I was quite shocked." Thus she was forced to construct her own meaning system, rearranging already existing filmic systems of signification into a personalized system of her own. Her mother, for whatever reason, was not able to adequately contain Mary's fears which remain stored in the viewing memory of this film. What is interesting and is a mark of Mary's resilience is that, left with no other option, she made the story and the particular moment safe by inserting it into a self-created narrative structure she could cope with.

The Singing Ringing Tree

Fairy tales and myths provide symbols for dreams in a range of psychic processes (Freud, 1919; Warner, 1995). *The Singing Ringing Tree* (Francesco Sefani, 1958), an Eastern European fantasy fairy story shown on British children's television in the 1960s and repeated in the 1970s and 1980s, is known to have frightened a generation of children.[8] However, I want to use Mary's case to suggest that we must look not just to the form and narrative of the text to understand why this is a scary program for children. The "fear," as in the case of *The Birds*, results from viewing the text within the reality of Mary's experiences which she could not fully comprehend. Her memories are the result of external reality and unconscious fantasy and are thus psychosocial.

Mary remembers the story featuring a handsome prince being changed into a bear. She links this to a persistent memory of being "terrified" at night in her bedroom where she would frequently see "a man changing into a bear from his feet up":

> A big man-sized bear who almost seemed like to the ceiling standing in my bedroom and he'd *always* (interviewee emphasis) be in the same place in the corner of my room. It was the process of metamorphosis that was frightening. He changed from the feet up. But that part of him was bear and part of him was man. And then the man bit disappeared and the *man* (author emphasis) bit arrived.

Here is an example of an interesting parapraxis, as there is some slippage between the bear and the man. In addition, this memory is associated with bedtime and suggests some possible conflation between waking and dreaming states. In the program the man disappears and is replaced by a bear but in Mary's narration the beast that is the end result of the metamorphosis is a man. There is some possible slippage between the bear and the man and both are frightening to Mary. Parapraxes are regarded as analogous to the dream as they also involve repression, displacement, condensation, and symbolization

(Freud, 1900, 1901). The story that Mary sets out consciously to tell mirrors something in the text (a man changing into a bear), but the slippages point to the confusion, as in Mary's dream the thing to be feared is a man who represents a beast. Thus these "errors," as I have suggested previously, are significant. I want to pursue an examination of the symbolism taken from the program, and its appearance in Mary's imaginary world, in the light of her awareness of adult sexuality precipitated by the birth of her siblings.

Historically, in fable and myth, bears have signified many things including sexual predators; they have also been associated with protective mothers, which would also seem pertinent with regard to Mary's current fears about her son (Warner, 1995; Dream Dictionary, 2015). In this memory Mary encounters a bear of whom she is afraid, and fear of bears in dreams is associated with troubled elements in waking life (Freud, 1900). Mary recognizes this, associating it with being "often distressed" and doing "extraordinary things" such as sleepwalking. Primal scene associations frequently feature beasts and fantasy creatures. Most notably, this is found in Freud's (1918) case of the *Wolfman* where he theorized the connection between trauma and the primal scene. Traditionally the bear is "the beast who walks like a man" (Warner, 1995, p. 301)[9] and in Freud's patient Wolfman it was not the wolf *per se* in his dream that generated fear, but rather the wolf's "standing upright and striding along," which related to his father's role in a primal scene.

I suggest it is plausible to link Mary's father to the bear, particularly as narrative events in *The Singing Ringing Tree* are set in motion by an absent father who then returns, and one of Mary's strongest memories of childhood is of spending time keeping her mother company because her father was frequently absent, being at work or in meetings. The fact that the bear changes from the feet up is another possible link to the primal scene, as this would be the way in which the scene would be encountered initially by the child before their presence is noticed. Note also that this position of a female at the bottom of a bed was how Mary remembered (inaccurately) the "lady" at the bottom of a bed with her eyes pecked out in *The Birds*. Freud analyzed the symbolism of feet in relation to sexuality, as the child will often experience looking at genitals from below before moving the gaze upwards. It has also been noted that there is a relationship between narratives involving animal bridegrooms, such as the bear, and the acceptance of sexuality (Warner, 1995; Bettelheim, 1976).

So far I have focused on issues around identity development, sexuality, and repression. However, I want to add that other developmental accomplishments also generate anxiety and unconscious fantasy. One such turbulent but developmental milestone is the relinquishment of omnipotence. At this stage of development, the child learns that the world and all the objects (people and things) in it are not under the infant's magical control, which is a feature of earliest life when the child is unable to differentiate between self and other[10] (see Hinshelwood, 1989; Winnicott, 1971). The anxieties around this are reactivated and intensified when an only child loses its status when siblings arrive.

Mary explains the narrative (which involved a prince being turned into a bear because he did not get back from a quest in the time specified by the magical Singing Ringing Tree. The princess was the only person who could reverse the transformation of the bear back into the hero Prince, but this could only be done with love and kindness) in the following terms: "The princess was spiteful and selfish and full of her own importance and the prince was very lovely and kind and he got turned into a bear. And she had to learn to love somebody other than herself." The omnipotent and narcissistic princess has to be displaced and learn to love somebody other than herself, which is another necessary developmental achievement but one that is also painful. Mary had been her father's "princess," and her centrality in the attention of both her parents is lost at this time due to the arrival of her siblings. She was presumably required also to love her siblings, which would have been difficult. This representation of the father-daughter relationship in popular culture often revolves around the idea of daughters as princesses or fantasy creatures such as fairies (Walkerdine, 1997). This narrative typically features a prince who fails to get back in time, as well as an absent father, rather like Mary's father who was often absent and late home. This prince, who was "lovely and kind," is condemned to remain a beast because of the self-centered actions of the princess who, as a consequence within the narrative, loses her beauty. The bear/prince tells her that this is because the animals see her "true" nature: selfish and spiteful. The princess has to learn humility and kindness in order for her outer beauty to return. Consequently, it can be asserted that the bear is also a reminder of her own omnipotent, destructive, and aggressive phantasies, possibly towards her much adored father, which in turn precipitated some guilt that is characteristic of the Kleinian depressive position[11] where the infant learns to feel concern for loved ones that they may have hurt or harbored destructive thoughts/ fantasies towards.

Vamik D. Volkan and Gabriele Ast (2014) have also argued that anxiety and conflict, caused specifically by sibling rivalry and the primal scene, can take a symbolized form, and it is common for this to be in the shape of animals and birds. In particular, the wounded birds seen in *The Birds* can be associated with separation from loved ones and concerns about errant offspring, both of which Mary was only too aware of at the time of the interviews as she feared for her son's happiness. It would be normal to feel narcissistically wounded at her replacement by another woman and fearful for his future. She remembers a powerful memory associated with her marriage which comes back to mind now she is facing the prospect of her son leaving to get married:

> I can remember the night before *I* got married. I remember hearing my Dad—you'll understand what I mean but the only word I can use is *howl*. It was a cry like an *animal*. And I can remember him just *sobbing* in his bedroom and me not daring to go in because I couldn't face it. [...] I understand how it was. Because often I find myself in tears when I think about him leaving, I know it's gonna break my heart when he goes.

Again there appears some interesting animal symbolism involving her father, in the form of what sounds like a wolf-like creature, and then her own inter-generational identification with this. This again suggests how fantasy beasts appear in Mary's personalized signification system that she returns to in situations of emotional turbulence.

Conclusion

A long-standing tradition of media research has been concerned with the "effects" of television on children, and the watching of material that is not age appropriate. In particular, television is always liable to be figured as a transgressive medium because of its location in the private sphere where it can never be fully regulated, and where the "watershed" remains something that can be ignored—even more so now in the age of on-demand television. My argument here is that "effects," or the fear and corresponding affect associated with a frightening text, must be understood psychosocially in relation to context and environment. Certainly "adult" texts will contain material that is frightening to children, but children's fairy stories are equally terrifying. In both cases it is important to recognize the *personalized* nature of fear and how particular television texts provide symbolic materials that chime with the normal, ordinary, and yet tumultuous life experiences of children. Children are able to take up and work with the symbolic materials the texts provide, and these must therefore be understood within the wider biographical context. This is something that a psychoanalytically informed method like FANI can facilitate. The complex imaginary work associated with *The Birds* and *The Singing Ringing Tree* can be seen in the context of negotiations made as part of normal psychosexual development that takes place in relation to unique family relationships and circumstances. In particular I note that the birth of siblings can, in particular sets of circumstances, set in motion momentous and traumatic changes in individual identity.

Roger Silverstone (1994) argued that the "box" was a pre-packaged complex communication of sound and image that makes powerful claims on reality and emotion. In this study I have explored the imaginative agency of the viewer and the psychic uses to which television can be put. Screen Memories are important as they are a special kind of representation, formed by individuals under the normal but immensely difficult strains of life, which at the time "might potentially overwhelm the individual and the capacity to make sense of experience" (LaFarge, 2015, p. 43). In this study the texts viewed on the television were taken up and used defensively for emotional survival. The memories are examples of this resilience that allowed Mary to handle emotional material that she was not mature enough to process, particularly when she could not always rely on her parents to offer her the explanation and reassurance she wanted. Thus television images, to use Mary's words, allowed her to "make up the story for herself" with the result that she was able to "escape the disaster of having been alone and helpless" (Guignard, 2015, p. 182). The interviews have allowed Mary in later life to explore her feelings of loss and in that sense, as Florence Guignard (2015, p. 183) has argued, we need not worry about the repressed nature of the content of Screen Memories because ultimately their most enduring qualities are that they enable the subject to produce a "tentative explanation" of their personal inner and outer worlds, which certainly seems clear from this case study. While we recognize that television memories are inevitably biographical, it is fascinating to explore what the nature of the biographical components of memory might be, and the role television provides as a psychosocial resource.

Postscript

Mary married a man who was the only son with six sisters. On their first child being a son they made the decision not to have any more children as they "didn't want to share him." Both shared such an antipathy to sisters that they didn't want to "inflict" siblings on him.

Notes

1. From Kate Morton's 2008 novel *The Forgotten Garden*, p. 128.
2. The ethics associated with the use of psychoanalytically informed methods I have explored elsewhere, see Whitehouse-Hart (2012, 2014).
3. This was a study of 12 in-depth biographical interviews with white working class British men and women aged between 29–65.
4. Free Association Narrative Interview is an interview method that is informed by the psychoanalytic principle of Free Association. Open questions are designed which generate narratives about specific events and experiences, with the assumption that these narratives will be more revealing of the emotional relevance than a generalized account. In this study the request was "tell me about … favourite films and television programmes…. And anything that comes to mind." "The principle of Free Association is based on the idea that it is the unconsciously motivated links between ideas rather than just their contents, which provide insight into the emotional meanings of interviewees' accounts. Therefore, it is particularly appropriate for exploring questions about interviewees' identities or that touch emotions and personal experiences" (Hollway and Jefferson in Lewis-Beck et al., 2004, p. 56).

5. Notable studies which place "scenes" at the center of trauma were analyzed by Freud; for example Oedipus, Leonardo's Dream, Hamlet, Wolf Man's dream.

6. I have presumed that to a young child the perception was the "middle of the night," but this is likely to have been 10 or 11 o'clock.

7. For an introduction to this school of thought see Melanie Klein Trust http://www.melanie-klein-trust.org.uk/ and Hinshelwood (1989).

8. The program was voted 20th spookiest program of all time by the *Radio Times* readers' poll in 2004. See also Denofgeek (2015) Scariest Kids TV Show: available: http://www.denofgeek.com/tv/19267/the-singing-ringing-tree-scariest-kids-tv-show-ever. (Accessed April 5, 2015).

9. Mary also explained that she was often terrified as she was convinced she could see snakes in her bedroom. Freudian theory would also link this with sexuality.

10. For accessible introductions see: http://www.melanie-klein-trust.org.uk/paranoid-schizoid-position.

11. The Depressive Position is a mental assemblage that occurs in early childhood but which continues to occur throughout adult life. It is characterized by realization of aggressive and hateful fears and phantasies about loved objects (usually parents) which generates feelings of guilt and concern for the other. This is felt to be a developmentally mature position as in earlier life the child is only concerned with survival of the self (see Melanie Klein Trust, 2015).

REFERENCES

Bettelheim, B. (1976) *The Uses of Enchantment: The Meaning and Importance of Fairy Tales*. New York: Random House.

Bion, W. R. (1962) (1984 edition) *Learning From Experience*. London: Karnac.

Bollas, C. (1992) *Being a Character: Psychoanalysis and Self Experience*. London: Routledge.

Cowie, E. (1997) *Representing the Woman: Cinema and Psychoanalysis*. Basingstoke: Palgrave Macmillan.

Denofgeek (2015) Scariest Kids TV Show. http://www.denofgeek.com/tv/19267/the-singing-ringing-tree-scariest-kids-tv-show-ever. (Accessed April 5, 2015).

Dream Dictionary (2015) www.dreamdictionary.org. (Accessed April 2, 2015).

Elliott, P. (1974) Uses and Gratifications Research: A Critique and a Sociological Alternative. In: Blumer, J. G. and Katz, E. (eds.) *The Uses of Mass Communications*. London: Sage, pp. 249–68.

Erikson, E. (1959) *Identity and the Life Cycle*. London: W.W. Norton.

Fletcher, J. (2013) *Freud and the Scene of Trauma*. New York: Fordham University Press.

Freud, S. (1899) (2003 edition) *Screen Memories*. Trans. by McLintock, D. *Sigmund Freud The Uncanny*. London: Penguin.

_____. (1900) *The Interpretation of Dreams*. Trans. by Strachey, J. first published in *The Standard Edition of the Complete Works of Sigmund Freud Vol IV and V* Hogarth Press (1991 edition). London: Penguin.

_____. (1901) (2002 edition) *The Psychopathology of Everyday Life*. Trans. by Bell, A. *Sigmund Freud The Psychopathology of Everyday Life*. London: Penguin Books.

_____. (1909) (2003 edition) *Family Romance*. Trans. McLintock, D. *Sigmund Freud The Uncanny*. London: Penguin.

_____. (1918) (1991 edition) From the history of infantile neurosis. *Standard Edition of the Complete Works of Sigmund Freud Vol xvii*. London: Penguin.

_____. (1919a) (2003 edition) *The Uncanny*. Trans. by McLintock, D. *Sigmund Freud The Uncanny*. London: Penguin.

_____. (1919b) *A Child Is Being Beaten: A Contribution to the Study of the Origin of Sexual Perversion* in 2013 edition Person, E. S. (ed.) *On Freud's A Child Is Being Beaten*. London: Karnac.

_____. (2011) *Three Essays on the Theory of Sexuality* Trans. James Strachey. New York: Martino Fine.

Grinberg, L. Sor, D. and Tabak de Bianchedi, E. (1993) *New Introduction to the Work of Bion*. New York: Jason Aronson.

Guignard, F. (2015) Screen Memories Today: A Neuropsychoanalytic Essay of Definition. In: Reed, G. S. and Levine, H. B. (eds.) *On Freud's "Screen Memories,"* pp. 172–85.

Hawke, C. and Alister, I. (2001) *Jung and Film*. East Sussex: Brunner-Routledge.

Hinshelwood, R. D. (1989) *A Dictionary of Kleinian Thought*. London: Free Association.

Hollway, W. and Jefferson, T. (2000) *Doing Qualitative Research Differently Free Association, Narrative and the Interview Method*. London: Sage.

_____. (2004) Free Association Interviewing. In: Lewis-Beck, M. S., Bryman, A. and Futing-Liao, T. (eds.) *The Sage Encyclopedia of Social Science Research Methods Volume 1*. London: Sage.http://dx.doi.org/10.4135/9781412950589. (Accessed June 12, 2015).

Kegan, P. (2002) Introduction. In: *Sigmund Freud: The Psychopathology of Everyday Life*. London: Penguin Classic, pp. vii–xlii.

LaFarge, L. (2015) The Screen Memory and the Act of Remembering. In: Reed, G. S. and Levine, H. B. (eds.) *On Freud's "Screen Memories."* London: Karnac, pp. 36–57.

Laplanche, J. (1992) Notes on Afterwardsness. trans. M. Stanton. In: Fletcher, J. and Stanton, M. (eds.) *Jean Laplanche: Seduction, Translation, Drives*. London: ICA, pp. 217–23.

_____. (1999) Notes on Afterwardsness. In: Laplanche, J. (ed.) *Essays on Otherness*. London: Routledge, pp. 260–6.

Lapsley, R. and Westlake, M. (1988) *Film Theory*. Manchester: Manchester University Press.

Melanie Klein Trust (2015) http://www.melanie-klein-trust.org.uk/depressive-position. (Accessed April 4, 2015).

Modleski, T. (1982) *Loving with a Vengeance: Mass Produced Fantasies for Women*. Hamden, CT: Shoestring Press.

Morton, K. (2008) *The Forgotten Garden: A Novel*. New York: Atria.

Mitchell, J. (2003) *Siblings, Sex and Violence*. Cambridge: Polity/ Blackwell.

Perelberg, R. J. (2008) *Time Space and Phantasy*. London: Routledge.

Rosenbaum, M. (1998) Childhood "Screen Memories" are they forgotten? *Psychosomatics*, 39 (1): pp. 68–71.

Silverstone, R. (1994) *Television and Everyday Life*. London: Routledge.

Sutton, P. (2004) Afterwardsness in Film. *Journal For Cultural Research*, 8 (3) pp. 385–405.

Volkan, V. D. and Ast, G. (2014) *Siblings in the Unconscious and Psychopathology*. London: Karnac.

Walkerdine, V. (1997) *Daddy's Girl: Young Girls and Popular Culture*. Basingstoke: Macmillan.

Warner, M. (1995) *From the Beast to the Blonde: On Fairy Tales and Their Tellers*. London: Random House.

Winnicott, D. (1971) *Playing and Reality*. London: Routledge.
Whitehouse-Hart, J. (2012) Surrendering to the Dream: An Account of the Unconscious Dynamics of a Research Relationship. *Journal of Research Practice*, 8 (2).
_____. (2014) *Psychosocial Explorations of Film and Television Viewing: Ordinary Audience*. Basingstoke: Palgrave Macmillan.

"Whispers of escapades out on the 'D' train"

The Entangled Visions of Cindy Sherman's Untitled Film Stills

VANESSA LONGDEN

"More photographs than bricks"

In 1976, critic and curator John Szarkowski wrote, "The world now contains more photographs than bricks, and they are, astonishingly, all different" (Szarkowski, paragraph 6, 1976; 2002). The camera as a documentary tool for recording the changing physical and cultural landscape became more ubiquitous. By 1976, America had experienced the loss of Diane Arbus, whose photographs inspired a whole new photographic interest in the unusual American life—"in life at the margins not usually represented in mainstream publications—life beyond the margins of Life" (Goldberg, 1999, p. 156). The likes of Danny Lyon's *The Bikeriders* (1968), Bill Owens' *Suburbia* (1973), and in the 1980s, Nan Goldin's *The Ballad of Sexual Dependency* (1986) were just some of the contributors to this peripheral perspective. Their subjects were brought to the fore from the margins of society in the midst of vast political, social, and cultural transformation. By the late 1970s mass media was challenged by counter culture, while performance and cinematic representation made impressions on some artistic practices and academic literature. Postmodernism entered the aesthetic discourse and challenged the traditional conventions of modernism; disciplines and visions melded and fragmented, challenging society's conventions and offering multiple perspectives on everyday life.

American photography critic and historian Vicki Goldberg spoke of post-modernism's influence on photographic practice: "Photography, once hailed as the great conveyor [of] truth and reality, was now said to have replaced reality itself […]. There were said to be no more authors, no true creators, no single dominant ethos, only pastiches of the past […]. The separation of culture into high and low was now regarded as just another instance of one class asserting its authority over another" (Goldberg, 1999, p. 204). By the 1980s Cindy Sherman was situated as an iconic feminist artist. She was hailed as a proponent of women's experience due to both her success in photography and her association with film. In his publication *Race, Sex, and Gender in Contemporary Art*, Edward Lucie-Smith called Sherman "the most celebrated feminist artist working in the United States" (1994, p. 156).

The "second wave" of the Women's Movement peaked in the late 1960s and early 1970s. The organization aided the development of feminist discourses, centering upon the importance of communicating women's experiences and their everyday lives. Women were no longer solely defined by the domestic sphere; their occupations, sexuality, beliefs, and aspirations were also intrinsic to their identities.[1] Here political conclusions were made from personal realities. The movement sought to improve women's place in society through judicial interventions and legislation. There was a growing dissatisfaction among some women over gender disparities regarding equal pay for equal work, the lack of opportunities to advance within the workplace as well as issues over racism, sexual harassment, domestic violence, and societal expectations over child-rearing. The Equal Pay Act was passed in 1963, the same year that American physicist, Maria Goeppert-Mayer, won a Nobel Prize. She was the second female laureate after Marie Curie. Lesley Gore's hit song "You Don't Own Me" (1963) climbed the charts and in the same year Betty Friedan published *The Feminine Mystique* (1963). The influential work sold five million copies by 1970 and was one of many contributions towards the modern feminist movement. The author described the boredom of the American housewife as "the problem that [had] no name," which "burst like a boil" (Friedan, 1965, p. 7) through the happy yet narrow image that was imposed upon her. Friedan and other feminists went on to found The National Organization for Women (NOW) in 1966, which sought to end sexual discrimination through legislative lobbying, litigation, and public demonstrations. In 1968, the New York Radical Women assemblage protested the Miss America Pageant in Atlantic City on sexist grounds. By the end of the '60s, more than 80 percent of wives of childbearing age were using contraception after the federal government approved the birth control pill in 1960. This not only gave women a choice of when or whether she wanted to start a family, but crucially enabled her control over her own body (Walsh, 2010).

The discursive feminist action pursued by Sherman's proponents contrasted the tangible change sought by the Women's Movement.[2] By taking patriarchal discourse as their subject of investigation, these writers and critics sought to question, challenge, and disrupt traditional narratives and representations. The latter was the key to women's oppression and their emancipation. Moving from the physical materiality of the body, Laura Mulvey (1991) has expanded upon the idea of bodily expression. She believed a new conceptual vocabulary was required to express the relationship between body politics and its politics of representation. Similarly, Teresa de Lauretis (1984) described women's experience as a process through which all social beings are subjectively constructed and expressed. "Experience" is not used in the individualistic sense of "something belonging to one and exclusively her own even though others might have 'similar' experiences" (de Lauretis, 1984, p. 159). Instead, de Lauretis argues that subjectivity is an ongoing process of development, and "not a fixed point of departure or arrival from which one then interacts with the world" (de Lauretis, 1984, p. 159). Another way to express this alternative vocabulary was through taking up the camera. Images like Sherman's continue to play an integral part in structuring and shaping society, building our physical surroundings and saturating the everyday environment.

Sherman's *Untitled Film Stills* (1977–80) features 69 images in which the artist herself appears as characters influenced by the post-war black and white film heroines from the 1940s and '50s. Sherman was born into a media-rich world and chose to be her own subject as artist, model, and film-star combined. It has been argued that Sherman consciously repositioned these figures in an attempt to subvert the male gaze and challenge the historically-imposed social category of the "feminine." Mulvey's renowned essay, "Visual Pleasure and Narrative Cinema" (1975), remains significant. While the gaze attempts to pin down and objectify the subject through voyeuristic desire, Sherman has been said to resist the classification by dictating how she wants to be seen. In front of the camera, Sherman metamorphoses from various female stereotypes—from heroine to femme fatale, from housewife to schoolgirl, and so on—depicting the everywoman in mass media. These transformations not only allow her to refuse fixity but also to stipulate that she wants to be seen in numerous ways, while blurring the boundary between fiction and reality. Meanwhile, in "The Discourse of Others: Feminists and Postmodernism" Craig Owens (1983) has positioned Sherman as a postmodern feminist. Examining the *Untitled Film Stills*, Owens believes that semiotically, each of Sherman's characters signifies male desire and does not have a voice outside of that representation. To say *Untitled Film Stills* are about the objectification of women is too simplistic: that is only a part of their intrigue. Visually, compositionally, and culturally, there is much more beyond the confines of the male gaze. While the knowledge of Owens' interpretation is largely known and accepted, it is also very much of its time.[3]

Her Products and Projections

Sherman's photographs were and will continue to be used as critical devices prompting questions about sexual difference and the visual representation of women. Images are not necessarily inscribed with a message. Instead they assume[4] the cultural and political ideologies of their viewers, and, consequently, "meaning" is also subjective and multifaceted. The borrowing, exchanging, and re-interpretation of material culture are the only ways in which new perspectives can be achieved on that which is deemed to be familiar. As for Sherman's work, it ultimately came at the right time: the *Untitled Film Stills* absorbed the influences which saturated Sherman's era. They exhibited a mediated past to onlookers which simultaneously did and did not exist in the minds of a collective cultural consciousness. A feminist stance was apparently not Sherman's original intention; she has spoken of her artistic process, admitting that she had no films in mind at all when staging the *Film Stills*. She merely saw it as an opportunity to "get dressed up" and experiment with different costumes and styles while questioning a woman's character in light of socio-cultural and media expectations. At the time she was wrestling with her own understanding of women. Sherman attempted to understand their levels of artifice and jumbles of ambiguity, of being torn between societal expectations of being "natural" or "getting dressed up" (Respini, 2012, p. 30).

"Representation," as described by Judith Butler, is a double-edged sword:

> representation serves as the operative term within a political process which seeks to extend visibility and legitimacy to women as political subjects; on the other hand, representation is the normative function of language which is said either to reveal or distort what is assumed to be true about the category of women. For feminist theory, the development of a language that fully or adequately represents women has seemed necessary to foster the political visibility of women. This has seemed obviously important considering the pervasive cultural condition in which women's lives were either misrepresented or not represented at all [Butler, 1990, p. 1].

While the *Untitled Film Stills* are static, their interpretations are not. It is therefore imperative to revisit these photographs and challenge existing perspectives of these mediated pasts.[5] According to Cruz (1997), "Sherman never considered these outings 'performances' in an artistic sense because she was not maintaining a character" but simply "getting dressed up to go out" (Cruz, 1997, p. 1). Cruz's use of the term "outings" followed by "performances" is interesting, as these words trigger associations to gender performativity, homosexuality, and of potential revelation or exposure—of "coming out" to society. Conversely, and in contrast to Owens, Kuspit (1988) does not see Sherman's work as feminist but suggests her work is pre-gendered. Sherman "shows the disintegrative condition of the self as such, the self before it is firmly identified as male or female" (Kuspit, 1988, p. 395). Yet gender is a "phenomenon that is being produced all the time and reproduced all the time [...]. We act and walk and speak and talk in ways that consolidate an impression of being a man or being a woman" (Butler, 2011). Thus, Butler states, there are no pre-existing identities. Rather, our gender identities are stipulated through institutionalized and routinized social practices and ideologies: gender is a performative construct. Similarly, Waters (2012) draws parallels between Sherman's characters and a drag act, from which she strives to keep a certain level of detachment: "I take [the picture] out if it looks too much like me," says Sherman. "Generally I feel somehow removed from the characters, but sometimes they do sort of hit too close to home, where it just seems like me on a bad day" (Sherman interviewed by Waters, 2012, p. 73).

Sherman is one we recognize but do not really know, whether as B-movie heroines, historical figures, and more recently the stuff of sardonic nightmares: surrealistic clowns and fairy tales gone wrong. The artist's work has been classed as too abstruse: it does not say or reveal anything and is merely "empty entertainment." Speaking of her 2012 retrospective at the Museum of Modern Art (MoMA), New York, American art critic Lance Esplund writes that here, "ambiguity is mistaken for art. Revealing virtually nothing in her photographs, Sherman turns self-portraiture on its head" (Esplund, 2012). Sherman has always subverted traditional self-portraiture in that it has neither been herself nor her face that she has portrayed (if she shows her face at all). Here it is important to question why "artistic revelation," "clarity," and "authenticity" are so important to the viewer in addition to who orders and prioritizes these values.[6] The problem extends to "viewership expectation" in contrast to "actuality"—what viewers want to take from an image as opposed to what they actually receive, which are more questions than answers—the latter are entangled in the desire for authenticity. Spectators want to know more but end up knowing less—or what they end up knowing is not what they expected to learn—and that is unsettling because not only does it suggest that there is no singular or unitary "truth" to be taken from an image, but it destabilizes the notion of "reality" itself and what spectators expect from it. The faces Cindy Sherman portrays to society are not the only ones which cover contradictions and multiplicities. Everything is open to critique.

The Vital Lie

Sherman's offering of so many characters undermines this attempt to fix her image according to our desires, Judith Williamson (1983) argues.[7] While words like "characters" or "subject" replace that of "the individual" in poststructuralist discourse, their usage reduces the idea of human agency.[8]

Moira Gatens and other feminists have quite rightly asserted that there is no one body; the body is an illusion. Sherman brought the fragility of identity into focus, highlighted its continual development, and challenged its (mis)-representation: that "the self" existed as a single unitary entity, a notion which endorsed the Western enlightened liberal subject and the "superiority" of the male rational mind over the "natural" and debased feminine body. Descartes' "logical" subject and woman's one-dimensional representation are decentralized by the sheer number and variety of Sherman's images which offer a multidimensional portrayal of woman instead. Sherman's transient characters allow the artist expression: she is at once all of these women and none of them, as the status of "woman" is not all encompassing or universally recognized (Gatens, 1991). "Woman" itself is a contested category which not only raises the question of what terminology we are to use in its place but also demonstrates that identities are temporarily "occupied" and are never fully "owned." While Cruz believes this is the nostalgic allure of the *Untitled Film Stills*—that viewers' desire "for the woman depicted as well as desire to be that woman, during that time" (Cruz, 1997, p. 4)—the problem, as Butler argues, is that "the presumed universality and unity of the subject of feminism is effectively undermined by the constraints of the representational discourse in which it functions" (Butler, 1990, p. 4). Women are trapped within their own idea of representation. Sherman's work exemplifies this and her lack of fixity applies not only to her art-form but to the notion of desire itself. We cannot fix Sherman to our desires, as Williamson states, partly because desire itself is not fixed. It is a constant projection which bathes the surface of forms and spaces. Desire clings for the briefest of moments before flitting away, and never penetrates: it is always elsewhere. Our detachment from these images and the anticipation of their possession fuels longing for the object in question. If the viewer were offered a definitive reading of Sherman's images, then desire for them would be extinguished; whether one would return to her images is then open to debate. These are mediated times which never actually existed; the photograph may exceed the limits of fantasies but by framing these scenes all Sherman is left with are reproducible interruptions: uncanny images dislocated from time.[9]

Sherman's work as postmodern may also be argued in terms of components. However, there is a danger here of not only interpreting postmodernism as a "pick and mix" theory—from which elements can be adopted and others discarded—but also of viewing Sherman's work as fragmented. The artist once commented, "I divide myself into many different parts. My self in the country [is one part] […]. My professional self is another, and my work self in the studio is another" (Sherman, 2003b, p. 7). The trouble is that the notion of fragmentation connotes shattering, violent breakage, and damage. Writing on psychoanalysis, trauma, and testimony, Suzette Henke argues in *Shattered Subjects* that women have often used writing in order to heal the wounds of psychological trauma. She refers to Shoshana Felman's argument that "a surrogate transferential process can take place through the scene of writing that allows the author to envisage a sympathetic audience and to imagine a public validation of his or her life testimony" (Henke, 1998, p. xxi). This extends Freud's initial suggestion that it takes two to witness the unconscious. The act of writing and the production of the written piece replaces the other witness and transforms the unconscious into a conscious testimony. Henke refers to this as the act of "scriptotherapy," which enables women to write out trauma as well as write through traumatic experiences as a process of therapeutic re-enactment. As Henke writes, "authorial effort to reconstruct a story of psychological debilitation could offer potential for mental healing" (ibid.), yet this desired outcome cannot be ensured.

Unlike Henke, I am skeptical that narrative recovery in any textual form ensures healing. Henke's belief that "the process of writing out or writing through traumatic experience in the mode of therapeutic re-enactment," to "heal the wounds of psychological trauma" (Henke, 1998) implies that woman is a fragmented (shattered) figure and needs to be "fixed"—in both senses of the word: mended and anchored—to a prior state. While autobiography offers a system of control it is rooted in the phallocentric notion of self-unity and wholeness; this "prior state" resides within the parameters of Lacan's Mirror Stage, that which is formative to the construction of "the self" (otherwise known as "je" or the I). Lacan argues that the human subject is always divided from the outset. The child's recognition of itself in the mirror is but a series of méconnaissances (misrecognitions) of a unified ego. The image of the I is empty and is only established by an imposed language, a language which Luce Irigaray argues serves only the male subject. Women have no alternative language with which to articulate themselves and are therefore un-representable. This subjectivity is formed and reformed continuously through thought and speech, but "in order to function as an effective being in the world, one must necessarily cling to this Lacanian mensonge vitale ('vital lie') as an enabling myth of coherent identity, despite its status as a fictional construct" (Henke, 1998, p. xvi). The vital lie, Henke argues, places the woman writer at the center of her own story, recast as the protagonist. But if this myth is constituted in a language she did not choose, how would her self-articulation be any more fulfilling than that of a mythic, fragmented, or ventriloquized subject who adopted a male discourse?

Historical Imaginings

The viewer adopts the position of the camera when they witness a woman walking down a dimly lit street. The character turns her coat collar against the wind and her gaze lies slightly off-center beyond the borders of the frame. Her platinum blonde hair is swept back, skimming her jawline in loose waves. It frames her face, an iridescent halo against the depth of night. She could resemble a Hitchcock heroine or even Marilyn Monroe; either way, the blonde wig "seem[s] very actressy" (Sherman, 2003b, p. 9). But *Untitled Film Still #54* is just one of many semblances. "People have told me they remember the film that one of my images is derived from," Sherman said in an interview, "but in fact I had no film in mind at all." It is with this knowledge that spectatorship of Sherman's images becomes unclear. If there ever was a line between fiction and reality it has since blurred. Remembrance becomes contested and the viewer is faced with the startling realization that we may know nothing after all. What they merely possess is an illusion of knowing (Jones, 2002). Henri Cartier-Bresson believed that "movies tell a story visually. Photography is an immediate reaction, drawing a meditation" (Cartier-Bresson, 2004, p. 45). But with Sherman these categories are indistinguishable: the photographer composed her characters and surroundings, arranged props, applied make-up, and recorded their development. Viewers are given a story which may be more akin to rumor—a snippet of conversation—than a linear narrative, and it is reflected upon during the editing process. These moments can be likened to interims, pauses or "prolonged encounters" in time and history (Proust, 1925).

But this is purely subjective: no actual film took place. Sherman's photographs are the outcome of a production which never existed, staged mediations which the artist planned in advance. "I'd carry around a suitcase full of wigs and costumes," Sherman told John Waters (2012, p. 70), "planning the characters in advance, going behind a dumpster to change, then yelling to Helene [Winer] or Robert [Longo] to start shooting. I would just do a few poses" (ibid.). These images transcend time and assume significance from those who view them. Amelia Jones describes this as a technology of embodiment, where the viewer re-connects with the image's depth by assigning meaning in light of our own time. This self-superimposure alters the tense of the photograph from the "having been" into the "not yet" of future possibilities (Jones, 2002). But time increases the ambiguity of events, actuality is blurred and there is a sense of lingering nostalgia, despite Sherman's movement and transformations. The uneasiness is not that viewers may not be able to distinguish an "objective truth," but that they are left with an image which becomes one of many (un)truths.[10] Just because these images are part of a historical imagining does not mean they are any less relevant or untrue. While "Marilyn [Monroe's masquerade] was like a trademark [which] had to always be absolutely identical [as] an instantly recognizable sign of 'Marilyn-ness'" (Mulvey, 1991, p. 149), the thought of Monroe stooping behind a dumpster to change diminishes the nostalgic glamour of the film star. But it also makes the thought of her more accessible.

The over-staginess of Sherman's images is enhanced by their lack of captions or descriptive titles. The images are untitled and numbered but do not follow a sequential order. The viewer is not dictated by the written word but by a visual language which opens up the possibility of multiple readings and interpretations. These are snapshots of anonymous moments which could be applicable to anyone in any location. While the artist captures an instant suspended in time, her images are just as much about the thought of what came before and after the single frame. Sherman's images are not only familiar because of the cultural connotations viewers assign to them but also due to the photographic techniques employed and the place in which they are set. All interior shots up until 1979 were taken in her apartment on John and South Street in Lower Manhattan and she rarely used flash, instead opting for regular electric light bulbs screwed into clip lights—nothing fancy but rather understated. Other images were taken outside on the streets and alleyways of New York City, or submerged in water where the body physically disappears. Sherman used strong chemicals and a high development time to achieve the images' "cheap" grainy quality, this prolonged process does not correlate with suggestions that her work is superficial. Careful thought went into the composition and production of her images yet her effort and lengthy developmental practice are not accounted for by her critics. What goes on behind the scenes of the *Untitled Film Stills* is overlooked.

Framed by the hazy backdrop of New York skyscrapers stands the figure of *Untitled Film Still #21*. The building's façades are clothed by geometric shadows and stretch beyond the frame. The camera tilts upwards, adding to the dizzying depth, creating an almost overwhelming claustrophobia. Yet it is the figure that dominates and focuses the gaze; she is too close and almost upon the viewer. She invades the viewer's personal space, like a crisp paper cut-out montaged against the dissolving buildings. The viewer finds themselves looking past her, above her, to the small square of open sky. The image is reliant on subject-centric lighting and the camera's low angle gives the sense of a panning close-up shot—frozen in the midst of action, the viewer is uncertain of the image's preceding or subsequent moments. Here, Sherman's film still physically deconstructs the notion of a traditional narrative.[11] The viewer is uncertain of what they are witnessing due to the extreme focus on the character's face in addition to the lack of identifiable landmarks around her. These factors add to the intensity of the image and emphasize the character's anxious gaze—which viewers presume is a reaction to something or someone beyond the border of the frame.

Like the majority of Sherman's film stills, this is reminiscent of Film Noir and the French New Wave films of Jean-Luc Godard. This, in Roland Barthes' (1977) words, is my studium. The studium is an element of the image which draws the viewer to look upon it and through looking they become implicated. It is an "enthusiastic commitment" (Barthes, 1977, p. 146) which requires little effort or interaction other than observation. In contrast, the punctum is the detail which "pierces," "pricks" or "wounds" the viewer, it is an element that demands attention and evokes an emotional response. When facing *Film Still #21*, I recall the actress Jean Seberg playing Patricia Franchini in Godard's film, *Breathless* (1960), and assume a Jean-Paul Belmondo–esque character lies off screen. In the film, Belmondo plays the role of Michel Poiccard, but incidentally mimics the mannerisms of 1940s actor, Humphrey Bogart (*Casablanca*, Michael Curtiz 1942 and *The Big Sleep*, Howard Hawks, 1946).[12] Compositionally, there is a similarity between Sherman in *Film Still #21* and Seberg in the closing scene of *Breathless*, but it is due to the shooting technique as opposed to exact resemblance or mimicry. The close proximity of the heroines and their wistful expressions, the contrast of light on dark and the grey areas in between, or even the disparity of space which is captured wide open, or restricting the gaze and confining the figure to the edges of the frame. Sherman's and Patricia's isolation and self-reflexivity is emphasized in bewildering vastness or enclosed space but nowhere in between. Of course, by this point in *Breathless* Patricia has picked up Michel's habit—of touching his lips with his thumb—a mannerism again borrowed from Bogart. What we have are entangled associations: Seberg playing Patricia emulating Michel played by Belmondo mimicking Bogart; and of Sherman, who may or may not have been consciously imitating them all.[13]

The fact is that Sherman and the characters of *Breathless* are self-conscious. They are all too aware of themselves, their presentation—both Patricia and Michel are aware of their physical appearance throughout the film—and of their limitations. Michel considered himself the suave American gangster until he lost his cool and killed a police officer while the aspiring journalist, Patricia, doubts her own loyalties to Michel once she learns of the incident. By focusing on the artist's physical location, Sherman successfully transcends both her physical appearance and limitations as her appearances become palpable and increasingly believable. While Tschumi believes bodies have always set limits in architecture and space, manipulating and dictating their function, images, people, and the spaces they inhabit (or are enticed to) are not static. They are all receptive and transform through time and geographical space. We are always beyond ourselves, living in retrospect of what has been or what may develop: of what I have done or what I am going to do. Surroundings will adapt and blur once the body leaves its space, just like the edge-lands where reality meets fiction or the borders of a photographic frame.

Interestingly, if one were to type Sherman's name into Google Images, *Untitled Film Still #21* is the first image one would encounter. We do not see an image of Sherman herself until the 16th image. Her creations absorb the attention away from the artist; it may not be such a paradox that she retains her privacy through her own exhibition. Photographers and their images are the mirrors and mouthpieces of society and the built environment witnesses their expressions. Exploring the photograph as a site of (dis)location and investigating its influence on the photographer is integral to understanding her expression. Amelia Jones was correct when she said "much ink has been spilled over Cindy Sherman," (Jones, 2002, p. 33) but I would add that it is rarely over the places in which she locates herself. Aside from Sherman's numerous characters and ambiguity, her refusal to be tied down is perhaps the most interesting aspect of her work, of where she chooses to place herself. Doreen Massey has argued in her publication *Space, Place and Gender* that "gender has been deeply influential in the production of 'the geographical'" (Massey, 1994, p. 177). But this is deeper than a dualistic relationship between body and space, it is a field in constant fluctuation and re-development. When recounting Sherman's performative identity and its extended movement across and between varying articulations of social relations, the symbolics of space must also be considered. Multiplicities, self-expression, and social relations cannot be created in isolation.

Burning in Space

To look at Sherman's stereotypes as a collective opposed to isolated snapshots is not enough either. Space must also be accounted for as it "give[s] us the flexibility to capture all the multiple dimensions of subjectivity, while also providing the means of theorizing subjective mutability" (Kirby, 1996, p. 154). Kirby continues, "We plot ourselves a destination, and inevitably find ourselves caught up in following the very outline we thought delimited ourselves" (1996, p. 154). Similar to identity, space and the structures which inhabit it are open to reinterpretation. Places have their own cultural identities and hold many histories. Bodies fluctuate in relation with space, the boundaries of which are never fixed. They constantly shift, but do not necessarily accommodate one another. As Longhurst writes: "Bodies and spaces construct each other in complex and nuanced ways. It is impossible to talk about bodies without talking about space, and vice versa. Bodies are performed, resisted, disciplined and oppressed not simply in but through space" (Longhurst, 2005, p. 93).[14] Spaces and their inhabitants are flexible sites; space envelops, manipulates, and adapts. Even in mediated worlds concrete offers little stability.

For Sherman, interior personal space and external physical spaces meld to become work spaces and dreamscapes, sites of creativity and experimentation. Her characters and their surroundings feed off and grow into one another. In Trinh T. Minh-ha's words: "The work space and the space of creation is where she confronts and leaves off at the same time a world of named nooks and corners, of street signs and traffic regulations, of beaten paths and multiple masks, of constant intermeshing with other bodies'—that are also her own—needs, assumptions, prejudices, and limits" (Minh-ha, 1991, p. 26). Here, the numerous spaces of work and creation, the physical, imagined, named and un-named intersect and entangle to create a rich and diverse setting; despite the chaos of the city and the elements which mark it—the street signs, regulations, everyday monuments (of worship and orientation), and the many bodies—there is a sense of (in)organic cohabitation. So place becomes just as important as the characters who prescribe the notion of societal and artistic performance. The built environment may be enacted upon but it is also enacted within. For this reason, it is not a stage, as these performances of everyday life are simultaneously engrained within the city's physical structure, but their execution can also be fleeting or unconscious. Encapsulating architectural weight is a difficult task, especially in images. Tschumi (1996) writes that "there is no way to perform architecture in a book" (Tschumi, 1996, p. 93) because architecture "is not a dream (a stage where society's or the individual's unconscious desires can be fulfilled). It cannot satisfy your wildest fantasies, but it may exceed the limits set by them" (Tschumi, p. 96). In this sense, the photograph is no different, as it always highlights a lack, the trace of an absence which can never be fully retrieved. But it is also a site of possibilities. What Sherman creates is an imaginary paper space: an image. Her collection is a series of geometrically self-contained spaces that are simultaneously strange and familiar. By moving beyond the framed figures viewers acknowledge that the

> fragments of architecture (bits of walls, of rooms, of streets, of ideas) are all one actually sees. These fragments are like beginnings without end. There is always a split between fragments that are real and fragments that are virtual, between memory and fantasy. These splits have no existence other than being the passages from one fragment to another. They are relays rather than signs. They are traces. They are in-between [Tschumi, 1996, p. 95].

The viewer finds themselves constantly in-between images. Both space and "architecture play[s] the seducer" (Tschumi, 1996, p. 90). They entice the artist and draw her in to pause and pose, and these sites become pregnant with ideas and inspiration as well as people. And the outcomes, the images, entice the viewer to look differently. They are invited to question its representations of body boundaries and how one (un)consciously presents and conducts oneself. But also how they themselves interact with the built environment and with its images. Photographs are microcosms of the artist's envisioning and these mediations constantly change, challenge, and exceed the onlooker's expectations with subsequent revisits. "Though all kinds of theoretical interpretations have been applied to Sherman's work over the years," writes Phillips, "what remains are her searing images that continue to burn in our memory years after they were made" (cited in Sherman, 2003a, p. 41).

Dark Side of the Road

But what comes around goes around. Despite the sense of lingering nostalgia, Sherman has moved with the times. The artist ended the film series in 1980 when she began to duplicate some of the stereotypes and realized that the work "was looking a little too fashionable" (Sherman, 2003b, p. 16). The creations had served their purpose, they had manifested from Sherman's imaginings and populated the art scene and now they were getting tired and a little too familiar. Sherman started thinking about how she could create images if she no longer wanted to be in the frame but also did not want to depend on other actors. It was going to come as a challenge for the artist who had been her own best and most reliable resource. Perhaps one should not try to place Cindy Sherman but instead ask which location will draw her in next. Dark skies overshadow the young hitchhiker (*Untitled Film Still #48*), the road dominates the frame arching wide and disappearing out of sight and there is no sign of a vehicle.[15] The girl has her back to the camera, her suitcase (perhaps full of costumes and wigs) is to her left-hand side. If Sherman has taught us anything, it is that we must always re-create; as Minh-ha (1991) states: "You must re-create reality because reality runs away; reality denies reality" (Minh-ha, 1991, pp. 40–1). Any notion of "representation" is bound to be paradoxical: partial and incomplete, multiple and superfluous. Representation is a "boundary notion" (Söderström, 2005, p. 11). To understand this is to recognize that the camera does not permit unmediated access to reality. Sherman is all too aware of this and in turn offers the viewer a type of reality.

The work of Cindy Sherman continually challenges and questions the viewer upon subsequent meetings.[16] Despite the artist's intentions, her images have assisted in subverting the traditional notion of the liberal enlightened subject along with other countless feminist readings. Sherman does not profess to have the answers, in creating artwork for her own inquiry and personal attainment she also demonstrates how women can use photography to express and articulate themselves within society. Women are still dealing with the anxiety of representation, but these images are multiple and can be reclaimed and appropriated (Butler, 1990). But as Sherman's photographs have highlighted, these self-made representations can become uncontrollable, changing, and mutating over time, just like the built environment and physical surroundings which are so often overlooked within Sherman's collections. Representation, like criticism, often prioritizes a static or definitive understanding over a fluid account of development, experimentation, and re-interpretation. This stance is not only restrictive but also reductive. Sherman performs, leaves her trace on a virtual landscape, but she does not take herself too seriously either. These visions of Sherman are now all that remain; perhaps the image of the hitchhiker encapsulates Sherman best, not in retrospect of where she has been but of where she is going.

NOTES

1. For more on American women's history and second wave Feminism, see Baxandall and Gordon (2005).

2. It is important to note that feminism was not considered (and is still not) a unitary movement, nor do I want to assert that there are many "feminisms" as this not only undermines the solidarity which the Women's Movement advocated but it also suggests that one approach could be prioritized over another, thus subordinating some feminists to the beliefs of others. The Women's Movement has a vast history, moving through numerous waves—first, second and third-wave feminisms—and has confronted various splits, conventionally between liberals, socialists, and radicals. Its outlook has also evolved from being Western focused to being international. During the mid-'70s the Women's Movement moved into mainstream UN activities, combining with the postcolonial movement and the human rights movement which led to 1975 being designated as the International Year of Women. Yet the rise of the global Women's Movement has not been without its own problems, how far the claims of Western women can associate, empathize and be linked with those of non–Western cultures and the experiences of "third-world" female subjects (who are often viewed as the victims of circumstance) has been questioned, while women of color, queer feminisms, transfeminisms, and countless others who have been silenced or marginalized in the conversation about women's rights continue to seek a space for discussion. For more on the globalization of the Women's Movement see Plummer (2015). It should be noted that Friedan's stance on women's rights is rooted in a liberal, white, heteronormative Western discourse which is a long way from de Lauretis' trajectory, whose work concerns issues of subjectivities, semiotics, literary theory, psychoanalysis, lesbian, and queer studies; yet I position these authors to show the development and divergence of feminist thought from the '60s to the contemporary day. This does not mean that feminism or its discourses follow a linear trajectory; these narratives weave, intersect, and influence one another at different times and in different spaces, they co-exist.

3. See Craig Owen's renowned 1983 paper "The Allegorical Impulse: Toward a Theory of Postmodernism Part 2."

4. In both the sense of "taking on" and "presupposing" their viewers' positions.

5. By "mediated pasts" I mean that these images have depicted a type of historical past—I do not believe there is a definitive past—one which is entangled with nostalgia and has been heightened by mass media, digitization, increased communication, and knowledge production.

6. Esplund's comments display a problematic understanding of self-portraiture: that a unitary self must be presented. A self-portrait does not have to be of the face, but instead could be an object of identification. Our possessions, fashions and cultural expressions are just as much a part of our person. To think the self-portrait is simple about the face excludes the materiality of the subject and reduces their self-expression. I would also question why Sherman should reveal anything in her images, if this is really about "genuinity" I wonder whether art has ever been sincere.

7. See Williamson (1983). This article is based on a talk given at the Watershed Gallery, Bristol, on May 18, 1983.

8. While the term "character" may not be commonly used in contemporary post-

structuralist discourse, I invoke the term to question its concept. I also make reference to the language of Sherman's proponents as the term was used during their time, in order to avoid ahistoricism.

9. My use of the "uncanny" is a reference to Freud's "The 'Uncanny'" (1919; 1955).

10. I use the term "(un)truths" to represent the uncertainty of dualist terms such as truth/lie, fiction/reality, past/present. When in fact they are an entangled entities and draw their references from far reaching spaces.

11. "Subject-centric lighting" is when the photographer positions light fully onto the subject in order to draw attention to them.

12. *Breathless* (1960) was loosely based on a newspaper article that French film director and screenwriter François Truffaut read in *The News in Brief*. The character of Michel Poiccard is based on the real-life Michel Portail and his girlfriend, the American journalist Beverly Lynette. In November 1952 Portail stole a car (an action which is directly paralleled with Belmondo's character) to visit his sick mother in Le Havre. In the process, Portail ended up killing a motorcycle cop named Grimberg. The storyline was initially dropped when Truffaut and Claude Chabrol could not agree on the narrative and it was later taken up by Godard. See, the Criterion Collection (2007) *Breathless*, Special Features, disc 2.

13. This is an example of "intertextuality," a term first coined by the poststructuralist Julia Kristeva in 1966. The term "intertextuality" has assumed numerous meanings as it has users. On the one hand, intertextuality has come to be thought of as a literary device which creates a complex related understanding between various texts. In literature, this can be achieved through (but are not limited to) references, allusions, pastiche, parody, and quotations. On a deeper level, intertextuality asserts that no piece of work—whether it is written, visual or material—is ever wholly "original," that texts (un)consciously draw upon the works of others to create meaning which is ultimately enmeshed. Meaning is not transferred directly from the author to the reader, as Ferdinand de Saussure believed; instead, meaning is mediated through numerous "codes" (here, Kristeva was challenging and expanding Saussure's study of semiotics, arguing that intertextuality replaced the notion of intersubjectivity, the psychological relationship between subjects) this suggests that meaning not only resides with the reader (as Roland Barthes asserted in his 1967 essay, "The Death of the Author") but that the reading process also evokes a complex network of texts. In other words, a text never stands by itself.

14. For more in the context of bodies and space, see Hayles (1999).

15. The figure in *Untitled Film Still #48* could be thought of as both a "hitchhiker" and/or a "runaway." These two words hold very different implications: the hitchhiker is usually associated with exploration and migration, of being "on the road" while the figure of the runaway is usually thought of as an escapee or victim. Both of these roles depend on the trust of strangers.

16. But subsequent re-readings are dependent on the arrangement of the images, their juxtaposition to other artists' work, as well as their positioning to the curator, critic and the viewer. New interpretations cannot arise from the images alone but are always situated to the trends of their time.

REFERENCES

Barthes, R. (1977) *Image, Music, Text*. Trans. Stephen Heath. London: Fontana Press.
_____. (1967) "The Death of the Author." *Aspe n5–6* (n.p.).

Baxandall, R. and Gordon, L. (2005) Second-wave Feminism. In: Hewitt, N. A. (ed.) *A Companion to American Women's History*. Oxford: Wiley Blackwell.

The Big Sleep. (1946) [Film] Directed by Howard Hawks. USA: Warner Bros.

Breathless. (1960) [Film] Directed by Jean-Luc Godard. France: Les Films Impéria, Les Productions Georges de Beauregard, Société Nouvelle de Cinématographie.

Butler, J. (1990) *Gender Trouble*. London: Routledge.

_____. (2011) [Video] Your Behavior Creates Your Gender. *Big Think*, February 19. http://bigthink.com/videos/your-behavior-creates-your-gender. (Accessed May 17, 2014).

Cartier-Bresson, H. (2004) *The Mind's Eye: Writings on Photography and Photographers* (1st edn). London: Aperture.

Casablanca. (1942) [Film] Directed by Michael Curtiz. USA: Warner Bros.

The Criterion Collection. (2007) [DVD] *Breathless*. Special Features, disc 2. Chambre 12, Hôtel de Suède.

Cruz, A. (1997) *Cindy Sherman: Retrospective*. London: Thames & Hudson.

de Lauretis, T. (1984) *Alice Doesn't: Feminism, Semiotics, Cinema*. Bloomington: Indiana University Press.

Dylan, B. (1964) [Song] The Times They Are A-Changin.' *The Times They Are A-Changin.'* United States: Columbia Records.

Esplund, L. (2012) Cindy Sherman Self-portraits Offer Empty Entertainment: Review. *Bloomberg Business*, February 27. http://www.bloomberg.com/news/articles/2012-02-27/cindy-sherman-self-portraits-offer-empty-entertainment-review. (Accessed April 4, 2015).

Freud, S. (1919; 1955) The "Uncanny," *The Standard Edition of the Complete Works of Sigmund Freud*, vol. XVII. Trans. from German Strachey, J. in collab. with Freud, A. assisted by Strachey, A. and Tyson, A. London: Hogarth Press.

Friedan, B. (1965) *The Feminine Mystique*. London: Penguin. Originally published: Gollancz, 1963.

Gatens, M. (1991) Corporeal Representation in/and the Body Politic. In: Diprose, R. and Ferrell, R. (eds.) *Cartographies: Poststructuralism and the Mapping of Bodies and Spaces*. Sydney: Allen and Unwin, pp. 79–97.

Goldberg, V. and Silberman, R. B. (1999) *American Photography: A Century of Images*. San Francisco: Chronical Books.

Goldin, N. (1986) *The Ballad of Sexual Dependency*. New York: Aperture.

Gore, L. (1963) [Song] You Don't Own Me. *Lesley Gore Sings of Mixed-up Hearts*. United Kingdom: Mercury Records.

Hayles, N. K. (1999) *How We Became Posthuman: Virtual Bodies in Cybernetics, Literature, and Informatics*. Chicago: Chicago University Press.

Henke, S. A. (1998) *Shattered Subjects: Trauma and Testimony in Women's Life-writing*. London: Macmillan.

Jones, A. (2002) The "Eternal Return": Self-portrait Photography as a Technology of Embodiment. *Signs: Journal of Women in Culture and Society* 27 (4), pp. 947–78.

Kirby, K. M. (1996) *Indifferent Boundaries: Spatial Concepts of Human Subjectivity*. New York: Guilford Publications.

Kristeva, J., 1966. Distance et anti-représentation. *Tel quel* 51.

Kuspit, D. (1988) "Inside Cindy Sherman." *The New Subjectivism: Art in the 1980s*. Ann Arbor: University of Michigan Press.

Longhurst, R. (2005) The Body. In: Atkinson, D., Jackson, P., Sibley, D. and Washbourn, N. (eds.) *Cultural Geography: A Critical Dictionary of Key Concepts*. London: I.B. Tauris, pp. 91–96.

Lucie-Smith, E. (1994) *Race, Sex, and Gender in Contemporary Art.* New York: Harry N. Abrams.

Lyon, D. (1968) *The Bikeriders.* New York: Macmillan.

Massey, D. (1994) *Space, Place and Gender.* Minneapolis: University of Minnesota Press.

Minh-ha, T. T. (1991) *When the Moon Waxes Red: Representation, Gender and Cultural Politics.* New York: Routledge.

Mulvey, L. (1975) Visual Pleasure and Narrative Cinema. *Screen* 16 (3), pp. 6–18.

_____. (1991) The Phantasmagoria of the Female Body: The Work of Cindy Sherman. *New Left Review* 1 (188): pp. 136–50.

Museum of Modern Art (MoMA) (1978) [Online image]. *Untitled Film Still #21.* http://www.moma.org/interactives/exhibitions/2012/cindysherman/gallery/2/#/23/untitled-film-still-21-1978/. (Accessed July 10, 2015).

_____. (1979) [Online image]. *Untitled Film Still #48.* http://www.moma.org/interactives/exhibitions/2012/cindysherman/gallery/2/#/50/untitled-film-still-48-1979/. (Accessed July 10, 2015).

_____. (1980) [Online image]. *Untitled Film Still #54.* http://www.moma.org/interactives/exhibitions/2012/cindysherman/gallery/2/#/29/untitled-film-still-54-1980/. (Accessed July 10, 2015).

Owens, B. (1973) *Suburbia.* San Francisco: Straight Arrow Press.

Owens, C. (1983) "The Discourse of Others: Feminists and Postmodernism." In: Foster, H. (ed.) *The Anti-aesthetic: Essays on Postmodernism.* New York: Bay Press.

Plummer, K. (2015) *Cosmopolitan Sexualities: Hope and the Humanist Imagination.* Cambridge: Polity Press.

Proust, M. (1925) *The Guermantes Way: Remembrance of Things Past, 5:1.* Trans. Charles Kenneth Scott-Moncrieff. New York: Modern Library.

Respini, E., Burton, J. and Waters, J. (ed.) (2012) *Cindy Sherman.* New York: Museum of Modern Art.

Sherman, C. (2003a) Centerfolds. In: Phillips, L. and Luce, H., III (eds.) *New Museum of Contemporary Art.* New York: Skarstedt Fine Art.

_____. (2003b) *Cindy Sherman: The Complete Untitled Film Stills.* New York: Museum of Modern Art

Söderström, O. (2005) Representation. In: Atkinson, D., Jackson, P., Sibley, D. and Washbourn, N. (eds.) *Cultural Geography: A Critical Dictionary of Key Concepts.* London: I.B. Tauris, pp. 11–15.

Szarkowski, J. (2002 [1976]). *William Eggleston's Guide.* New York: Museum of Modern Art. http://www.egglestontrust.com/guide_intro.html. (Accessed July 5, 2015).

Tschumi, B. (1996) *Architecture and Disjunction.* Cambridge: MIT Press.

Walsh, K. T. (2010) The 1960s: A Decade of Change for Women. *US News,* March 12. http://www.usnews.com/news/articles/2010/03/09/the-1960s-a-decade-of-promise-and-heartbreak. (Accessed April 12, 2015).

Waters, J. (2012) Cindy Sherman and John Waters: A Conversation. In: Respini, E., Burton, J. and Waters, J. (ed.) *Cindy Sherman.* New York: Museum of Modern Art, pp. 68–79.

Williamson, J. (1983) Images of Woman: The Photography of Cindy Sherman. *Screen* 24 (8), pp. 202–06.

Space and Place to Remember

Television's Double Articulation in the National Space Centre

HELEN WOOD *and* TIM O'SULLIVAN

This essay contributes to a growing interest, also signaled by the presence of this book, in the relationship between television and memory. Television in this regard is curiously contradictory: it is a medium which both constantly reasserts the present, and is thus mythologized as an instantaneous, ephemeral medium for forgetting, while at the same time, it is increasingly obsessed with the past and is therefore a significant medium for collective, as well as biographical, remembering. The key debate in this terrain reproduces this contradiction. On the one hand, more abstract philosophical debates see television as a negative force in producing cultural "amnesia" as part of a broader critique of postmodern culture where television is responsible for "the annihilation of memory, and consequently of history" (Doane, 1990, p. 227), or contributing to "memory collapse" (Hoskins, 2004). On the other hand, recent studies have called for more sustained and sophisticated empirical accounts of the sites, artifacts, texts, and audiences through which television has a more nuanced set of relationships with memory practices (see, for example, Holdsworth, 2008, 2011; Bourdon, 2003; Bourdon and Kligler-Vilenchik, 2011; Keightley, 2011). This essay therefore takes up the challenge set out by the latter list of scholars and responds to the call to "pay specific attention to media forms and the operations of a contemporary media culture" (Holdsworth, 2008, p. 138). It does so by considering the place of television in what might at first sight seem an unlikely location: the National Space Centre in Leicester in the United Kingdom.[1] This essay considers the various ways that television is used in the Space Centre galleries to consider the broader role of television in "place-making" activities and in the recreation of nostalgia and memory.

The National Space Centre opened in Leicester in June 2001 and its slogan reads: "The National Space Centre will capture and inspire the public imagination in all aspects of space and demonstrate its relevance to life on Earth in the 21st Century." The Centre has been described as a "surprise hit" (Adam, 2004) with around a quarter of a million visitors each year since opening. There are six themed galleries within the Space Centre, housed inside a large structure known as the Rocket Tower, as well as in adjacent buildings. Some of these galleries include the Sir Patrick Moore Planetarium; the "Tranquility Base," which offers an experience of astronaut training; and "Orbiting Earth," which provides interactive exhibits around satellite technology and includes the opportunity to present a "televised" weather forecast. Its educational activities have been shown to have a positive effect on enthusing children about the value of science and of being a scientist (Jarvis and Pell, 2005). What this essay is most concerned with, however, are the ways in which television and television culture are used to demonstrate the relevance of space to "life on Earth in the 21st Century." In this regard space and television have become closely allied companions. Cultural imaginings of space are often evoked at the Centre, including *Doctor Who* and *Star Wars*, as well as through special themed events such as a "*Back to the Future* Night," which also signifies the relationship between space and imagined time travel. At its core the Centre also offers an exploration into the history of actual, documented space exploration developments. The address to visitors in the galleries of the Centre deploys the modality of the museum, and as such we now consider the ways that television has previously been figured in relation to the contemporary museum.

Television in the Museum

Previous analyses of television in the museum have often been very critical of its mode of articulation. As such, they form part of the broader critique of television for its postmodern emphasis upon signification at the expense of substance: television is accused of being unable to convey actual or authentic materiality because of its emphasis upon the constant present. It is therefore identified as another part of an illusion of the memory boom as a direct response to the "spread of amnesia" in Western society (Huyssen, 1995, pp. 16–17). Indeed, television has been used as a metaphor for what is wrong with the contemporary museum more broadly, as in Jeudy and Baudrillard's description of the museum as "just another simulation machine: the museum as mass medium is no longer distinguishable from television" (1995, pp. 30–31;

cited in Holdsworth, 2011, p. 134). Analyses of contemporary museums which have drawn upon the simulations of events afforded by the effects and use of television have sometimes followed a similar critical tack. For instance, sociologists Lisus and Ericson (1995) describe the Museum of Tolerance in Los Angeles[2] as having misplaced history and memory by its deployment of what they term "the television format." They go further to suggest that the use of special TV effects for the viewer experience is a form of social control whereby "the visitor is entertained into submission. The aesthetics of emotion become the aesthetics of control" (1995, p. 8). Accounts like these draw upon impressions of television as a signifier of simulation. Like Baudrillard, they assume the language of media effects, whereby television itself is literally responsible for social amnesia, causing passivity, and securing social control. Yet, Lisus and Ericson repeatedly reference the Museum of Tolerance's appropriation of a "television format" as though there were only one. In essence, critiques like this use television itself as the symbol of the denigration of memory without any understanding of television *form* or of television studies. It is this frustration with which Amy Holdsworth (2011) asks us to reconsider not only television's seeming incompatibility with the museum, but also, following Huyssen, to reconceive its dialectical relationship between remembering and forgetting as much more productive and nuanced.

The museum is "both the space of the archive *and* exhibition, and it is the transfer of objects from one to the other, their re-contextualisation within the 'spectacular *mise-en-scène*' of exhibition, which marks their resurrection" (Holdsworth, 2011, p. 130). The use of television in the National Space Centre articulates much about television as inseparable from our understanding of space as culturally symbolic. Television, according to Roger Silverstone, has a "double articulation" (1994, p. 83): it must be considered both as an object of signification which produces texts and stories, but also as a material object directly connected to the time-space relationships of its settings. It is precisely this double articulation which powerfully connects the personal, intimate, and the everyday to the broader national, historical, and global landscape.

This double articulation marks the way in which television mediates both the terrestrial and the extra-terrestrial at the National Space Centre. In the galleries of the Centre, TV screens are everywhere, showing footage mostly of real space explorations but also of science fiction films and series which feature outer-space. In Figure 1, for instance, the retro television set, placed as though it has crashed through the living room wall, is playing scenes from the 1955 horror sci-fi film *This Island Earth,* where aliens come to earth seeking scientists to help them in their war. Of course, this draws attention not only to space, but also to *ideas* about space as a long-standing cultural signifier of fear, danger, and invasion which have variously been attached to specific moments in political history. Yet, equally important is the use of the retro

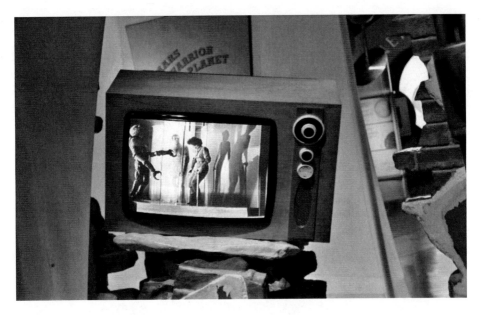

Figure 1. The Alien Invader.

television set, whose materiality cannot be easily separated from the ways in which cultural ideas about space have been imagined and communicated. The set itself is as much part of that nostalgic re-imagining as *This Island Earth*.

A similar retro television set is located close by, screening actual television news footage of the 1969 moon landings, a key defining moment in space exploration (Figure 2). The television set in Figure 1 is framed as though it has "crashed" through a wall as an alien invader, while here the set appears to have travelled to the moon and to have landed on the moon's surface, where we are reminded of the indelibility of human footprints. We are also perhaps reminded of the indelible inscription of television into cultural memories of the moon landings, as well as television's capacities for "mobile privatization" (Williams, 1974, p. 26), in which the technology can imaginatively transport its audiences to distant spaces. Indeed, while the television set in Figure 1 is coded as an invader into the home, importing "alien" images and ideas into the domestic sphere, the set in Figure 2 is coded as an apparatus of exploration, mobility, and adventure, enabling audiences to "travel" with it to worlds that would otherwise be out of reach. This cues us in to the ways in which television functions as a relay between public and private space, but also how it transforms the nature of both. Here, the material television set and the images it screens indicate the complex spatialities and temporalities of memory and popular visual culture; television simultaneously signals futurity, nostalgia, and otherworldliness as well as the home, domestication, and mobility.

Figure 2. The moon in the living room.

Of course, following Baudrillard, critiques would see the juxtapositions of film fiction with news footage and the material television set with the lunar surface as symptoms of "memory collapse," where science fiction is set up as potentially indistinguishable from TV news coverage, and the shallow seductions of the television screen overwhelm and contaminate the historical event. This type of analysis can only see memory as fundamentally and fatally tainted by its mediation and suggests that the still materiality of objects and artifacts offers some more pure route to authentic memory than does the moving television image. However, from the outset in the Space Centre, television is heavily codified as the object for both space and time travel; it can take us to imagined or real outer worlds, and it can also take us back in time. This essay argues that it is the play on this double articulation—television as both a material object in the space-time relations of the domestic, and television as an object of signification which produces stories and texts—that ignites memory as the site where the personal and global meet.

Television Culture as a Lingua Franca of Time

Many of the concerns over television's role in modern societies have related to its claimed part in what Anthony Giddens (1991, p. 24) calls "time-space distanciation," wherein the media, and television in particular, allow time and space to become dislocated and strangely insulated, set apart from one another, enabling us to experience the same event at the same time in different locales. There is more than one way to understand this in terms of our lived experience of time. Whereas for Giddens it might be seen as part of the drive towards increasing individualization, for others this experience has helped forge ideas about new kinds of "imagined communities" (Anderson, 1983). The rise of newer communication technologies has extenuated arguments about television's obsession with immediacy and continual presence, leading authors like Paul Virilio to worry over the "acceleration of real time" ceding "primacy to the immediacy of telepresence" (2005, p. 118) and relegating subjects to passive spectators without recourse to a sense of past, present, and future, constantly trapped in the "replay" of the temporal present. Emily Keightley (2011), however, asks us to reconsider some of the technological determinism (and, again, we would add assumptions of media effects) underlying these accounts of the experience of time. Rather, she suggests that media offer "imaginative and symbolic" articulations of temporalities as being particular, contingent, and "intermediate"; moreover, she wants to re-locate the human agent that has been jettisoned from these more abstract accounts of mediated time.

Figure 3. History, space and television timeline.

News, culture, politics, and social developments are used at the National Space Centre to help mark and plot time for the visitor. In its educational timeline of the developments of space travel, a process with which most of us are relatively unfamiliar, television programs are given the same status as social and political developments to stitch space exploration into our cultural memories (Figure 3). The timeline is suggestive of television's role in animating and invoking—rather than annihilating—memory. Again, this employs television's double articulation, foregrounding the development of the material technology as well as the significant texts that made a historic mark on the cultural landscape. For example, the timeline's flagging of the abolition of the "Toddler's Truce" (Figure 4), which was a nightly shutdown of British television with the intention of creating time for children to be put to bed, invites us to reflect on the changing ways in which television has been bound up with the quotidian rhythms of domestic life. Similarly, the timeline's plotting of *The Sky at Night,* a BBC television program on astronomy first broadcast in 1957, posits the central role of television in stitching outer-space into the national imaginary. The material development of the domestic VCR is also symbolic of notions of time as associated with progress and linear notions of history (Figure 5); as such, the domestic technologies of television and video recording become part of an over-arching story of technological and cultural advancement.

Jérôme Bourdon and Neta Kliger-Vilenchik (2011) in their audience research discuss the use of television programs in the construction of a particular Israeli sense of collective national remembering. In the National Space Centre, the use of key television programs to assist in memory production is similarly significant: there is mention of *Coronation Street, Doctor Who,* and *Monty Python* amongst others, all of which appeal to and embed a collective sense of time which is very evocative of the British national cultural imaginary. In Figure 6, for instance, the more familiar image of *Dad's Army* from the late 1960s is used to help us to locate in time and memory the failure of the Soyuz space mission. Since Britain has played little part in the major events of space exploration, and since imagery and ideas of space are not closely associated with the British symbolic imaginary, British television's promotion of a "national family" may be extremely important to the ways that memory and meaning are anchored and mobilized here. David Morley has pointed to the ways in which "the mediated public sphere constructed by the institutions of national broadcasting functions as a symbolic home for the nation's members" (2000, p. 105; see also Geraghty, 2010). Thus, the national story is made to seem cohesive at the Space Centre through the deployment of the historical markers of television's iconic texts; the signaling of its material presence in the home; and, more broadly, through its ability to invoke a sense of British national identity and belonging. The symbolic power of public

Figure 4. Television memories and history.

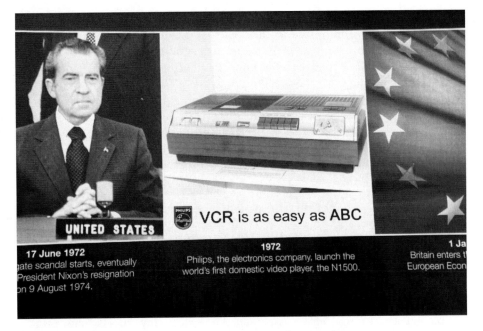

Figure 5. Television history and memories.

Figure 6. Television nostalgia and history.

service broadcasting thus forms a hidden but important context for cultural memory as it is mobilized in the Centre. Of course, television audience research has long investigated the nature of television as a source for collective identity and for shared senses of understanding and remembering (see for example Gillespie, 1995; Hobson, 1982; Gray, 1987). Tim O'Sullivan, for instance, has discussed how television programs often provide entry points for the discussion of memories, which "frequently fuse television programmes and experiences to the rites of passage of domestic biography, serving as markers for remembered people and situations of changing relations of kinship, lifestyle and shared experience" (1991, p. 163).

Television and Place-Making

Throughout, the Space Centre draws upon an implied common understanding of television as inextricably woven into national memory, inviting the visitor to plot their own cultural memories as part of its guided experience of learning about space. What has not yet been accounted for in the discussion of television as it invokes cultural memory is how it can also be a place-making activity. In *Ambient Television*, Anna McCarthy (2001) discusses the use of television outside of the home and domestic space: in the pub, the doctor's clinic, and the shopping mall, although not in the museum. However, her analysis is useful here since it helps us to understand the relationship between space and subjectivity afforded by the presence of television in public. McCarthy asks for a historically sensitive, *site-specific* discussion of television as it has moved beyond its traditional location in the domestic realm. In the Space Centre television is used, like in the shopping mall, as a "space-binding" object which is also "scale-shifting": "The fact that we can approach television as a spatial instrument that is at once a physical object in social space and a source of enunciations originating in, and displaying, other places, suggests that the screen not only exists in more than one place but also on more than one scale; it is the physical space where local processes meet the "global" determinations of the image" (McCarthy, 2001, p. 15). Of course, in obvious ways television is used to anchor and to institutionalize the very notion of space in the Space Centre. For example, television is used to imaginatively transport us to the scene of a Russian rocket launch, so that in a darkened room, real video/TV footage allows us to experience the excitement of take-off as though sitting with the astronaut (Figure 7).

The use of television in this exhibit attempts to give us some of the immediacy of "being there," a feeling of co-presence with the astronaut, and an embodied sense of partaking in an historic event. For some more pes-

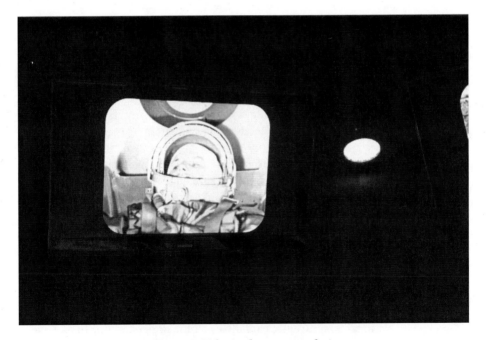

Figure 7. Televised space travel.

simistic accounts of television's role in memory, this constructed sense of first-hand participation dislocates our sense of "actual" history. Yet, this is part of what McCarthy calls television's "virtual mobility," its capacity to manipulate space and, here, to conjure the "actual" experience of the launch of a space mission. In McCarthy's analysis, this potential for doubling subject positions contributes to what she calls television's "subjectivization of public space" (ibid., p. 20) which, in her analysis of retail spaces, further reinforces rhetorical and ideological ideas about individual consumption. Here in the institutionalized space of the museum we might also discuss television's deployment in a rhetorical/educational mode, rather than as a method for distraction. The accounts of television that we discussed earlier understand the act of viewing as antithetical to active learning and knowledge retention, partly through the ways that television can be seen to "scramble"[3] historical time. However, we would suggest that the disruptions and reconfigurations of time and space that television provokes here have potentially more productive implications through their doubling of subjectivity. Indeed, the fact that the Centre successfully promotes an interest in learning about space and astronomy points to this, and we would suggest that the imaginative uses to which television is put in the Centre may not be separated out from this success.

Domestic Nostalgia

Television can privatize public space, to allow one to understand oneself within the institutionalized material space, but also to imagine oneself in another worldly space. Television is incessantly criticized for its role in memory production, for its ever-moving flow of simulation, and thus its inability to make memory stable for recollection, leading Susan Sontag (1977) to say she prefers the still image of the photograph. However, we might see this as part of Emily Keightley's (2011) discussion of the way in which collective and personal memories tend to be cleaved apart in analyses, with little empirical attention to the juncture between the two. Work on television and memory shows very clearly how memories of television punctuate the very fabric of remembering everyday life, where "identities can become 'concreted' into objectivized forms" (Keightley 2011, p. 397, discussing van Dijck, 2007; see also Collie, 2013). Such pessimistic accounts of the role of emotion in remembering tend to separate out the emotional from the cognitive, but we might want to consider the value of feeling and of the experiential to modes of understanding (see, for example, Mankekar, 2009; Berlant, 2011).

The National Space Centre capitalizes on the understanding of cultural memory as having the ability to concretize your own personal experience, and does so through a self-conscious exhibition which asks you to consider "where you were when" the first men landed on the moon. In the National Media Museum in Bradford, England, the moon landings of 1969 are screened on a loop with a large screen framed by the statement "You'll remember where you were and who you were with the first time you saw them" (cited in Holdsworth, 2011, p. 144). The moon landings are often collected together with other "flashbulb" memories in Jerome Bourdon's (2003) typology of television memories; these are usually bad news events which arrest us and thus stitch us in memory into a very particular time and place. However, the moon landings were also a particular television and media event; as such, we can only really ask the question "Where were we *when we watched*?" Given that the National Space Centre attracts visitors of all ages, and especially that it runs as an educational center for children and schools, this question might miss the mark for many of its younger visitors. What the Space Centre does, then, is re-create a late 1960s living room through which we are invited to transport ourselves back to a place for remembering and, as stated on the sign affixed to the wall, "Re-live the first moon landing" (Figure 8).

The reconstruction of the 1960s retro interior draws upon all the nostalgic iconography of the domestic styling of the era: the wallpaper, the clock, and the g-plan furniture. This is accompanied by technologies of the era: the

Figure 8. The lunar/memory module.

radio, the typewriter, the dial telephone, and—most centrally—the black and white television set which screens on a loop the newsreels of the moon landings from 1969. We might say that in this exhibit we can identify the creation of three layers of spectatorial and spatial figuration, from the museum to the living room to the moon. What we can clearly see, again, is how the television as a *material* object is also a *symbolic* object whose styling has become part of the very notion of remembering in contemporary media culture. Retro television sets form part of the current fascination with nostalgia and with nostalgic television. In the 1950s and '60s, the material design of the television set and that of other household appliances were strongly influenced by a trend for "space-age" styling, particularly in the U.S. (Chambers, 2011, p. 368), and so connotations of space travel might be already-inscribed in the materiality of television sets. This complicates the notion that television's double articulation can be easily divided into its material functions on one hand and its symbolic functions on the other: the television object is itself part of the cultural language of remembering, and of remembering particular periods of time. Additionally, so familiar are we now with the domestic styling of "the Sixties" or "the Seventies" that many younger generations will recognize the living rooms of decades ago from media depictions of the past and from the "regimes of repetition" of TV re-runs (Kompare, 1999). It is not that television merely mediates history, as though history can be extracted from it, but that history and television are doubly entwined in a more culturally dialogic and harmonious, rather than entirely contradictory, set of relationships between materiality and simulation.

The Terrestrial and the Extra-Terrestrial

Visitors, of course, do not experience this exhibition as a complex and contradictory articulation of spectator positions and material and symbolic space. They are familiar with the mediated notion of "where were you when" as a shorthand form of "where were you when *you watched*." In this space of a mocked-up living room, the National Space Centre invites visitors to write on postcards their memories of the moon-landings as well as their memories of the 1960s and '70s. It keeps hundreds of these postcards and we are grateful to the Centre's Director Chas Bishop for giving us access to a wide selection for analysis. They were hand-written by visitors at the moment of their visit, and while they give us some insight into how people experience the Centre, they cannot strictly be taken as audience research, especially as many of the cards give us very little access to the social or cultural identities of their writers. The postcards simply invite a response to "My strongest memory of the moon landings is…" and, at the bottom, "I was X years old at the time." Nevertheless, they do offer us some interesting insights into how this coming together of the material and symbolic relationship of television in the site of this museum evokes and stimulates subjective memories of a particular historical moment.

Most of the cards actually tell us of families, holidays, homes, and the ups and downs of domestic life. Very few tell us much about the moon landings, of course, as the concreteness of memory is personal and not so much related to the factual experience of the event. Absent from the written memories is a sense of the geo-political context in which the moon landings took place; while in its other galleries the Centre does explore the Cold War tensions in which space exploration was centrally implicated, the living room space invites memories through the modalities of the domestic and the personal. In what follows we present some of the key themes identifiable in the written memories, and consider the complex ways in which television is bound up with histories and temporalities that are personal and collective, public and domestic. They evoke both the symbolic and imaginative power signified by the television images of the moon landings, as well as the material organization of domestic space around the television set. Again, the memories reveal how these symbolic and material properties of television are inextricably bound up with one another.

Awe and Spectacle

While most of the postcards record memories of the broader contexts of personal lives at the time of the moon landings, some do foreground the event itself. They talk of their fascination and awe of the moon and the remembered spectacle of the event, and the negotiation of this within the domestic realm:

"Rushing to the landing window, staring at the stars desperate to glimpse the rockets going to the moon," age 5.

"I still remember the amazement that this was possible and how it would feel—still am!"

"Sitting in my living room watching the first man on the moon and being totally transfixed by it all."

"Everyone was so excited and knew that history was being made. We all watched in on the TV in wonder."

"I was in USA in Boston and was scared the world would come to an end."

These stories speak of the ways in which the event ruptured the spatio-temporal norms of the domestic sphere. The sense of awe in response to the television spectacle could veer into the realm of fear—in being "scared the world would come to an end"—but most often this rupturing was articulated as a sense of wonder and the infinite opening out of spatial possibility. The sense of "history being made" was produced by the collective experience of watching television, both through the gathering of families around their own sets, as well as in the binding together of the physically dispersed television audience through broadcast time.

Family and Home

Most of the memories, however, are about close personal details of family members, recalling the "who" and the "where" of domestic life. While the viewing of the moon landings was clearly an interruption to everyday life, the written memories nonetheless chronicle some of the mundane details and particularities of the quotidian and the domestic—furniture, curtains, sofas—and the relationships between family members. Because this event of profound public and international significance was for most people experienced through the television in the space of the domestic, it is etched into personal histories of the home. What might otherwise be remembered as a moment of technological and scientific triumph with significant geo-political ramifications is instead framed through the optic of family life. As such, the political history of the moon landing is remade as a social and cultural history.

"Came home from school with my mum and she closed the curtains and put the television on (to make the picture show up best) and told me to watch it. At night I looked at the moon thinking I would be able to see the people waving and didn't understand why I couldn't see them."

"My parents had a studio couch. My brother and I and my parents had a bed made up on it and we all sat up to watch history being made."

"Waiting for the astronauts to be woken up and actually step down on to the moon. Our youngest son was 6 months old and we tried to sleep when the astronauts did so we woke up very early to watch this 'Giant Step.'"

"I was a young girl. I was woken up and allowed to come down the stairs and watch. My mother told me to watch carefully, I sat with my family. I AM STILL WAITING FOR THE ROBOT I WAS PROMISED ON THE TOMORROW'S WORLD PROGRAMME."

The moon landings here are stitched to precise biographical details which recall domestic settings, siblings and family.

Many of the cards remember the breaking of traditional domestic routines and, in particular, *staying up late* as a real source of excitement:

"My parents let me stay up to watch the first moon landing on the TV. I can still clearly remember it."

"Staying up all night, fighting to keep my eyes open. Was annoyed to find the astronauts needed a rest before they got out to walk on the moon. Eventually they got out to walk and I watched them till the sun came up. Felt so tired all the next day."

"For the first time in my young life I was allowed to stay up late to watch it live it was amazing like Thunderbirds had become reality."

"I was allowed to stay up for the first time. We watched it at my Nan's with all the family and neighbours. It was really exciting."

The symbolic entwinement of television viewing and space travel—both of which have the capacity to transform normative conceptions of space and time—come though in a number of different ways here. The experience for children of "staying up late to watch," and therefore transgressing the usual temporal structure of broadcast television and family life, was clearly thrilling for many respondents, and intimately bound up with the thrill of the event itself. The simultaneity of the astronauts' journey into space and the children's formative foray into night-time viewing seemingly made the experience of the latter more intense. Thus, the private experience of "staying up late" was also endowed with a broader public and historic significance. The invocation of the British science-fiction series *Thunderbirds* (1965–66) in this context, as though it "had become reality," points to how the imaginative possibilities of television were viewed as somehow akin to the miracle of the moon landings.

There was also much remembered excitement about the landings rupturing the normal school day:

"For the first time we were allowed to watch the television during lesson time at school."

"We had a TV in the main hall at school and could watch at break and in free periods."

"Standing around a TV in school and being told this is the most significant thing the world had known."

"Sitting at school and having lunch as it was so special a television was put on."

The incongruous presence of the television set in this non-domestic setting is what signals the exceptionality of the event: its material presence also constitutes its symbolic resonance. The phrase that echoes in many of the written sentiments are of the notion of being a witness to history "in the making," which before the appearance of television did not have such resonance. However, the more widespread adoption of television ownership at this time allowed for a sense of shared history. The moon landings, like the 1953 Coronation in the UK, are often figured as synonymous with a process of televisual remembering.

There is also a sub-set of symbolic cultural memories which attaches to the cultural significance of the set's materiality:

"We bought a television especially for the landing on the moon. I stayed up but my husband went to bed."

"My father bought a brand new television to watch the moon landings and we watched through the night every night till they landed back on earth."

"We had just moved house and had to go and buy a television to see the moon landing."

"How could it be that we were able to land on the moon but only had black and white televisions?"

Buying a television was thus remembered as a conscious act undertaken in order to partake in this historic event. The act of private consumption was therefore connected to a more public and social process, which also troubles some ideas of television viewing as purely a form of individualistic retreat from the public sphere. Television viewing and consumption are here not suggestive of a withdrawal from public time and shared space, but rather of participation in a new spatialized configuration of the public.

For some, the TV technology is recalled as most central to memory, and these postcards include examples of television experienced beyond the domestic realm. For instance:

"My strongest memory of the moon landing was watching it on a giant TV screen at Jodrell Bank."

"Watching the moon landings on a portable black and white TV in a trailer tent built by my mum and dad on a campsite on a beach near Conway. The TV was connected to the car battery... as time went on the picture grew smaller and smaller! Fantastic to watch though!"

Not of all of these memories were positive, though:

"Watching the lunar landing on TV with my family on a rather temperamental telly."

"I remember watching it on my neighbours TV. We couldn't see much, it was in black and white and I was bored."

There were also recollections of trying to capture, long before the advent of VCR technology, the television footage:

"We were on holidays in Sandbanks and my dad cine-filmed the telly— it came out really well."

"Taking photos of the action on the TV screen with my camera—yes they came out!"

More recently, media studies have discussed the ways in which history is tied to the notion of the media event (Dayan and Katz, 1994), but these examples also articulate the other side of media orchestration. They explicate the ways in which the event is stitched into daily rhythms and everyday practices of the audiences, where the television's "double articulation" between the material and the symbolic is routinely in play in the production of memory.

Conclusion

In this discussion, we have presented a brief case study of a modern British cultural organization that is dedicated to the history of space exploration, in part a site of commercial leisure and related thematic entertainment and also a site of educational engagement with the recent past, underpinned by the mission to popularize and promote the public understanding of science and technology. We have argued that in achieving these ends, it employs television to *index* and to *anchor* popular, generational memory in a number of ways. In its early years, the appearance and spectacle of television, like film some 50 or so years before, was often hailed as a new form of miraculous "instant history," able to mediate "live" coverage of world events—sporting or cultural spectaculars, political tragedies or triumphs, technological breakthroughs, and so on—directly into the living room. These were epitomized by the TV coverage of the moon landing in July 1969. None of our examined memory card responses recorded in the Space Centre betray a hint of suspicion that what was presented on the television screen at that moment was anything other than scientific "fact," despite the proliferation of subsequent conspiracy theories that it was science "fiction." This was TV viewed by guileless, innocent audiences, the television of "witness," as aptly termed by Ellis (2000, pp. 6–38).

In the Space Centre, television's "double articulation" of the material and the symbolic is deployed in its reconstruction and appeal to the past. Old TVs as well as old programs are used to mobilize memories of the relatively recent past and act as generational markers, as short-cuts to biographical memories: "where you were," "who you were with," "what you were doing," and so on. Similarly, this double articulation is animated in visitors' written postcard submissions, where the symbolic and emotional resonances of television in cultural memory emanate not only from the historic footage that is broadcast but also from the materiality of the set in the affective space of the home. We have called into question some of the dominant conceptualizations of television as a technology that perpetuates the endless replay of the temporal present which militates against the possibility of memory, history, and polity. The more pessimistic accounts of television's use in the museum may conceive of the National Space Centre's multiple employments of television as part of "memory collapse" or a perturbing "scrambling" of historical time. However, we want to suggest that the diverse uses of television in the Space Centre set in motion dynamic, dialectical interactions between the material and the symbolic which conjure place, subjectivity, and emotion. Thus, it is the *uses* of television's "double articulation" and the way that those are experienced that are key to understanding television's function as an instrument of memory in the space of the museum.

Acknowledgments

Photographs, Tim O'Sullivan.

We are grateful to and acknowledge the continuing work of Chas Bishop, Director of The National Space Centre, and his staff for their assistance and collaboration in the development of this essay.

Notes

1. Leicester is a city of some 330,000 in the center of England.
2. The Museum of Tolerance, based in Los Angeles, is devoted to an examination of racism and prejudice, with a strong emphasis on the history of the Holocaust.
3. We are grateful to Jilly Boyce Kay for this observation.

References

Adam, D. (2004) Lost in Space. *The Guardian*, August 7. http://www.theguardian.com/travel/2004/aug/07/familyholidays.family.unitedkingdom. (Accessed June 13, 2015.)

Anderson, B. (1983) *Imagined Communities*. London: Verso.

Berlant, L. (2011) *Cruel Optimism*. Durham: Duke University Press.

Bourdon, J. (2003) Some Sense of Time: Remembering Television. *History and Memory* 15 (2), pp. 5–35.

Bourdon, J. and Kligler-Vilenchik, N. (2011) Together, Nevertheless? Television Memories in Mainstream Jewish Israel. *European Journal of Communication* 26 (1), pp. 33–47.

Chambers, D. (2011) The Material Form of the Television Set. *Media History* 17 (4), pp. 359–75.

Collie, H. (2013) "It's Just So Hard to Bring It to Mind": The Significance of "Wallpaper" in the Gendering of Television Memory Work. *Journal of European Television History and Culture* 1 (3), pp. 13–21.

Dayan, D. and Katz, E. (1994) *Media Events: The Live Broadcasting of History*. Cambridge: Harvard University Press.

Ellis, J. (2000) *Seeing Things: Television in the Age of Uncertainty*. London: I.B. Tauris.

Doane, M. A. (1990) Information, Crisis, Catastrophe. In: Mellencamp, P. (ed.) *Logics of Television: Essays in Cultural Criticism*. Bloomington and London: Indiana University Press and BFI, pp. 240–66.

Geraghty, C. (2010) Exhausted and Exhausting: Television Studies and British Soap Opera. *Critical Studies in Television* 5 (1), pp. 82–96.

Giddens, A. (1991) *Modernity and Self-identity: Self and Society and the in the Late Modern Age*. Cambridge: Polity/Blackwell.

Gillespie, M. (1995) *Television, Ethnicity and Cultural Change.* London: Routledge.

Gray, A. (1987) Behind Closed Doors: Video Recorders in the Home. In: Baehr, H. and Dyer, G. (eds.) *Boxed In: Women and Television.* London: Pandora, pp. 38–54.

Hobson, D. (1982) *Crossroads: The Drama of a Soap Opera.* London: Methuen.

Holdsworth, A. (2008) "Television Resurrections": Television and Memory. *Cinema Journal* 47 (3), pp. 137–44.

_____. (2011) *Television, Memory and Nostalgia.* Basingstoke: Palgrave Macmillan.

Hoskins, A. (2004) Television and the Collapse of Memory. *Time and Society* 13 (1), pp. 109–27.

Huyssen, A. (1995) *Twilight Memories: Marking Time in a Culture of Amnesia.* London: Routledge.

Jarvis, T. and Pell, A. (2005) Factors Influencing Elementary School Children's Attitudes Toward Science Before, During, and After a Visit to the UK National Space Centre. *Journal of Research in Science Teaching* 42 (1), pp. 53–83.

Keightley, E. (2011) From Dynasty to Songs of Praise: Television as Cultural Resource for Gendered Remembering. *European Journal of Communication* 14 (4), pp. 395–410.

Kompare, D. (1999) *Rerun Nation: The Regime of Repetition on American Television.* Unpublished Ph.D. Thesis. University of Wisconsin, Madison.

Lisus, N. A. and Ericson, R. V. (1995) Misplacing Memory: The Effect of Television Format on Holocaust Remembrance. *The British Journal of Sociology* 46 (1), pp. 1–19.

Mankekar, P. (1999) *Screening Culture, Viewing Politics: An Ethnography of Television, Womanhood, and Nation in Postcolonial India.* Durham: Duke University Press.

McCarthy, A. (2001) *Ambient Television: Visual Culture and Public Space.* Durham: Duke University Press.

Morley, D. (2000) *Home Territories: Media, Mobility and Identity.* Abingdon: Routledge.

O'Sullivan, T. (1991) Television Cultures and Memories of Viewing. In: Corner, J. (ed.) *Popular Television in Britain: Studies in Cultural History.* London: BFI, pp. 159–89.

Silverstone, R. (1994) *Television and Everyday Life.* Abingdon: Routledge.

Sontag, S. (1977) *On Photography.* London: Penguin.

Virilio, P. (2005) *The Information Bomb.* Trans. C. Turner. London: Verso.

Williams, R. (1974) *Television: Technology and Cultural Form.* London: Fontana.

About the Contributors

Rowan **Aust** is a doctoral candidate on the ADAPT Project (adapttvhistory.org.uk) at Royal Holloway, University of London. Her dissertation addresses editing practice in television during the transition from film to digital editing. She has contributed to *View: Journal of European Television History and Culture* and to the BUDDAH Project at the Institute of Historical Research.

Debarchana Baruah is a doctoral student at the Heidelberg Center for American Studies, Germany. Her dissertation explores the phenomenon of 21st century retro, using the television series *Mad Men* (2007–15) as a case study. Baruah teaches representations of the suburb in post-war American literature and representations of the self in 20th century African American literature at the Anglistisches Seminar, Heidelberg University.

Amy **Holdsworth** is a lecturer in film and television studies at the University of Glasgow. She is the author of *Television, Memory and Nostalgia* (2011) and has contributed articles on television theory and aesthetics to *Screen, Cinema Journal, Critical Studies in Television, Journal of Popular Television* and the *Journal of British Cinema and Television*. Her research mostly focuses on television theory and criticism.

Jilly Boyce Kay is a research associate in the Department of Media and Communication at the University of Leicester. Her work has been published in *Feminist Media Histories, Critical Studies in Television, Social Movement Studies*, and *Journalism: Theory, Practice and Criticism*. Her research interests are in feminist television studies, with a focus on factual and talk-based genres.

Vanessa **Longden** is a doctoral candidate in the Department of History at Durham University. Her research is in conjunction with the Centre of Visual Arts and Culture (CVAC) and the Leverhulme Trust. Her research interests explore the (re)construction of photographic space and changing perceptions and also the portrayal of performative bodies, gender, and identities within visual culture.

Cat **Mahoney** is a doctoral candidate in the Department of Media and Communications at Northumbria University. Her research focuses on representations of female participation in the Second World War on British television in a post–1990 post-feminist media context. Her work has been published in *Frames Cinema Journal* and she has presented at conferences.

Laura **Mee** is an associate lecturer in film studies at De Montfort University, Leicester, and a visiting tutor in media theory at Birmingham City University. Her research interests include adaptation, horror cinema and cultural recycling. She is the co-editor of *Cinema and Television History* (2014) and the author of a forthcoming book on *The Shining*. Her work has also appeared in *Horror Studies*.

Kaitlynn **Mendes** is a lecturer in media and communications at the University of Leicester. Her research interests include feminism, activism, and gender issues and she has published in *Feminist Media Studies, Media Culture and Society,* and the *Journal of Gender Studies*. She is also the author or editor of three books, *Feminism in the News, Feminist Erasures* (edited with Kumarini Silva), and *SlutWalk: Feminism, Activism and Media*.

Tim **O'Sullivan** is an emeritus professor in the Leicester Media School at De Montfort University, Leicester. He has written widely on aspects of British cinema and television cultures in the 1950s and '60s and he is a member of the Cinema and Television History Research Centre (CATH) at De Montfort University.

Claire **Sedgwick** is a doctoral candidate in journalism at De Montfort University, Leicester. Her research focuses on how *Spare Rib* and *Ms.* represented second wave feminism and how the magazines can help feminists understand feminist history. She has also presented research about feminism and the internet at conferences, including "Console-ing Passions" at De Montfort University in 2013.

Caitlin **Shaw**'s research interests include retrospective depictions of the 1980s in post–2005 British film and television and understanding them within the context of popular retro and nostalgic trends in British and global cultures. She also focuses on British film and television and nostalgia and memory in contemporary media. Her work appears in *Cinema, Television and History: New Approaches* (2014).

Christine **Sprengler** is an associate professor of art history at Western University in Ontario. She is the author of two books, *Screening Nostalgia* (2009) and *Hitchcock and Contemporary Art* (2014), as well as articles on British and American cinema and television, new media art, and the relationship between film and the visual arts.

Marta **Wąsik** is a PhD candidate in the department of Film and Television Studies at the University of Warwick. Her essay in this volume derives from her thesis research, which explores the history of home movies represented in fiction films. Her research interests include home movies and amateur film, residual media, representations of domesticity, and gender.

Jo **Whitehouse-Hart** is a lecturer in media and communication at the University of Leicester. Her research takes a psychosocial approach to the study of audiences, culture and society, and she studies the creative industries and performing arts, looking specifically at audiences who become performers. She has also explored the creative processes in advertising.

Helen **Wood** is a professor of media and communication at the University of Leicester and has published on television, audiences, class and gender. She is the author of *Talking with Television* (2009) and, with Beverley Skeggs, *Reacting to Reality Television* (2012). She edited *Reality Television and Class* with Beverley Skeggs (2011) and *Television for Women* (2016) with Helen Wheatley and Rachel Moseley.

Index